Briefly,
ABOUT THE BOOK

This is a fascinating chapter of autobiography in which Ivor Montagu collaborated with Sergei Eisenstein and Grigory Alexandrov on two original film scenarios written in Hollywood in the days when the world's film capital was at its most fantastic peak. *Eisenstein was the nearest thing to a universal genius ... that the cinema has yet produced,* Montagu writes in these highly personal memoirs of that time. They are told with humour and a wealth of anecdote. The Hollywood of the thirties drew people from all over the world interested in the new technique of sound film and within the pages of this book the reader will meet many of the famous of the day, working and playing together. Included in this volume is the first publication of the two film scripts, *Sutter's Gold* and *An American Tragedy*, which grew out of this collaboration. Why they were never produced is part of the story. However, the scripts alone are fascinating. They will be appreciated by the specialist as examples of Eisenstein's genius and will be enjoyed by the layman for the exciting story they tell ...

INTERNATIONAL PUBLISHERS
381 Park Avenue South
NEW YORK, N.Y. 10016

WITH EISENSTEIN IN HOLLYWOOD
by IVOR MONTAGU

Ivor in Grass.
Sketch by Eisenstein of the author working on the scenario of King Solomon's Mines, Moscow, July, 1936
(Coll. Eisenstein Archive).

With Eisenstein in Hollywood

A Chapter of Autobiography by
Ivor Montagu

including the scenarios of
SUTTER'S GOLD and
AN AMERICAN TRAGEDY

INTERNATIONAL PUBLISHERS
NEW YORK

85584

This Edition
is published simultaneously by
International Publishers, New York,
and Seven Seas Books, Berlin, 1969
Second printing 1974.

For Pera, Lyuba, Bianca
and Eleonora

Cover photograph:
Before Hollywood — the Schoolchildren of
La Sarraz. Front cover: front row (l. to r.)
Sergei Eisenstein, Janine Bouissounousse,
Hans Richter, Béla Balász. 2nd row left;
Ivor Montagu, Jack Isaacs.
Spine of cover: standing, Grigory Alexandrov,
seated Eduard Tisse.
Back cover: seated l. to r.: Walther Ruttmann,
Robert Aron, Leon Moussinac.

Copyright (c) by Ivor Montagu, 1967
ISBN 0–7178–0220–5
Cover Design by Lothar Reher
Printed in the German Democratic Republic

BY THE AUTHOR

Books:
: The Traitor Class
Plot against Peace
Land of Blue Sky
Film World
Germany's New Nazis

Translations:
: *(from French)*
Le Cocu Magnifique (Fernand Crommelynck)
(from German)
Heil!
The Yellow Spot
(from Russian)
Pudovkin on Film Technique
The Fiery Angel (Valery Bryusov)
A Subaltern in Old Russia (A.A. Ignatyev)
Tuatamur (Leonid Leonov)
Sot (Leonid Leonov)
Benia Krik (Isaac Babel)

Films:
: Bluebottles
Daydreams
The Tonic
Wings over Everest
Defence of Madrid
Man One Family

Film Script:
: Scott of the Antarctic

ACKNOWLEDGEMENT

The scenarios of "Sutter's Gold" and "An American Tragedy", written for projects never proceeded with, are included in this book by kind permission of the holders of copyright in the original novels, Blaise Cendrars' *L'Or* and Theodore Dreiser's *An American Tragedy* — respectively Madame Raymone Cendrars and *les éditions de noël* for the former and the Dreiser Trustees and World Publishing Company for the latter — who retain all rights in these novels, including film rights, except any that they may have specifically assigned.

Their inclusion also has the kind approval of Grigory Alexandrov and the Committee on Sergei M. Eisenstein's Literary and Creative Heritage, Moscow (Chairman, Sergei Yutkevich).

The author thanks also for cooperation the Museum of Modern Art, New York; the British Film Institute, London; the Eisenstein Archive, Moscow; Lawrence Bachmann, Paul Capon, Heinrich Fraenkel, George Hellgren, Naum Kleiman, Grigory Kozintsev, Jay Leyda. And Mrs. Kay Pankey for invaluable editorial advice.

CONTENTS

Why this Book? … 11

BEFORE HOLLYWOOD … 13
  Meeting at La Sarraz … 13
  Mission … 17
    Interlude for Dead-end
    Go West, Young Men
    Off

TRANSATLANTIC … 37
  The Scout … 37
    Terra Nova
    Ace of Trumps
    A Job
    Bull's-eye
  Men at Work … 75
    Rooftree
    The Fleshpots
    Fairy Gold
  Denouement … 110
    Sudden Death
    Tidying-up

AFTER HOLLYWOOD … 129
  Mexican Postscript … 129
  Conclusion … 138

Appendix 1.
The Scenario of *Sutter's Gold*   149

Appendix 2.
The Scenario of *An American Tragedy*   207

Note on Scripts   342

Notes to pages   345

Select Bibliography   350

Index   353

Photo pages *facing pages*   24, 72, 312

Eisenstein's sketches for
Sutter's Gold   153, 167, 173, 189, 190

An American Tragedy facing page   313

Why this Book?

Eisenstein has been a long time dead. The events this book describes took place a generation ago. Perhaps it now comes too late.

The author has been pressed to write of his time in Hollywood for many years. American scandalmongers, friends and contemporaries of Eisenstein in several countries, more youthful worshippers of the legend, have all requested it — but altogether these do not add up to an excuse. Perhaps nowadays there are not very many left who are still interested in this story.

Nevertheless there were reasons why it could not be written before. One was moral, the other practical.

Europeans have always felt that there was something comical and rather undignified in Hollywood in its heyday. We would arrive, adventurous flies ready to grow fat on the rich carrion we anticipated, and then, if something went wrong, we could always come back and raise a laugh about the foibles of our hosts. I felt this acutely. After all, many ridiculous things happened and I could not see any way of telling of them without appearing to be disagreeable to those who, after all, had only been kind to us according to their lights.

Now, with distance, the risk of pain to anyone is much abated and age has taught me that we, rather than playing heroes, will look as absurd as anybody else.

Second, if there has ever been any reason for recording the story it must have been to include the scenarios we all three wrote together. They, after all, are the essential part, without which nothing else can be clear, and — so far as that nebulous quality 'Film Art' is concerned — they are the whole fruit of the enterprise.

We wanted to publish them in 1931. Dreiser wanted us to. So did Cendrars. Paramount had no objection. But the respective publishers who at that time controlled the English-language copyrights of the original novels on which the scenarios had been based would not agree. Until now access to them has only been available to scholars, either at the Eisenstein Archive in Moscow, or at the Museum of Modern Art in New York where Eisenstein deposited such copies as we co-authors did not take away.

Today, a generation later, this obstacle has been removed. The appropriate thanks and acknowledgement for permission is included on another page.

I suppose there is still a reason for setting it all down. What does it matter what was written and never came to fruition, all so long ago? Has not cinema moved on? Are the scenarios, never made as films, worth reading and visualising for themselves, as stories? This last question the reader will have to decide for himself. But anyway the "cultural record" is incomplete without them. Scientist, philosopher, innovator — Eisenstein was the nearest thing to a "universal genius" of the type of Leonardo that the cinema has yet produced. What he tried to do, and what happened, is a part of film history and therefore a part of its treasury of experience for the future. I make no apology for telling it as autobiography for the better you know the witness the more truly you can judge the tale he tells.

I. M.

Before Hollywood

MEETING AT LA SARRAZ

The place is La Sarraz, in the foothills of the Alps on the borders of France and Switzerland near Geneva. The time is the late twenties of this century. The scene is the chateau, the hostess its chatelaine Madame de la Mandrot. The occasion is a meeting of the élite and not-so-élite of *cinéma de l'avant-garde*. The happening is an irruption. The irruption is the appearance of three young men dressed in blue, not exactly from outer space but from its then spiritual equivalent, the U.S.S.R. And the result? The result — that in a few hours all the priceless treasures of the castle, the medieval furniture, culverins, gonfalons, greaves, pikes and battle-axes were now strewn about the lawn. We were busy making a film.

I shall assume a few explanations are in order.

The conference was, I suppose, the very first precursor of all the festivals of cinema which are now such a familiar feature of the landscape, such an occasion for manoeuvring and junketing. But we were rather different. "Art" had not yet been annexed by commerce as a term to justify the deshabille of starlets and a gloss to throw over every production costing several million dollars. "Film Art" in those days had something at once priggish, monastic and exciting about it. Those were the days of "Little Theatre" and "Little Magazines". We were even proud to be in a minority although we certainly did not intend to remain one.

The idea of the conference had come from a young Frenchman, Robert Aron, who had sent out the invitations and now ran about anxiously, despairing of the disorder and trying to soothe Madame de la Mandrot. The experts and *aficionados* included a spattering from all sorts of countries. Walther Ruttmann, who had already set us by the ears with his feature documentary "Berlin — the Symphony of a Great City". Hans Richter, who had imported surrealism into cinema by trick photography in his bowler-hatted joke "Vormittagsspuk". A young Parisian, whom few knew to be Brazilian, Alberto Cavalcanti. An old theoretician, exile from his Hungarian homeland, Béla Balász. All kinds of sparklers and luminaries from all over Europe were there, even an American admirer of the arts with a Welsh label, Montgomery Evans. The "we" of this company were we two delegates from the Film Society in London, granddaddy in its day of all the innumerable progeny since spawned by its example — Jack Isaacs, later Professor of English Literature at King's College in London, and its Chairman, still more or less juvenile at twenty-five, myself.

At first all had gone fairly steadily and staidly, as had been planned. We showed one another films. We praised one another and admired one another. All was plain living and far from plain speaking, indeed an elevated and enervating atmosphere of high polite discussion.

The invasion of the three men in blue quickly put a stop to that.

The newcomers were Sergei Mikhailovich, Grisha and Eduard. Otherwise, S.M. Eisenstein, G.V. Alexandrov and their cameraman Tisse. The two last-named were slim, strong, handsome, fair-haired and golden-skinned. They wore their blue boiler-suits with an entirely appropriate engineering flavour.

The third was shorter, a barrel-shaped torso, small limbs and tiny, delicate hands — surmounted by the gigantic head, the dominant forehead, the abundant quiff, the mischievous (and sometimes malicious) piercing eyes already familiar from his portraits.

For these men were already known to the film world, and especially to coteries such as ours. Were they not our heroes? We were not "Reds" — the epithet was little used then — but we adored experiment. Convinced, and not incorrectly, that the great cinema of those days, the cinema of industry and prosperity, was too complacent, we all sought at once to save it and incidentally carve a niche for ourselves, by ingenuity and innovation. S.M. and his associates had already made themselves, by the fame of "Potemkin" and the rest, a world-banner for our movement. Were they not the supreme experimenters, not artists alone but scientists, and had they not stormed the citadel by their success? It is doubtful whether any other Soviet film-makers touring Europe would have been such natural invitées for La Sarraz. But their arrival was at once its highlight and its justification.

At that time Grisha and Eduard were deaf and dumb to our communication except by signs. They were almost exclusively limited to Russian. Quickly they picked up bits — Eduard in a restaurant could smile blandly and ask for "pineapple", the two caused consternation on a railway platform in England trying to enter a door whose legend they read as "Laddies". Later both managed fair English, Eduard German, Grisha good French and Italian — he is now a suave and experienced diplomat on the cultural circuit. But at La Sarraz and for long after they were wholly tongue-tied compared to Eisenstein, who scintillated polylingually, word-perfect in English, French and German, competent in Spanish; he could even manage something in Japanese.

S.M. revelled in the situation and immediately took command of it. Our academic mutual admiration society was smashed into smithereens, the idols that had contented us hitherto were mocked. "Pick and Pabst" appeared in the vocabulary as a term of disdain for all that, however worthy, was unadventurous. When I ventured to protest the blanket condemnation of a director

— I saw a distinction between a short and jerky mannered comedy he had made and a more leisurely and pictorially evocative semi-documentary (both on offer at the conference) — I was firmly put down by Eisenstein with a devastating: "So there is a difference between dog-shit and cat-shit". But swiftly he tired of all discussion. We must be practical. Action must replace theorising. The castle possessed appropriate resources in properties and costume. Therefore a film must be made to express our theme. Aron and our poor hostess were left groping in the flood.

S.M. was diplomatic enough not to appoint himself director. For this post, Richter was conscripted. Joint cameramen Tisse — who, of course, had not come without a camera — and Ruttmann. Grisha, general dogsbody and factotum. Sergei Mikhailovich just ran about everywhere and, if anything, was prop-man.

There was a role, dramatic or technical for everyone. Janine Bouissounousse, the muse and adjutant of Aron, representing the Spirit of Cinema in flowing cream-coloured shift with, as huge breastplates, empty thousand foot film spools, was confined somewhere under the eaves of the topmost tower. Jack Isaacs' substantial profile qualified him for the casting as Commerce, her gaoler. Encased in armour cap-a-pie, he hurled defiance through his visor on the hosts below. Every variety of period was portrayed in the columns and weapons of the advancing liberators. At their head Moussinac, a tall black-moustached figure in leather thigh-boots, sash over shoulder and plumed D'Artagnan hat. Everything seemed chaos. I, as Richter's assistant, was perfectly satisfied to let things slide.

Where is that film now? Who knows? Some say that Richter took it away to cut in Germany and it disappeared. Others that pieces turn up from time to time. Probably its loss was an impoverishment of film history rather than film art.

But there was other fruit from La Sarraz. I got on with

Grisha and Eduard. I had twice been to the U.S.S.R. already, I had a smattering of Russian — it was said then (as I learned later) at the Soviet Embassy in London that "if you talk to Montagu in baby-language he understands" — so that I was able to mollify their incomprehensions. I got on with Eisenstein, too. Although he had heard my name already and been told by Pudovkin to look me up in Europe, this did not diminish my inclusion in his general mockery, but we found we could laugh at the same things and that is a fair start to friendship. Anyway, before Jack Isaacs and I left, we had fixed for the three to come to London and for Eisenstein to give a course of lectures to the Film Society.

MISSION

Interlude for Dead-end

At this stage it is necessary to digress from this meeting with Eisenstein and tell here what I was doing at the time so that the reader can see how our paths came to run together.

I had been in cinema professionally for about four years, drifting there through my connection with the Film Society. But round about now I had reached a dead end. The ambition of most people in films is to be a director. You can do other things well for years — editor, cameraman, art direction or script — but director is the real breakthrough. In cash and in prestige. And you do not go backwards. Once a director, always a director (usually). That is, producers setting up a production think of you as a possible.

With me it had not worked out that way. I had broken

through, made my three short comedies and they had fallen flat.

These three short pictures were the H.G. Wells' comedies. I had done most things in the business apart from camera, and including direction of reshot sequences for other people's failed or limping product. The little company I ran with Adrian Brunel we, and others, considered the best editing and titling medium for foreign imports in the whole country. A third partner was Frank, H.G.'s younger son, with whom I shared a past in zoology which we had both deserted.

We got our breakthrough from a dapper American who did something no one could be quite sure of on the fringes of Wardour Street. He had the reputation (I have not the slightest idea if it was well-deserved) of sitting at the window of his West End flat and sending his valet after passing beauties who aroused his romantic imagination. Like the similar man at the corner of the crossroads he (or rather his valet) must have got a lot of metaphorical slaps but they were said to get other results too. Anyway, he was always extremely nice to me and the only thing I really knew that counts against him was that he was the worst lawn tennis player in the world. Nothing would persuade him to give up trying to learn, he must have poured buckets of gold into the pockets of professionals in England and the South of France; he tried Heirons and he tried Kozeluh, but somehow, however correctly he arranged his feet and whatever the motions he made with his arms and with his legs, the ball and his racket were never there at the same time.

Some people do seem to have this insuperable difficulty with a moving ball.

This nice man said that he would find the money for three comedies if H.G. would write original stories for them. It was not a lot of money — five thousand or six thousand pounds for the three I think — pictures did not cost so much in those days. He had common interests with

Ideal Films, whose head was Simon Rowson, a leading figure in trade circles of the day. We had edited films for Rowson, my wife (Hell) at one time worked as secretary for him, and he as renter agreed to put up the necessary guarantees of distribution. It all worked out very well.

H.G. was quite willing. He was very keen that Frank and I should make a career in films together and spoke about it several times. He thought we would get on with one another. (He was right about this, we always have, but wrong about the career, for when later on the trade union was formed I joined at once, but Frank would not and so we separated.) H.G. made only one condition. The comedies must launch Elsa Lanchester as well as ourselves. She must be the star. This suited us all right for we both admired Elsa as much as he did. We knew her not only from the theatre but from the Cave of Harmony. Elsa brought in Charles Laughton, whose only film effort up to that time had been a bit in one scene as a restaurant guest in a film called "Piccadilly" made at Elstree. He was to play villains in all three stories and for hero we had Harold Warrender, one of our dearest cronies at the Soho restaurant where we always lunched.

The only thing left was to get the stories. Easier said than done for H.G. was always writing something else. But at last I ran him to earth in a flat in Paris (it was the "Dolores" period by then). I came straight from the overnight train and roused him out of bed. He gave me breakfast while, in his dressing gown, he wrote down "Bluebottles". The other two "Daydreams" and "The Tonic" were more difficult but I dug my heels in. Finally they emerged as about a paragraph each and I flew back triumphant to London on the afternoon plane.

As assistant we had Lionel (Tod) Rich, one of our Brunel and Montagu boys, who fortunately knew more about work on the floor and costing than either of us, and was one of the most sensible if mock-lugubrious men I ever met. While we were desperately working on H.G.'s scraps of paper, trying to think up visual jokes and turn them into scripts, he would occasionally say, "Tee-hee". This fatal comment meant that, in his opinion, if there were any laugh there it was certainly a small one, and he was usually right. Woe betide us (as we afterwards found) if we were stubborn and insisted on keeping in the gag he thus condemned. It was "Tee-hee" also when the audience saw it, if as much as that.

We took the floor in the old Gainsborough studio in Islington, now a warehouse. We had a happy ship, with Freddy Young as first cameraman, Roy Kellino as his first assistant and Hell as continuity girl. There were the usual misadventures associated with most film production. Laughton, who was just at that period clinching the name he was making for himself at the Court Theatre, took his parts as earnestly as all his professional work, that is, he put his whole self into them, however short they might be. A deputation from the gantry boys came to me to complain that he was giving them the creeps. In "Daydreams" he played a rajah in a turban and to be very sinister he would prepare himself by going behind a flat and shaking his head and shuddering to get the right expression, only poking his face out when we were ready for the shot. He had thought he was invisible but unluckily these antics had caught the eyes of the electricians alert up among the lights. In another scene Elsa was kidnapped and we shot it as a night shot from the studio roof in order to follow the car carrying her as victim along several alleys in one take. The thugs, who had been told to punch the unresisting dummy, dressed and made-up to represent Elsa, never heard the cry "Cut" and drove half round Islington battering it to the scandal of the neighbourhood and confusion of the police.

"Bluebottles" is a story in which Elsa finds a police whistle on the pavement and blows it, and the battle that ensues ends in the rounding-up of a gang.

These were the days before the Film Artistes Association rightly established a closed shop and the casting of the plug-uglies made parts for many of our friends. Charles Laughton looked gleefully murderous, Joe Beckett plausibly muscular if too benign, Norman Haire with shirt tail hanging out of a hole in his trousers carried away a body quite effectively. Frank incautiously revealed a talent for falling downstairs, so we dressed him in a striped jersey and killed him many times, each time having a chandelier collapse on his head as soon as he reached the bottom.

There is always trouble with animals. In "The Tonic" Elsa is a maid who, when her mistress faints, reads in *Block's Medical Dictionary* that an unconscious person can be revived by burning feathers and approaches the caged parrot with a determined air. There was only one way to play this. We advertised for what is called a "feather-eater", that is, a bird that through some dietary deficiency or quirk of its imagination has denuded itself by eating its own feathers; and a beauty as bare as a plucked chicken was brought in by an old lady from Pimlico.

The scene cut as follows: Elsa advancing determinedly; the parrot (a different and intact parrot of course) eyeing her apprehensively: Elsa wrestling with the out-of-picture cage and returning to revive her mistress; the denuded and miserable result. Alas it became quite apparent that the old lady dearly loved her parrot. She had thought we wanted it to make a complimentary photo or at least a scientific record and I have never forgotten (it is an unhealed scar upon my conscience) her distress when she learned that, for the trifling sum that we had advertised, she had betrayed her heart's companion to be laughed at.

Worse still was the shark. After a shipwreck Elsa, Harold and the rajah all find themselves on a raft. A shark is in attendance, a *deus ex machina* to eat the rajah eventually. The shark was represented easily by a wooden property fin on a wooden segment of back. We finished shooting in autumn, but the cutting took several weeks and when it was completed in January with the trade show only a few weeks off, we discovered to our horror that in the director's inexperience we had shot the fin too small for it to achieve its menacing effect.

Nothing for it but for a retake unit to hurry down to Southend and for the director himself, as penance, to impersonate the shark. The struggle to keep wholly under the icy January water (there were no snorkels in those days), and hold the too buoyant shark dummy firmly and precisely on the surface while the necessary shot was put "in the can", was dreadful; and I burned my overcoat on a stove trying to stop shivering in the cafe where we all tried to roast ourselves to normal blood temperature afterward.

The tryout in North-East London went down splendidly and the trade show itself was a fair success. One circumstance, however, caused me worse twinges than the parrot. At that time Charles Laughton had been playing in Arnold Bennett's "Mr. Prohack" and his make-up in it as the author had had a great success. He wanted to keep the same successful make-up in "The Tonic" and I passed it as not inappropriate to the suburban father of a family, the most considerable of his roles in any of the films. But Bennett, who was a friend of the Wells family, came specially to the trade show in compliment to Frank and I could see the caricature hurt him, especially the stutter. It was one thing for him to approve the imitation in his own play, under his own control, quite another for us youngsters unthinkingly to take it over for a film of wide distribution, without asking him and so to speak behind his back. I have always felt he was right and been ashamed.

Why then, after all, did the films fall flat? If one looks at them today one can see blank spots where they contain in-jokes, allusions that have dated or others that never were very funny ("Tee-hee"), but they are not as bad as all that. In Germany, where Lotte Reiniger's husband Carl Koch distributed them they were a great success, especially "Bluebottles" (as *Pfiffe in der Nacht*).

At least partially responsible was the fact that the distributors' programme meant holding their release up until nearly a year after shooting had finished. Conception occurred in a world of silent films. Parturition in a world already invaded by sound, when programmes, including shorts, were being given away gratis to exhibitors in return for buying the sound reproduction apparatus marketed by the distributor controlling it. In Germany the talking film conquered just a few months later than in Britain. In Britain, anyway, the comedies died the death.

Once a director, always a director, even if unemployed. I could not go *back*. Adrian and I, both out of work, felt proud that every person who had received his training on our staff had found good jobs in the new industry. Only we could not. In attempting to set up another picture I found my scientific turn of mind a handicap. I knew too much, I was my own worst enemy. The prospective angel, impressed by the proposition, would ask: "Can you guarantee that this production will make a profit?" I always felt I had to reply: "Certainly not. A director can only hope to guarantee about his film that audiences will enjoy it, *if* they see it. I cannot guarantee that exhibitors will book it to show it to them." (I never learned how to get on well with exhibitors.) "Nor can I or anyone guarantee against a royal scandal or other national calamity occurring unexpectedly to hit it on release date." For some reason this did not encourage the angels. What was I to do?

It was about this time that I began to think of Hollywood.

As it turned out, the same target was beckoning the three men in blue.

Go West, Young Men

At this stage we should tell something more about our principals. In the months that followed, and years afterwards, I learned a good deal. Some is on record, some things I judged from observation, some they told me, but Eduard was always reserved, Grisha moderate and modest, Eisenstein loved dramatising and pulling everyone's leg.

Sergei Mikhailovich was the spoilt child of reasonably well-to-do parents. His architect father, a jovial man, was of distant Jewish origin. His mother was Russian, not Latvian. There are photographs of his father straw-hatted, black-bearded, every inch the Riga business man. He was evidently a man of some humour. The boy's mother may be seen in "Battleship Potemkin", portraying one of the citizens of Odessa who go out in small boats to greet the rebel vessel. She is the ample lady who hands a goose up over the side. In later years she used to live with her son in their one-room-plus-kitchen flat in Moscow and look after the enormous dog which had alas to be put down at a time of the shortage. (Not the first, post-civil-war, but the second, collectivisation-struggle shortage.) As a teenager he made his way to Petrograd, studying civil engineering at first and, despite his unathletic figure and personality, joined the levies hastily recruited to withstand the advancing counter-revolutionary troops.

Grigory Alexandrov on the contrary was a handsome athlete, a Lothario, with some Kazakh admixture despite his blondness. He had run into Eisenstein as an actor and they had become in some sort part pupil and teacher, part partners. Those were days of frantic experiment in art, when all doors were open to youth and the barriers of the arts dissolved so that one flowed into another. (Indeed nothing more clearly highlights the defects of *Dr. Zhivago* as an historical novel — I say nothing of its merits or deficiencies on other planes — than its author's

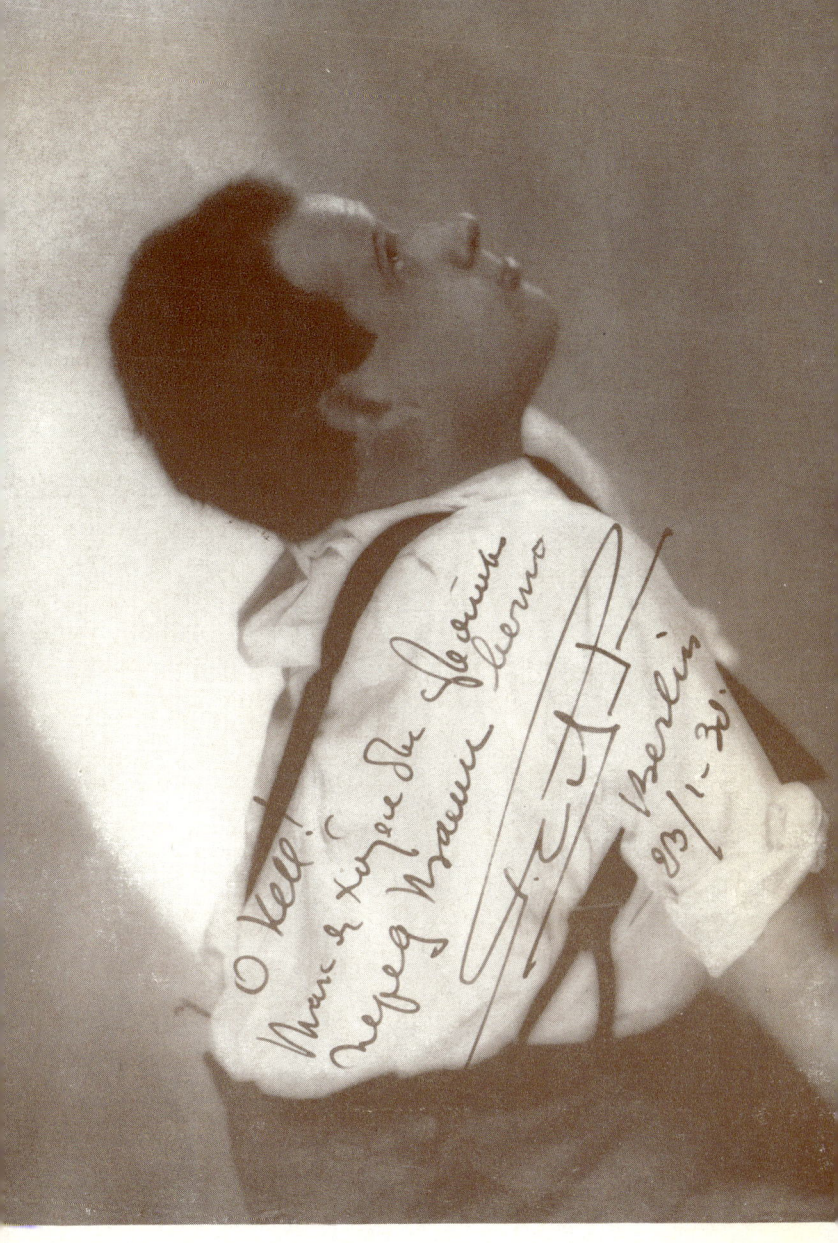

S. M. Eisenstein:
O Hell, that I might sit thus gazing up at you forever.

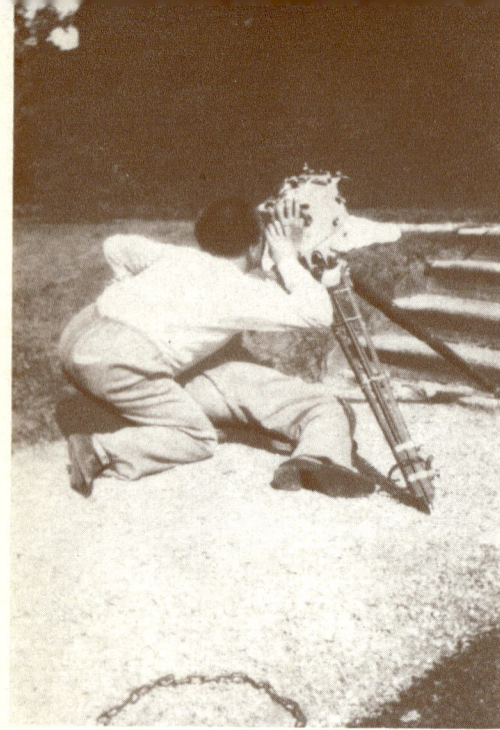

Liner-Upper: Eisenstein and Alexandrov at La Sarraz.

On Shore at Shoreham: Production still from "Daydreams". l. to r.: Charles Langhton, Hell, I.M., Renée de Vaux, Freddie Young (camera), Elsa Lanchester, Frank Wells, Lionel Rich, Walter Wichelow (make-up).

Plug-Uglies Unveiled: Still from "Bluebottles".
l. to r.: Sergei Nolbandov, Joe Beckett, Dr. Norman Haire.
Foreground: Elsa Lanchester

confusion of the drabnesses and orthodoxies of a later period with what happened in those early post-revolution days, perhaps the most hectic and the freest for the arts of any time anywhere.)

Eisenstein and Alexandrov became moving spirits in a young group that staged satirical burlesque, compounded of melodrama, farce, dance, acrobatics, clowning — a sort of "with it" fringe of that day and age. The story is well-known of how, in trying to lend their topical themes and interpretations a greater realism, Eisenstein tried to use actual scenes and settings to play in, staging a strike in an actual factory and the like. He found it didn't work and this led him inevitably to film.

Here is where the older member of the trinity, Eduard Kasimirovich Tisse, son of a Swedish sea captain long settled and naturalised in Russia, came in. He had been a newsreel cameraman long ago and used to tell how in early revolutionary days he might be handed a small roll of film — then not manufactured in Russia and rare as platinum — and feel the responsibility of recording some historical event, such as Lenin addressing a great demonstration, without a foot to waste. As Eisenstein's collaborator he was to prove himself a genius among exterior cameramen. He it was who in "Potemkin" contrived to make the unexpected scenes of mist — a phenomenon of course unforeseen and unprovided for in the script and usually regarded as making conditions impossible for photography — a treasure of the film canon. He also mastered the art of achieving unprecedented depth of focus, thus giving Eisenstein a third dimension for the compositional "conflicts" in which the graphic elements of his images were relationally arranged. At first, no doubt, as the only one at that time with film experience, he had been brought in to hold the others on a technically even keel.

Each of these men supplied a quality that the others completely lacked, their abilities perfectly dovetailed.

Their temperaments might clash. Living and working with Eisenstein anywhere must have been a strain. Doing so abroad must have been exceptionally trying for the other two — for S.M. with his mastery of foreign languages and cultures could fit in anywhere as easily as into a glove and did plunge into the lionising as a fish into water, while Grisha and Eduard were necessarily cut off and so had extra worries.

But when they worked together, each was so completely devoted and necessary to the enterprise, each so naturally allotted to his slot that they seemed less three separable persons than the integrated parts of one creator. Indeed, I think it was the experience of working with them that first undermined my youthful egoism and taught me the *social* nature of man, the impotence of genius, however towering, to achieve, unless it has the good fortune to meet, and the talent to inspire, and carry with it, suitable others in the realisation of its plans.

These were the three whose films had made such a world-wide impact and who were now outside their country. They had been given a year's leave and they had wanted to leave for a year. Why the latter, should be explained. At that time the creative cinema in the U.S.S.R. was — like myself in my tiny way — partly stuck and undergoing crisis. And basically for the same reason; the advent of sound film.

Not that Soviet film-makers did not have ideas about sound film. Witness the famous manifesto on sound of Eisenstein, Alexandrov and Pudovkin. For historical reasons, which I will not go into here, the sound revolution in the U.S.A. and its dependent markets had developed at first as an all-singing, all-talking picture, made appealing by its novelty, but none the less slow by reason of its rigid association of the image of the natural causative agent with every sound employed. The manifesto called for exploration of the marvellous new powers given to cinema in their full fluidity, the employment of every sound, natural and arbitrary, and their association with whatever image best suited the expressive purpose of the film. They had ideas but they could not use them.

It was not because the Soviet authorities underestimated cinema that the film-makers could not at once get the opportunity and that sound and talk came to the U.S.S.R. later than to any other film-producing country. Had not Lenin himself said: "Of all the arts cinema is for us the most important"? The trouble was that sound film came into the rest of the world just as the Soviet Union had got well into the Second Five-Year-Plan. Part of this plan was designed to widen enormously the Soviet film industry and make it independent. Up to that time cameras (Debrie) had come from France and film stock (Agfa) from Germany. Now the Soviet film industry was to manufacture its own cameras and stock and other equipment that it needed, as well as multiply the number of cinemas and the network of screens in clubs, factories, travelling to villages, et cetera many times. Such an undertaking cannot be suddenly interrupted in midstream and changed over to sound. And it is of no use just making a sound film, with specially imported apparatus, if all your screens are still silent and there is nowhere to show it. So the change-over in the U.S.S.R. had to wait several years.

Meanwhile what were the film-makers to do? Films had to be made but how could any ambitious creative artist be content still to work in silent film while the rest of the world, including his special rivals abroad, was already exploring expression in this new means? It took the heart out of the job. And matters were not made much better for those proud of their profession and the great name the Soviet cinema had earned in its pictorial aspect, by the fact that the reliability of the first Soviet-built cameras and the speed of the first Soviet-made film stock were varying and undependable so that the photographic quality became a matter of chance.

Various of the young directors faced this problem in different ways. Some took sick-leave for a time, hoping that the teething troubles would be over by the time they must return. Others, more subtle, got trilogies accepted for production, and then had to take a year or two off to prepare all three scenarios fully before the first could be thought of for the floor. Eisenstein, Alexandrov and Tisse were lucky. They had just finished three tremendous films, one after the other, that the government had been grateful for. All three pictures had had matchless prestige success and the first was a smash-hit with the public too. Their makers had become world-famous. Had not Douglas Fairbanks and Mary Pickford on their trip round the world seen "Potemkin" in Moscow and lauded it to the skies on their return?* The boys deserved a holiday and, since they must face handicaps and delays by waiting at home, why not put the opportunity to profit and learn what they could abroad of the new ways coming in. Eisenstein could look after them with his languages. Perhaps they might even find they had an earning capacity in the capitalist jungle. If so, they would not need valuta.

So the three quitted Soviet territory and crossed the border (we had not yet learned to call it a curtain) with a year's leave and twenty-five dollars each.

At first the expectation that they could gather their expenses did not work out too badly. Not only their reputation as film-makers but Eisenstein's brilliance as a lecturer made them the lions of the day. They were welcome among the intellectual coteries in every country. Universities, including the Sorbonne, film institutions competed to learn from them. Notabilities in literature, the arts, academic circles, society who were just beginning to be interested in the cinema, and there were many at that time, were all eager to meet them. Few visas were refused to them. They did have trouble with Switzerland,

* When Fairbanks saw "Potemkin" in Moscow he immediately said to S. M.: "How long does it take you to pack your bags?"

and in France too, but mostly they could pick and choose and travel almost anywhere in Europe.

Eisenstein's appetite for experience was insatiable. He must meet everybody, see everything that was going, anything that was unusual, perhaps one should say abnormal for he was particularly interested in oddities of behaviour. He linked a study of psychology with his study of rhythms in the presentation of his pictorial patterns to dictate, regardless of content, certain moods of responsiveness in his audience. We would run into him in a variety of places. In Paris he had just fulfilled an ambition by meeting James Joyce (at the film school in Moscow he used to set his pupils passages from *Ulysses* as prose exercises to be turned into script form). He told us of Joyce's gentleness, of his expressive voice that in reading parts of *Work in Progress* would make them seem beautiful and sound momentarily limpid clear however puzzling and impenetrable they might be in print. And of how Joyce had said courteously how much he would like to see "Potemkin" and wondered whether there was any way of making this possible (although, because of his near blindness, of course there was not).

Soon someone hauled us all (the three, Hell and myself) off to the rue Blondel to a special resort where the hostesses, all middle-aged and plain but with a special talent, sat beside us on the red plush sofas but without clothes, chatting calmly of their husbands and children and kitchens and how much they earned in the working day, until the time came to display this talent which was an ability to pick up coins from the edge of the table with an organ not usually so employed.

In Berlin we made up a party to visit the museum of *Sexualwissenschaft* run by Magnus Hirschfeld*, an extraordinary small ugly man with copious Emperor Franz-Josef whiskers, who showed us piles and piles of files each

* He later came to California and was billed by the Los Angeles newspapers as *the Einstein of love*.

about some great public figure, obviously his heroes, whom he had decided were homosexuals (Kitchener was top of the lot) and bread rolls which he said had phallic significance. Presently he asked us if we carried penknives and explained to us that no homosexual ever carried one. The men among us turned out their pockets and found we could not muster one among the lot. (By the way, I have since always carried one, as an alibi.) Presently we came to a glass case full of tiny coloured paper sailors nude except for their naval caps, boots, bandoliers, etc. and painted red as if bleeding from various wounds. Hirschfeld explained to us that naval uniforms, even — as here — only accessories, by implying "discipline", heighten the satisfaction experienced by sadists. "Oh," says Eisenstein, quick off the mark, "then you would perhaps attribute the success of 'Battleship Potemkin' in Germany to this fact and the naval uniforms?" *"Teilweise,"* (partially), firmly replied our host.

Britain was less exciting or, at least, more decorous. He gave the Film Society lectures. As usual he ranged widely over the sciences and drew his examples from the art and literature of many countries, obliging us to think for ourselves on many problems and give our filmic solutions of real events and literary passages. He often preferred as examples not so much the esoteric as the unexpected, liking Webster better than Shakespeare as a dramatist and Milton better as a poet. Coleridge was his favourite source of materialist aesthetics. He taught us to see much with new eyes, illustrating, for example, his theory that motion can be conveyed by a conflict of two states differing in time, by the Toulouse-Lautrec picture of Cissie Loftus, pointing out that the legs of this remarkably mobile figure are oriented in two directions, a position that could not possibly be assumed naturally by limbs at the same time. Among those who attended the course were several young men who have since become pillars of British film production. It is a tragedy that we took no stenogram and in those days there were no tape recorders. Nor do I know of any complete notes that were taken, but Nizhny's *Lessons with Eisenstein** gives something of their flavour.

Sidney Bernstein threw a party for him. Jack Isaacs took him to the theatres and browsing amid books. Herbert Marshall, just then beginning in cinema as an amateur, took him to see the City and the more ordinary sights. (Bert was later to become the only foreign student to go through the whole course of the Moscow Film School and graduate there, as an Eisenstein pupil. S.M. then thought highly of him as a comic actor — a talent Bert has since successfully concealed — but I remember that, at the time, S.M., who cannot be said to have exactly disliked admiration, nevertheless returned exhausted at the end of the day, exclaiming in wonder: "He is so *very* worshipping".)

The Film Society showed "Battleship Potemkin" for the first time in Britain complete and uncensored, with the mutineers' white-photographed flag handpainted red as it is designed to be, as a gala especially for him. We showed it with the Edmund Meisel musical score, which Eisenstein had never heard before though its power had contributed so enormously to the force of the film that in parts of Germany it was the music, not the film, that was banned as *staatsgefaehrlich* (dangerous to the state). But though the show was triumphant Eisenstein was in a bad mood, I think because, in spite of his blatancy and readiness to put up a show, he was fundamentally a shy and sensitive person, aggressive for defence. First he complained that our opening film — Grierson's "Drifters" — had given away all the best parts in "Potemkin". (There is some truth in this. Grierson had cut and titled "Battleship Potemkin" in New York and studied it carefully, admitting the debt he owed to it in his first and most famous film, which fathered British documentary.) Then,

* See Bibliography.

at the end, when everyone was applauding the great "Potemkin" climax he complained that, with the Meisel music, we had turned his picture into an opera.

I took him to Cambridge. He made friends with Dobb. I have described elsewhere* how Peter Kapitza invited us to High Table at Trinity and how J.J. Thomson, then Master, trying to be nice, turned to S.M. and said: "I understand you are connected with the *kye-nee-ma*. I saw a *kye-ni-mato-graph* performance once." At King's we saw a performance in college by undergraduates of an Elizabethan pastoral organised by Lopokova (Mrs. Maynard Keynes) with, of course, as is appropriate, the girls' parts taken by young men. After the play, the undergraduates sat around with drinks, sometimes on each others' laps. S.M.'s eyes goggled and he whispered to me: "The authentic atmosphere of Oscar Wilde." I had to put him right, the atmosphere was still entirely in period. Of course he loved the Fitzwilliam, but having trouble to get him up in time to lunch with the director, Louis Clarke, who had a marvellous personal collection of impressionists, I incautiously told him in haste and for shorthand that Clarke had a lot of French stuff. In consequence I had to endure the catchword "French stuff" as a gibe in difficult moments throughout the following months.

Back in London I took him to Shaw in Whitehall Court, who was, as ever, gentle and extremely hospitable. As he helped us on with our coats he told us a marvellous story against himself. He had entertained Einstein on the latter's first visit to London and, just as he was seeing his guest off, had confessed that he had never been able to make head or tail of the theory of relativity. Einstein had smiled benignly and put his hand on Shaw's arm: "Never mind, Mr. Shaw," he had replied. *"Ce n'est pas votre métier."*

But this sort of thing could not go on indefinitely.

* *Film World*, Penguin, London, 1964.

Somehow the tourists had to raise money, get an income. In France Eisenstein had a splendid idea. Why not set up a production of "The Road to Buenos Aires", Albert Londres' famous reportage of the white slave trade? After all, he (S.M.) was known as the master of typecasting and since, as everyone knew, French angels if they put up money would insist on their womenfolk being given leading roles, this would solve all problems simultaneously. Somehow it did not come off. Instead, Grisha managed to charm his way to backing for a short, "Romance Sentimentale", the first sound film the unit ever made, which starred one of the protegées and two large white grand pianos. The picture was sharply and not unjustly dismissed as rubbish by the critics when it was shown in London — one grand piano they might have passed, perhaps, but two!

One of the conditions of the arrangement had been that, whoever directed it, Eisenstein should be credited as director, and Eisenstein stood loyal to Grisha in this storm, never letting on, but writing fiercely to the papers to say that the film was an experiment and "if science was allowed its white mice why should not art have its white pianos".

Meanwhile Eduard was faring no better in Switzerland. The Swiss producer Wechsler financed him to direct a picture on abortion, which he did extremely well. The trouble was that the original idea was to make a pro-legalised-abortion film. It began with a series of views of monstrous births as a warning, showed several stories of the ruin of pretty girls by the usual means of Victorian melodrama (gilt restaurants and glasses of champagne, etc.) all of whom came to a bad end, and finished with one who got on very well by having everything done in a clean clinic. When all was finished, however, somebody somewhere got cold feet, stuck the end on the beginning and the beginning on its end and turned it into the opposite, i. e. anti any form of abortion.

These and like experiences in the feared jungle were sufficient. The time had evidently come to think of the Mecca of every *cineaste* — Hollywood.

Off

Let the record be straight. I did not go to Hollywood solely to get Eisenstein out there. I went to Hollywood because it seemed the logical thing to do and because my benevolent Uncle Lionel*, the racehorse owner, a partner in our family bank, offered to stake me five hundred pounds to keep me in the United States for a year while I was trying to find a job. It was not to be a gift, it was to be a loan, and I was to pay him back. But by it the venture would be made possible.

On the other hand Eisenstein and the boys also wanted to go to Hollywood. It was the logical thing for them too. Where else but where the sound film wave began could be so useful to the tourists from the U.S.S.R.? Indeed, if it had not been that S.M. had wanted to drink of Western Europe's cultural sources and exoticisms it should have been their target right away. At the same time, the position was complicated by the fact that if you want to go to Hollywood you must never on any account show you want to go to Hollywood. If you do, you will simply be devalued. If you are big enough, and it appears that you do not want to go, or at least do not care whether you go or not, then Hollywood will be after you with a cheque book. It was certainly so then. It is probably so even now.

We agreed that advantage should be taken of my pioneering to see, discreetly, if I could not get someone to nibble for the whole group. I was to play John the Baptist and put in a word here and there in the right quarters, singing the praises of Eisenstein, letting it be

* Capt. the Hon. Lionel ("Cardy") Montagu, D. S. O.

known that he *might* be free, that tact *might* succeed in inducing him, etc. etc.

If anything came of it S.M. would try to make the contract to cover the whole five of us, the three boys in blue, Hell and me. In the meantime I would try to lodge myself independently. And that, in both parts of the programme, is exactly how it worked out.

First of all I prepared carefully. I got together some more respectable clothes with creases in the right places and had a needed haircut. Then I accumulated introductions. The first was one from Uncle Lionel himself. It was to Adolph Zukor of Paramount whom he had met at the gaming tables on the Riviera. They had made friends and Zukor had of course asked Uncle Lionel to visit him at Paramount if he ever came over. The letter said Lionel was sorry not to be coming yet awhile but here meanwhile was his nephew and he hoped that Zukor would be good to me and show me the works. Then there was one from Basil Dean whom I had met down at Dunmow. Dean's was to David Sarnoff, head of R.C.A. R.C.A. was the *other* sound system, variable area, as opposed to the at-the-time more generally used system, variable density, of Western Electric, who were also responsible for synchronisation with discs. Variable area has since generally conquered, being much the better, but at that time only one American firm used it, R.K.O. (owned by R.C.A.), the rest being clients of Western Electric. Dean was going to become an outlet for R.K.O. in Britain and so perhaps was important for Sarnoff. Anyway, these gave me a sort of entry to both systems.

I also had nice letters of introduction from both H.G. Wells and G.B.S. to the Fairbanks and Pickford ménage and Charlie Chaplin. That ought to be a help somehow. And with an eye on the Eisenstein angle G.B.S. had promised me *The Devil's Disciple* for Eisenstein if an option on it would help to get him signed up, and H.G. had done the like with *The War of the Worlds*.

(It later turned out, by the way, that H.G. Wells had long ago sold the rights of *The War of the Worlds* in perpetuity to Paramount, and then forgotten, and this was to cause endless trouble to Frank and me when later on we wrote a script on it for someone else, not knowing it wasn't free, and Paramount wouldn't sell, but that lay in the future.) I chose these two subjects — which Eisenstein did not know well — because I considered that they would possibly suit best for films in the circumstances we could expect to meet.

And, finally, I had a destination to go to that would shelter me in New York while I was "looking round".

So I kissed Hell and we said our *au* we hoped shortly *revoir* .... In those days one did not yet fly to New York. People were still using liners. I embarked on the Majestic.

Transatlantic

THE SCOUT

Terra Nova

The family that was willing to welcome me and that took me to their bosom straight off the pier at New York was that of Mrs. Henry Moskowits.

The only member of it I knew, the daughter Miriam, I had left behind in England. She was married at that time to my cousin Cyril and was a round, pretty young woman. (She has since married the sculptor Naum Gabo.) She was the first person I met to wear contact lenses and I thought her for this very courageous.

The mother, an obvious head of the family, had the doubtless well-deserved reputation in the New York of that day of being the city's ablest woman citizen. She was a twinkling, humorous person, as small and round as her daughter — indeed they were all a small, round family — who gave the impression of immense latent power. A dynamo concealed in a plain deal box would have been the same sort of creature. No one would have expected from her modest, bustling demeanour the power she did in fact wield — she was Al Smith's campaign manager in New York state — and it was fascinating to observe the respect, even awe, with which her name was greeted in the most diverse circles whenever it came up.

Her husband, Dr. Henry Moskowits, devoted to her, of equal intelligence but deliberately self-effacing, was of the same shape and size. His great moment of glory came at mealtimes when with his own hands he mixed the salad like a true paterfamilias. At this he was a master.

He was her second husband. The first, an artist, Josef Israels, had died some time previously, leaving to his widow, besides Miriam, two sons. The elder, Carlos, was a lawyer, working for a Jewish charity that in many parts of Eastern Europe helped with machinery etc. for agricultural settlement. He became my guide and introducer to New York. The younger, Josef Israels II, with his first novel on the stocks, I saw little of at that time. He was off to Europe just as I arrived and I was given his room at the top of the tall, narrow house during my stay.

Under such patronage, equipped with the know-how the Moskowits family could give, it seemed I could not go wrong. I have never known a family that exuded such tolerance, good humour and beaming kindness.

There were things to see, people to meet. Mrs. Moskowits had strings that led everywhere. To a literary lunch at the Algonquin or, through an Afro-American police doctor, to a "drag", where every dancer on the floor was a transvestite. To a coveted seat at the crowded season of Mei Lan-fang or the cave of miracles of Dr. Langmuir in the Western Electric research laboratory where I saw his first device for television.

Carlos had been to the Soviet Union in connection with his philanthropic activities and had graphic comparisons to make between Soviet and American ways, as well as between American and English based obviously on arguments with my family, whom he knew through their bank. "Now if you are going to build a hospital on the top of a hill and a road up to it, which do you build first?" he asked, answering himself as he went on. "Of course the road. What is the use of a hospital without a road to it and, besides, making the road first means that you can get all the materials for building to the site with that much less effort. But in the Soviet Union they do things the other way round. I tried to show them, but they explained to me: 'If we asked the people round here to build a road before there was a hospital they'd never believe it was for anything and look on it as forced labour. But everyone wants a hospital and nobody objects to effort in building that. Once they've got the hospital they'll be keen enough to get the road'. Not so dumb, either. They told me: 'Give the youngsters in a village a few good motor cycles and they'll build a road to speed on for themselves'." I too was very impressed with this reasoning at the time, but now I must admit I find it rather Utopian.

The bank, on the other hand, he thought wrong. "Take Miriam's father-in-law and your people," he complained. "They have a snobbish attitude to charity work. Your people are tremendous supporters of charity but they would think it wrong to take money from it. This is quite a mistaken attitude, if on net balance the charity benefits. Better for the charity to pay ten thousand a year to a first-class man capable of raising a hundred thousand than to economise by a cheap man at a thousand, or even by voluntary treasurers, and never raise more than a few hundreds." I found this logic unanswerable, but equally must admit the soundness of his diagnosis of how we were all brought up, for, logic or not, I should find it embarrassing myself to earn my living by it.

He used also to inveigh against the English businessman's lunch. "Three hours out of the working day," he said, "while we go into a drug store and are through in twenty minutes." I remembered my father making the precisely opposite comparison: "Americans think our lunch time is waste time," had been his version. "It is often the most important business time of the day. If you don't hurry over your meal you can discuss things thoroughly and by the time you arrive at the cigars you have often reached an agreement that would have been impossible at a desk and in a hard-backed chair. American businessmen think they save time by snatching a meal at a lunch counter. They don't. When they get back to the office they have to take pills and put their feet up for an hour to save their ruined digestions." Nevertheless I became an addict of the drug store and if I regret one thing more than another at being denied return to the United States it is the tuna fish on rye and the chocolate marshmallow sundae.

Mrs. Moskowits took me to see Al Smith. A slight man of enormous dignity and charm. He was exactly as one imagined him. His wrinkled face oozed humanity and sympathy. His campaign for President, lost to Hoover because it was too early for the electorate in the United States to accept a Catholic in the White House, still lay ahead, but I understood why, when it came, so many of my Hollywood acquaintances ignored the aspersions about Tammany connections and saw in his defeat the loss of the chance of a move forward for their country.

One evening Mrs. Moskowits came in and said her office had had a call from Mrs. Roosevelt. The Governor had heard I was in New York and wished to show his appreciation of my mother's work for American naval officers and ratings during the war by inviting me to the Executive Mansion. (Among her multifarious other First World War activities my mother had promoted a sort of entertainment club for the U.S. Navy at Eastleigh near our house in Hampshire and Roosevelt had been Secretary of the Navy.) Franklin D. Roosevelt was then Governor of New York State and lived in Albany. I was received very hospitably by Mrs. Roosevelt and the first impression was of a number of very large and rugged youngsters, mostly boys, who shambled among the guests like Newfoundland dogs and were in and out constantly. They seemed to be the Roosevelt children. We did not see Roosevelt himself till dinner time, but then and after the meal he was in great form, his splendid torso resting regally in a lounge chair in the middle of the drawing room as he entertained his guests with a succession of anecdotes. His attitude to World War One was romantic and boyish. Most vivid was an account of the arrival of Joffre early in the war, and the French General's effect on a big meeting at which he was supposed to ask for funds and support but, such was his emotion and anxiety, he could only stand there with tears running down his face and unable to utter a word.

Most instructive, however, was a sidelight on his pragmatic view of government. Agitating New York at that time was a struggle around a question of stage censorship. The affair had caused a great excitement in the press, everyone had taken sides, and everybody was lambasting everybody else. Only the Governor could decide and tension was rising. "What are you going to do?" asked a guest, and I weighed in with observations, for censorship on film and stage had been a speciality of mine and I had already written on its incidence in London. "Nothing," replied Roosevelt, and went on to explain. "If I act at this moment I shall shock and disappoint half of the citizens whichever side I take. I know that people are clamouring more and more urgently, saying: 'He must do this, he must do that,' but I shall wait. Only a few days more and they will be sick of it. When they are bored most people will be so relieved when I do act and settle the matter that they will not mind which way it goes." I noticed later when he was President that he used exactly the same tactics over transforming the Supreme Court. People got so bored fighting over the issue of whether he was entitled to enlarge it or not that they hardly noticed when he got the same result by slipping his own men into some naturally occurring vacancies. This point about timing is often useful.

Meanwhile I was rounding off my own affair. At Paramount Lasky was just going off to Europe. He promised to see Eisenstein in Paris and I tentatively suggested *The War of the Worlds*. Zukor gave me a letter to the West Coast studios, and asked whether, while still in New York, I would like to visit their production here (they were the only major company with a studio, a small one, in the East). The methods of the director I saw working there astonished me. When preparing a scene he walked around the floor drawing in his wake a huge array of assistants and other technicians. Not once did he turn and look at a single one of them or address a word to one directly. He just went on speaking in a low voice, indicating his wishes, and the following flock was so perfectly organised that each knew and noted down what would affect himself.

At R.C.A. Sarnoff was less forthcoming and more highfalutin. The talk was more grandiose and mostly about how sound was going to affect films and the world in general which I could guess as well as he and neither of us could guess accurately. However he was polite and I received the usual buck-passing letter on to Hollywood. That left a few personal matters to tidy. I had a play translation, done at the Stage Society in London, to try to place. Everybody asked to read it and nobody put it on. Bennett Cerf nearly published it, but froze off at the last gasp. Next I had to interview a young man who had published an American edition of my translation of *Pudovkin on Film Technique* and not paid me a cent. He proved very nice, very crestfallen and promised the cash. (Ten months later, when I left America he was still nice, still more crestfallen and still promising. I never heard from him again.) Third, Shaw had recommended me to call on his copyright adviser, Benjamin Stern, reputed to be the greatest wizard on the subject. He proved to be small and neat and silver haired and sat behind an enormously solid desk in a cosy old office inspiring absolute liking and confidence at first sight. Finally, I was flattered to be commissioned by an eminent publisher, Simon & Schuster, to write a book, and an eminent journal, the *Saturday Evening Post,* to write an article on, of all things, ping-pong. (I have no doubt I had to thank Mrs. Moskowits' surreptitious strings for this.)

On the wings of this minor triumph I left for Hollywood. Literally on wings for I had a passage on the very first plane of a new airline instituted by Lindbergh which for the first time did the coast to coast trip in thirty-six hours. (We spent a night on the way in Kansas City.) I am, or rather was, a terrible air passenger. (Since then, airsickness pills have saved me, and now pressurised aircraft make even these unnecessary.) But my peculiar form of airsickness always operated so that, thoroughly queasy in the air, the actual calamity would not occur until after I had reached the ground. Here the P.R.O.s of the new company had arranged that at every stop there would be a mayoral reception. The dignitaries would advance, a band would play, Lindbergh would come forward to accept the plaudits, the passengers would be forced to descend — by officials who did not know what had happened at the previous stop — and there, with the cameras whirring, alas would be me, advertising the amenities of the new line by being sick in the background. The only joy of the trip was that I made the acquaintance of an enchanting fellow-passenger who turned out to be Charles MacArthur, co-author of the then *succès fou*, a ruthless play of newspaper life called "The Front Page". (He delighted me by giving me a copy, inscribed — for some reason — *From the grateful schoolchildren of Liège*.) Worse was to come, however, in Arizona. Here in the desert, with a shade temperature of 103, I gasped for a drink after landing. I asked for "soda water", not knowing that what I required is known there as "White Rock". I noticed that this evoked an old-fashioned look, and it produced a mixture of *soda* and *water*. Conclusive disaster followed.

On this inauspicious note my career in Hollywood began.

Ace of Trumps

I took a small room on an upper floor of the Beverley-Wilshire Hotel, went through my pockets and examined the cards I found there.

Many books have been written about the Hollywood of those days and I do not therefore have to give much physical description. Suffice it here to know that its lineaments were exactly as have been so often and so vividly described in other books and to repeat a minimum of details in case there may be in the present generation a reader who may happen never to have met any of them.

Hollywood, as a film colony, was at its fantastic apogee. It was, *is* if it has not yet been swallowed up, a suburb of the city of Los Angeles. Founded by monkish settlement in the days of Spanish rule of California, the territory was part-seized, part-purchased by the young United States not long before the civil war. Here, you are on the Pacific coast. Confronted by these enormous blue billows the European can go no farther. In a beeline nothing is in front of him, nothing solid between him and China. If he dare go on, geography begins to bring him back to the Old World again. This is a remote exile. For the intellectual what the Black Sea coast was to Ovid. In those days the two newspapers, the *Los Angeles Times* and the *Los Angeles Examiner* were purely parochial. You would search them in vain for news of learning, news of home, news of the big world in which a variety of mankind thought and argued and decided peace and war. In fact, if you wanted to find out the latest beyond the boundaries of the parish pump you could find it better in the weekly journal of the entertainment industry of exactly that name, *Variety*. Wise writers from the East Coast, to preserve themselves from the stultifying effects of isolation, would, if their eminence enabled them to dictate the terms of their contracts, insist on an intermittent engagement, six months here, six months back in the seething, polyglot East. The foreigner felt himself a floater, and the native beside him no less a spiritual castaway than he, for Americans insisted that their true land was neither its East nor its West, nor could it be judged by either. The true America lay in that endless intervening Middle West, faceless to the visitor for he had overflown it or passed it in the prison of his Pullman dining car or sleeper.

It was on this separation that the fantasy of the film world, the self-sufficiency and gaudiness of its life, as well no doubt as the remoteness from reality of its films, were built.

The famous climate, the ever-blazing California sun, are what had attracted film-makers initially to make Hollywood. I have heard that once or twice in a generation bad weather has come to California, mostly since our visit, that Edgar Wallace caught a chill and died and others fall victim to a killer smog. This I find hard to believe. The joy of sunshine soon wears off. You will hardly credit how desperate grows the plight of the Englishman who wakes each morning to the same unpitying, unvarying sun. He sighs for — if only for one day — a nice wet mist or spell of lashing, driving rain. What is there to talk about? A friend of mine, a shoemaker, had the same trouble in South Africa. Visiting customers to sell shoes he would begin with the usual gambit he had learned at home "Fine day today, isn't it?" and be stared at as if he were mad. Oh, the monotony of a climate where every day is fine.

Los Angeles itself, the dense-packed teeming city, the film colony and its passing visitors seldom penetrated unless, greatly daring, on a slumming visit to an exoticism like the Holy Rollers, or the ultra-Brighton beachfront and fun-fair at Venice esplanade, or a part-phony Mexican restaurant with burning dishes so sticky that, once in your mouth, the other end could never be disentangled from your fork.

Hollywood lay inland, a wilderness of blocks of white suburban villas in a pseudo-Spanish style, each fronted by the same lawn kept green by a revolving spray, indistinguishable one from another by confusing four figure numbers. The blocks are patterned in such exact rectangles that their separating straight roads can only be kept from becoming deathtrap race tracks by being cambered so sharply that if you do not slow down to cross an intersection your neck is in danger of being broken as you bump up to hit the roof.

At every corner miniature golf shouted its temptations, with the same watertraps, bridges, arches and tunnels and decorative gnomes in rival crimsons, yellows and bright blues. Here and there rose the absurd outline of some cinema or restaurant in a quirky shape, one of the three skyscraper hotels, or the forbidding white fortress walls of the studio compounds, enclosing glimpses of the high corners of standing sets conventionalising every quarter of the globe and constituting the *raison-d'être* of the entire mess. Right through the suburb ran the tawdry grandeur of Sunset Boulevard, with its night spots, shops and drugstores.

Others have written of how this confusion by day, viewed from the hills above by night — distance lends enchantment — became by some miracle an exquisite and interwoven lace of dotted lights.

In a sector of those mountains above, far from the madding crowds but beset by the danger of fires and earthquakes (of which several a year, but strictly unreported unless the magnitude of the calamity defeated all suppression) nestled the larger and more comfortable mansions of the rich, the houses of the successful and the stars. This was Beverley Hills. A further, separate, suburb, over airport way, was Burbank, to which few ever went, reputedly, like Bournemouth, the dwelling place of the middle class in retirement, waiting for death. Far off to the south sparkled the legal, if morally illegitimate, delights of Tia Juana and Agua Caliente, brothels and gambling dens, the edge of prohibition territory. Eastward the desert intervened to separate all from any other humanity. Northward, the stars kept sea bungalows at Malibu Beach and, still further off, the state capital of Sacramento and the comparatively "cultured" island of San Francisco (which had theatre, Hollywood had none, only a Bowl) interested no one.

All distances were so enormous — between studio and studio, between suburb and suburb, between any two addresses one was doomed to visit, that walking was impossible, to be carless was to be legless. No one, be he magnate or proletarian, was without personal transport, the broad highways were nearly invisible beneath the moving mass.

Here I, a pedestrian, must plan my campaign, and in my bedroom I studied maps, read through introductions, counted resources.

Of friends and predecessors from the old country I knew but three. Charles Lapworth, best of men, mild but eccentrically determined, who had quitted an editorship on the *Daily Herald* for a brief frustration in British films, sold up, carried his family to America, purchased a second-hand Ford and in it crossed the continent to set up house, or rather tent, in the hills where, on the first day, the twelve-year-old daughter, left in charge while the others went for stores, had had the good luck to kill a rattlesnake. Cedric Belfrage, whom I had known in Cambridge, and whose avenue of approach was to act as gossip correspondent for some of the film-fan magazines then proliferating in Britain. I nearly bought the old car he was getting rid of, but I astonished him by suddenly halting as I was writing the cheque. All at once I remembered that I had inherited from him a university journal when he left Cambridge and had made a mess of trying to run it. So, irrationally, I thought I might do better to buy someone else's car. Heinrich Fraenkel, author, journalist, would-be film writer — our old acquaintance is another story — the most "in" of the three but clinging by his eyebrows to the fringes of the Central European immigration. None of these had influence, though all had useful experience to relate and by which to be warned, and Heinz and I could lend each other a hundred dollars or so at bad moments as well.

It was clear that the solution must lie in the papers from my pockets. I studied them carefully as they lay spread out on the counterpane of the bed. All of them were mere politenesses of one kind or another. Obviously I would present the letters to Fairbanks and Chaplin at once. But I began to concentrate upon the letter from Adolph Zukor. It was addressed to B.P. Schulberg, head of the West Coast studio of Paramount, and it had been rather vaguely worded. It ran something like this: *This is to introduce* etc. etc., *who is connected with persons important to this company. I shall be obliged if you will help him to achieve his purpose during his visit to Hollywood.* Something like that. This was obviously the one.

A Job

Douglas Fairbanks received me immediately and within a few minutes I was in his Turkish bath.

This was a sort of club for the male members of high Hollywood society. I had never experienced a Turkish bath before, and was surprised to see how small and unswimmable-in was the "plunge". It was a place where one lounged and steamed and heard the gossip. That day besides ourselves there was Jack Pickford, Mary's brother, pale and slightly puffy but otherwise unmistakably a Pickford, a strange reputed Red-Indian being called Chief Longlance and a number of the great moguls who shall be nameless because they were unbeautiful. In fact their sedentary and successful lives had made them old and fat as I am now. Douglas was superb and brown.

It was a dreamlike atmosphere. The array of bodies recalled a medieval Last Judgment or a Cézanne bathing composition. In how many instances, later meeting some principal of a giant corporation, was I in the situation of the classical prostitute who incautiously exclaimed "I hardly know you with your clothes on". However, I must have acquitted myself correctly, for I received an open invitation to return and did several times. Indeed, most of my conversations with Douglas Fairbanks were conducted nude.

Charlie was more difficult of access. He had his own studio, address Hollywood-La Brea. This was quite unlike the others, low and mock-Tudor. I handed in my letters to the Cerberus and was told that I should certainly be written to.

Now for Paramount. I telephoned and soon received an appointment that opened for me gates and a forest of salutes, hands to peaked caps. His secretary ushered me into the office of B.P. Schulberg. This was the head of the studio, you could go no higher. (Zukor was head of the company, Lasky the head of production — that is, overall planning head both of the East Coast and Hollywood studios — Schulberg the boss of the West, this was the hierarchy of power.) He was a strong-looking relaxed man, who resembled an amiable efficient crocodile smoking a large cigar. After a pleasant exchange of courtesies, some gossip in which I tried to touch, not too obtrusively, on my previous travels and experience, Schulberg leaned back and delivered the crucial question: "And what can we do for you? What would you like to do?"

This was the moment that I had foreseen ever since I studied the ambiguity of the introduction. Quite obviously it had been intended as the minimum of politeness, the usual run-around on the red carpet. It was now or never. If I answered as I was supposed to: "I should very much like to see over the studio," that would be that. I should have lost the letter, it would have passed out of my hands, Schulberg would have done his duty in giving orders for me to see round and, though he would no doubt have greeted me if we had afterwards encountered each other at parties, I should probably never pass through those gates again. Instead I said: "I should like to follow some production through here, to learn from it how you work." I explained that I had experience of every phase of production in England, but that there, though we did not think our pictures were bad, we thought (as indeed we did) that American pictures had something ours hadn't got. They were faster, had more speed. It was how they got that speed into them I should like to learn. B.P. Schulberg chewed his cigar, twisted it, then took it out and blew a puff of smoke. "I don't see why you shouldn't," he said.

He pressed a bell and then sent for an Associate Producer. (It was before the days of intercoms.) While we waited, he asked: "Do you want a salary?" Lying, I said that the money was of no consequence to me at all, I did not need it, but that as a matter of principle I should feel it wrong to do work for nothing for which another would have had to be paid. "Whatever you think proper and appropriate for whatever work I do," I concluded.

The Associate Producer, not so broad but dark and a little like Edward G. Robinson, came in. He was accompanied by a modest person, the writer Albert Shelby Levino. "This is Mr. Montagu from England," said Schulberg. "Introduced by a friend of the company. Tell him that story you're working on — the one we changed yesterday from Hungary to Russia. Mr. Montagu has been to Russia and I'm sure he will be very helpful on the writing of it."

The modest man cleared his throat and began: "Moscow, August 1914, the eve of the Great War. It is night, the lights are glittering on the snow and the droshkies. . . ."

I interrupted. "One moment. There's no snow in Moscow in summer," I said. "On the contrary, it is very hot." For this was something I had noticed in 1925.

The three men looked at each other. Schulberg gave another twist to his cigar.

"That's a new angle," he said. "Moscow without snow. The public will like that." I was in.

I think in the upshot I was paid two hundred dollars a week. According to my calculation the general level of costs and wage rates in the U.S. at that time was just about double that in England. It was good enough, if I were careful.

An Associate Producer, I should explain to those not familiar with the workings of the film industry at this period in its history, was reputed the lowest form of animal life. He was neither quite one thing nor the other. He partook of the character of a boss, because he gave orders, and was responsible for the pictures of which he was in charge. But on the other hand everyone knew that he must tremble, just as you had to, before the head of the studio, who gave him orders. He came about, as an institution, in those studios which made too many pictures a year for the studio head to watch every picture made, once he had approved its general idea and setup, in its every detail from egg to fledgeling so-to-speak.

The Associate Producer himself would probably be responsible for from two or three to six or seven pictures every year. He really needed, to be good, to understand everything in cinema, imposing on the director the business aspects which he had agreed with the administration, and defending to the administration the creative aspects he had agreed with the director. Where things went wrong were if he were an ignorant dunderhead who made the director's life an unpredictable hell, or a weak-kneed jackass who acted merely as a transmission belt for a tyrannical and interfering head. On the other hand, if he was good and the head was good, it worked well. I know all about this for it was my fate when I returned to England to spend most of the rest of my stay in the film business as an Associate Producer. Whether I was one of the good or bad ones is not for me to guess.

Paramount was one of the places where the system worked reasonably well. Schulberg, though he did not escape occasional arbitrariness and unpredictability — no man with such power as that exercised by a studio head in those days could avoid it — was able and intelligent and knew how to make his authority respected. And the Associate Producer, J.G. Bachmann — he had been a boyhood friend of Schulberg and his wife was a bosom friend of Mrs. Schulberg — was kind and intelligent too and extremely considerate.

Mr. Bachmann led me to an upper floor where a large office near his own was already being made ready for me. The legend is quite true, and I have seen it happen, that sometimes a member of the staff is unaware that he has been sacked until he returns to his office and finds another name painted on the door. On this occasion I reached the door in time to see the previous name being painted out, but mine had not yet been begun, perhaps because the lettering artist was a little uncertain about the spelling. A personable secretary appeared with notebook and I began to chat with her. After a short while there was a knock at the door and a man came in with a brisk and business-like manner.

"I am the studio bootlegger," he announced. (I had forgotten to mention earlier that the era of all this was that of Prohibition.) "Mr. Bachmann asked me to call and see if there is anything you would like."

This was embarrassing. I rarely drink. I did not like. How not offend him? My secretary helped me to disperse this problem.

Further time — not long — passed. Another knock. The newcomer was much more furtive.

"Mr. Bachmann asked me to call. The walls are rather bare, don't you think? I can supply you with pictures, the best quality. I have supplied them to most of the people on this floor. One over there, about three feet by two will be right, and one here, rather smaller perhaps."

He had his tape out and was already measuring. My admirable secretary helped me to get rid of him too but she was rather astonished, I think, that I did not want his services either.

Lunch took place in the studio restaurant. In many British studios the bosses eat (when they are not engaged elsewhere in what my father defined as a "business" lunch) in a private room. At Paramount, the country being a democracy, everyone in the studio ate in one enormous hall. But perhaps it was not quite such a democracy after all, for V.I.P.s were segregated in a corner behind a sort of wooden fence such as marks out the private frontage of a suburban garden. On this occasion I was admitted through the little wicket gate.

In the evening I dined with the Bachmann family, and a very nice and united family they were. The dark and pretty daughter, Lily, and a great husky tennis-playing schoolboy son with a terrific wipe, forehand and backhand. Mrs. Bachmann (Bea) was cosy and comforting, so was the furniture. We talked of Eisenstein, and also of Russia, which was the birthplace of the Bachmann forbears.

It may seem strange to readers brought up in the Cold War generation that my travels had brought me this unexpected bonus, in the United States of all places. But although there were no diplomatic relations in the nineteen-twenties and nineteen-thirties between the U.S.A. and the U.S.S.R. the atmosphere was totally different then from what it afterwards became, in the McCarthy era. There were McCarthy precursors, as we shall later see, but by and large they were looked on as a lunatic fringe. Russia was not a menace. Of course one disapproved of it but one lost no sleep over it. It was a mystery, maybe, but to that degree romantic. It may also seem a puzzle that three able and intelligent men, even in the

United States of nineteen hundred and thirty, had not themselves combined to squash the snow in Moscow in midsummer. I have not the least reason to suppose they were ignorant that it was wrong. It is much more likely that they had never thought about it. They had trained their minds — and this no doubt was part of their value to the system — to see things as they supposed (no doubt correctly) the majority of the public saw them.

Already that afternoon I had been out to the home of my colleague-to-be, Bert Levino, and we had got down to work. Albert Shelby Levino was very exceptional among writers in Hollywood and I was lucky to be allotted to him. Most writers would be outsiders from beyond the film industry. Some would be authors of famous novels or successful playwrights, purchased sight unseen on their reputation and brought over to Hollywood on the principle that if they had "had it in them" in one medium, they should be able to knuckle down to it in another. Some of these liked the exile and found a way to stay, others fled with an unhappiness that gold could not console. Another kind had been tough newspapermen, these were good on gangster stories. Others, the young, would be as it were imported briefly for a tour of duty, then replaced. As a Paramount executive once said in my presence: "We like to keep fresh blood filtering through the writing department."

It was very rare, in those machine-production days, for the same writers to begin, and carry through to the finish, any story. Yet everything was perfectly reasonable, that is, if one looked at it from an unfamiliar point of view. A young writer, a friend of the Moskowits family — we will call him G. — came out while I was there to M.G.M. That studio was a coveted goal in those days for its young head, Irving Thalberg, had a great reputation for enterprise, and it was also the scene of the elegant activities of Paul Bern, whose walking stick was an intellectual symbol.

G. was greeted warmly by his Associate Producer, told not to hurry, but to go away and acquire atmosphere and come back in three weeks. In three weeks he came back only to be sent away again with a few scripts to read. G., who had arrived full of genuine enthusiasm, was disappointed at this. He knew that the studio had been having difficulty finding a subject for Greta Garbo, whom it held under contract, and he begged to be allowed to try his hand at an original. The Associate Producer indulgently agreed. G. went away, worked night and day, came back in ten days with his outline all complete. The Associate Producer frowned. He had not expected him back so quickly. He read through the outline. When he had finished it, he spoke.

"This is very good, very good," he said. "I can see you have studied our pictures with Garbo. This would probably make an excellent picture and suit her admirably."

He dropped it in the wastepaper basket.

"Now, let me see, how much do we pay you a week? One hundred and fifty dollars? And you have taken ten days? That means your story has cost us less than three hundred dollars. If we do not make it we shall be only that much worse off."

He pulled out a drawer of his considerable desk and took a script out of it.

"Now this is a story which has cost us thirty thousand dollars. We cannot afford to ignore or discard an investment of that size. This is the story we shall have to use for Garbo. Take it away now and have a shot at seeing if you can adapt it so as to make it suitable for her."

On this plane, how can you counter such reasoning?

The subject to which I had been assigned, as I now learned from Bert Levino, had already undergone its first vicissitude. It was to survive many more.

Its origin was a play called "The General", the sort of play which is put on and runs for three nights in Budapest and, so far as I could learn, something of that sort had been its fate. It had the kind of plot which, when you read it, you imagine must be turned down immediately by every management in stage and film, but, apparently, no.

The action was as follows. In the First World War the dearly-loved husband of the heroine, an unworldly professor whose researches are of value to humanity, is conscripted to serve at the front. His desperate wife learns that only a particular General, in command of that sector of the frontier and of dour and strict disposition, can excuse her husband his active service and makes her way with iron resolve to the front as a nurse, determined to beard the General and beg her dear one's life for her own and science's sake. The General is wounded, of course, taken to the hospital where she works, they meet, fall in love, and this new-assorted combination lives happy ever after.

(A few years later, we in Britain obtained from Hollywood a marvellous book called *Plotto*, listing and arranging all the possible plots that have been, or indeed can be, used in one guise or another. You will certainly find some like this in the index.)

It appears that the Hungarian author of this play had visited Hollywood, lunched at Paramount, talked casually about his ewelamb and, however strange this sounds, sold it immediately. Anyway, here it was, scheduled as the next picture for Rowland Lee when he had finished the one he was engaged on, with Walter Huston (the father of the current Huston, John) as the General and Kay Francis as the heroic nurse.

The first writers who received the job of adaptation were an experienced pair, accustomed to work together. Not long before, their improvisation had saved a misadventure. They had separated on receiving an assignment and gone their separate ways toward enjoyment, each relying on the other. When the time came to be recalled to Schulberg's office to tell him how they had been getting on, both had found themselves empty-handed. Immediately one had started improvising on the subject. When he ran dry, the other took it up, and when the second's imagination faltered for the moment, the first came to his rescue. So it had gone on, like a relay race or the game of "Consequences", and it had served very well. On "The General", however, they had come a cropper.

After due time, the usual verbal report in Schulberg's office had had to be made and the two had repaired there full of confidence to retail their "treatment".

They began in the usual way.

"August 1914, the eve of the Great War, Budapest...."

Schulberg stopped them.

"Has nobody told these guys the story has been changed to Moscow?" he enquired.

This had stumped the pair for this time their version had been rich in carefully mugged-up local colour, and Bert Levino had been sent for to start it all again. As I later learned, Schulberg had explained.

"The story is all right. There's nothing wrong with it. But who in America has heard of Hungary? Most people who have heard of it think it is a city. Now Russia is in the news...."

Evidently I had turned up just at the right moment.

Most of the time we worked not in the studio but at the Levinos' flat. Unlike my friend the neophyte Mr. G., we did not hurry. (Levino knew too much to allow us to do that. Our labours would be valued by their apparent thoroughness.) The gestation took several weeks and it was thorough. The atmosphere was pleasant, though the Levino couple, long married and much in love, had a deep sorrow. They had had two young children, not quite in their teens, and one, just before I came, had been carried off suddenly by some dread illness. Bert, who, slight as he was, was tough and leathery, would break off when the surviving boy came into the library in a way that was painfully touching. I have said that Levino was an exceptional man as a film writer. He was at once a complete professional — having worked in Hollywood from the very earliest days — and a well-read man specialising in early American history. His shelves of books upon the subject were *not* supplied by the yard by the studio bookseller. It was from him I heard the story of how they had made the first New Testament picture when everybody had doubled the roles of actors and technicians, and Jesus — doubling as principal and assistant director — had been seen with a lamb in his arms, crook under his armpit, kicking the remaining sheep into their positions. He was perhaps somewhat exceptional in his long marriage too. Mrs. Levino showed me a letter she had received from one of her two sisters. *What an old stick-in-the-mud you are,* the letter said. *There you are — still married to Bert, while X* — the other sister — *has been married twice, and I've married three times, and every time we've bettered ourselves.*

The treatment progressed as treatments do. Bumpily at first, while you argue over whatever issues you get it into your head are fundamental, more smoothly afterwards.

The opening precipice was obvious. To knock any seeming sense at all into the story you had, obviously, to account plausibly for the lady's change of love-object. A love powerful enough to induce her to embark on a sort of Joan of Arc rescue journey — not of her country in this case but of her husband — must fade to be replaced by love for the man who was the hated symbol of the very factors that had enforced their separation, and this chameleon change must appear sincere enough and justified and inevitable enough to the audience to evoke their sympathy. How?

The solution my co-conspirator accepted was my proposal. I can scarcely claim originality for it. I went to Shakespeare for help, to *Much Ado*. What is the classic case of convincing true love between characters who begin by detesting each other? Benedick and Beatrice of course. The gruff, grumpy General and the resolute nurse-wife might each resent the other as intolerable, but they were to be the only outstanding personalities in the hospital, gravitating together because of their distinction from the mediocrities in their surroundings, until their reciprocal rudeness turned to teasing and they finally found each other indispensable.

This idea was helped by the proposed casting — Huston, an oldish actor at the time, was a man of outstanding personality and dignity, Kay Francis a woman also dignified and handsome, radiating intelligence and poise.

We finished the treatment on these lines and the scheduled report to B.P. Schulberg took place in his office. This was the first time, save for a handshake in passing, that I had seen our destined director, Rowland Lee. Naturally, as soon as I had been put on our assignment I had wished to meet the director. It had seemed indispensable that, before we got too far, indeed at the outset, we must meet him and find out his ideas so that we could develop the subject with a knowledge of them. But no. It had never happened. He was always too busy on his current production.

Now the production was finished and he sat in at the conference.

The conference was a disaster. Rowland Lee simply iterated and reiterated that the script was impossible, he could never shoot such a treatment, etc. Schulberg did not say much, but he did not contradict him. We retired in poor order, I veritably shattered. In the corridor outside Rowland Lee asked me to lunch. After a pleasant lunch he asked me to his office.

Here he in turn resorted to a cigar, put his feet up on the desk, made himself comfortable.

"You know — this is not at all a bad treatment," he observed complacently, flipping its pages.

I was startled and taken aback.

"What do you mean?" was all I could manage.

"Yes, not bad at all," he repeated.

"Then why did you tell Mr. Schulberg you thought it impossible?"

"Oh, I always do that," replied Rowland Lee. "You may have wondered why I refused to talk while you were working on it. I always refuse to talk to writers while they are working out treatments for me. You see, if I did talk to the writers and work with them while they are preparing the story, it would be my story and I should have to defend it to the company, see? This way it's the Company's story, and it has to defend it to me. It's the only way you can get changes. In this one," he flipped the pages again, "I don't think we shall have to alter much."

He then proceeded to outline the "not much".

"There's not much that's wrong here except the casting and the way he falls for her," he said, mentioning the two principal features of the enterprise to date.

"How can you expect a man to fall for a woman who's so rude to him? It's not natural. You know: the way I see it is that he has a headache and she stands behind him and" — suiting the action to the word — "strokes his brow, like this, see. That draws them together.

"And another thing," he went on, "Kay Francis is wrong for the woman. Who would want to hump Kay Francis?"

I could have made a suggestion, but I forbore.

"What we want for that part," he concluded, "is a girl, fresh, full of the joy of youth."

He mentioned a young actress, pretty and talented, who was appearing in his current picture and whom I thought insipid, but who later confirmed herself as a rising star. As a matter of fact, granted this premise, he was quite right about the treatment. If this new girl was to play the part, this was the only way it could be written.

It did not take long for the new casting to be agreed by head office.

But twenty-four hours later everything was in the melting pot once more. "Have you heard the news?" Bert Levino asked me as I came into the studio. The Rowland Lee picture had been sneak-previewed the previous night, at a cinema in the suburbs, and had turned out a disappointment. Its reception had shocked the studio. Rowland Lee was immediately taken off "The General".

About that time, as I shall relate later, news came from the East of the meeting of Lasky and Eisenstein in Paris and Levino and I were taken off "The General". It was handed on again.

It had been my first Hollywood job, however, and I was still anxious to follow it through and learn as much as possible. Johnny Weaver was assigned to write the dialogue. Who was Johnny? He was a young poet whose long satirical poem about the New York social whirl had been the rage in intellectual circles there — and with the public — as I was passing through. As a success, irrespective of the genre in which he had achieved it, he had been at once snapped up and brought out to the West Coast, where he had since languished. I went to see Johnny Weaver in the "writers' block", a rectangular white building for their segregation consisting of similar small rooms on several floors. We might nowadays say it reminded us of Kafka or a concentration camp.

He told me he thought the dialogue good. This gratified me, although if so it owed most to Bert for dialogue has never been my strong suit as a film writer.

"Then you will not be changing much of it?" I asked.

"On the contrary, I shall change it all from beginning to end."

I was by now learning to be less surprised, but still I asked why and once more the explanation was irrefutable.

"You see, I have been here six months and during that time not one line I have written has been used. Suppose

I return this script now and say that there is not much I can do to improve the dialogue, head office will say: 'What do we pay this man for?' To save myself I must rewrite it."

I have only two further episodes to recount to finish the story of "The General". I had better relate them, because, although they happened later, the subject's total adventures may help to set the scene for the Hollywood of Eisenstein's visit as nothing else could do.

Several months later I heard by chance from J.G. Bachmann that Mrs. Patrick Campbell was in Hollywood. As we now know, recent times had been hard for Mrs. Campbell and the sally Hollywoodwards had been somewhat of a desperate throw. I told him what a giant she had been upon the English stage. She must not be allowed to leave without Paramount using her in something suitable. Harry Herzbrun, in charge of contracts, had interviewed her. Later I asked Bachmann what came out of it. "Nothing," he replied. "Harry had it all fixed up and then he asked her: 'What salary do you want?' Mrs. Campbell told him she did not know, but what did George Arliss get?" George Arliss at that time was getting thirty thousand or forty thousand pounds a picture — a lot for those days — he was at the top of his profession as a drawing card. How was poor Mrs. Pat to know that she, unknown to the film world, could not be at least on a level with one who in his old days on the stage had been but a support while Mrs. Campbell ruled the roost?

I asked what she had been going to play. I was told: "The brothel-keeper in 'The General'." "But there is no brothel-keeper." Oh, yes, there was. A brothel scene had now come in. In its present stage of preparation the current director-in-anticipation was a Frenchman.

The narrative shifts yet several months on. The contract between the Eisenstein group and Paramount had been dissolved by mutual consent. Everything was very friendly. With full studio approval we were being done the honours of a final go-round the studio, so that we might pick up any little bit of knowledge that could help the Soviet cinema on the boys' return. They picked up bits of the sound-proofing too, discreetly off the walls behind their backs. Is this what is called 'economic espionage'? Perhaps not. By this time such materials were no great secret. (Many years later, when I took the first Soviet sports delegates to Britain to Wembley and to Wimbledon the visitors had full consent of their hosts to dig up with their penknives cubic inches of the sacred turf of football field and centre court as samples for their own groundsmen back home.)

First we visited the mausoleum of dead tunes. In the music department stood rows and rows of files, painstakingly arranged and labelled: *Mother Music, Infant Music, Battle Music, Sad Music,* skinned and extracted from the living originals like the rows of mice in the cabinets of the British Museum (Natural History) at Cromwell Road. Last in this belated Grand Tour came a visit to the trick stage. Here I was particularly interested in a giant glass backing representing a night scene of a city under snow, a wide river wending its way between classic buildings. "And what is that for?" I asked. "The opening scene of 'The General'. It is St. Petersburg," was the reply.

The snow had come back.

I never saw the picture when it was released.

Bull's-eye

It was not to be thought that I did not have any social life while all this was going on.

It seems that the Fairbankses had asked Shaw for the film rights to *Caesar and Cleopatra* — this was long before the days of Gabriel Pascal — for G.B.S. wrote asking me to discourage them. They had just shown *The Taming of the Shrew* in London and Shaw did not think much of them as talking actors. As a result of conversations I was able to write to assure G.B.S. that, if the rights were granted, Douglas at least had no intention of playing in the film. But this put G.B.S. in no way at ease. I received the reply that, as for Douglas not participating, it was unlikely to matter what he wanted, but only what Mary wanted, and that not for the world would G.B.S. have him play Caesar. "His voice is rather like the howling of a wolf."

Douglas was just off to Britain for the Open Golf Championship (under the tuition of, I think, Gene Sarazen he had become an addict) and when I conveyed Shaw's continued refusal to him he said loftily that he would make the time to see Shaw and talk the matter over.

In the meantime, Mary asked me to lunch. The lunch was a curious affair. Included in our select company were a visiting English peeress and her lady companion. Mary did her best to induce me to persuade G.B.S. that, if *Caesar and Cleopatra* was ever to be filmed, and only Hollywood *could* provide the necessary resources of course, no one but she could play it.

"After all," she said, "Mr. Shaw is most insistent in the play that Cleopatra, when it opens, is only a young girl just starting on her teens. Well, I am the only actress in Hollywood who is capable of playing a really young girl and also accustomed to act as a Queen."

As she said it, it was perfectly easy to understand what she meant. In fact, I am sure she was right.

This was the signal for the peeress to start gushing about how dear Miss Pickford was such a wonderful actress. There was no one like her, no one in sight who would ever be to films the same as she was.

Mary smiled with — shall we say "Queenly" — condescension.

"You forget our younger generation," she said. "You forget Miss Twelvetrees." Helen Twelvetrees, a budding lead of the period, whose competition the reigning monarch certainly did not fear, remained dumb and embarrassed as, indeed, she did throughout the meal.

However, when Douglas came back the matter had advanced no further. "I had fixed up to meet Mr. Shaw," he told me in the Turkish bath when once again we had our clothes off. "But just an hour before I was due to call somebody rang up. Your prince (this was the Prince of Wales) wanted to play golf with me."

I think in this case G.B.S. was mistaken and Fairbanks was indeed no danger to *Caesar and Cleopatra*.

Fairbanks was a wonderful figure of an athlete, a wonderful colour of health, and what he brought to films in the silent days of sweeping, almost balletic grace of movement and gesture is without equal. But this weakness of his was a byword. Charlie once greeted him with the exclamation: "Hullo, Douglas, how's the duke?"

"What duke?" came the reply.

"Oh, any duke," countered Charlie.

I heard from one present of the embarrassment of those in Hollywood who were invited to attend Douglas' and Mary's showing of the film they had had made of their voyage round the world — the trip on which Douglas had turned up at the old Wimbledon and asked what they would like him to do, "go on the centre court holding a racket or something?" and while in Moscow had seen and lauded "Potemkin". They had been made the centre of demonstrations of spontaneous enthusiasm and affection wherever they went and naturally the royal Hollywood couple wished to share their pleasure with their friends and show them the scenes shot by the accompanying United Artists cameramen as soon as possible. Unfortunately there had been time only to sling these together, and the cameramen had concentrated on what they thought would please their employers best. The travellers were shown arriving in Paris to the plaudits of the crowd, receiving the same cheers outside their hotel, the same in London, in Berlin, in Moscow, in Tokyo and so on. As the outside of every main railway station and every luxury hotel looks almost exactly the same everywhere, picture after picture seemed identical and the voyagers, for all anyone could see, might almost never have left home.

When the royal marriage at last ran on the rocks and their long and beneficent reign seemed over, Douglas came to Europe.

He took a large country house near London. Here an emissary from Hollywood called and tried to talk him out of finalising the divorce and to have him drop the fresh alliance he was contemplating with Sylvia Hawkes, due to become the next Mrs. Fairbanks. Douglas lay full length on his stomach on a sofa in the middle of the vast drawing room while the emissary tried to remind him how injurious the affair would be to the repute of Hollywood, how it would tarnish what was then not yet called its "image", etc.

"It would not be so bad," the emissary cried, "if Miss Hawkes had not been just a mannequin — a mannequin!"

This was too much for Douglas. He raised himself on one elbow and turned upon his tormentor.

"Mary sold bananas in Toronto," he interrupted.

With Charlie matters were still entirely blocked. I used to call often at the studio to ask about my introduction, but there was never any reply. "Mr. Chaplin has not forgotten," the studio manager, Mr. Reeves, used to assure me. "He wishes to do something for you. He is anxious to show his deep respect for Mr. Shaw and for Mr. Wells. Only at present he cannot think what to do."

Mr. Reeves was one of two Englishmen who had been with Charlie almost ever since he had left the Karno touring company to stay, and achieve fame and fortune, in the film colony. The other, Mr. Robinson, had quarrelled with Chaplin at the time of the latter's world tour, been dismissed, and written an unkind, though in some ways percipient, account of their association published in France not very long before. Reeves remained ever faithful.

We became close as a result of a remarkable coincidence. Mr. Reeves was a South Londoner, like Charlie. Despite his fifteen years and more residence in California with Charlie, he had never become acclimatised in the slightest degree and he was desperately homesick. Hell is a South Londoner, too. One day I said to him: "I know exactly where you come from. You come from Camberwell just where it borders on Brixton. My wife comes from there, too, and you speak exactly the same." I am no Professor Higgins and my ear is usually not very good but even to me it was clear in their every intonation.

This made Mr. Reeves sympathetic towards me. I so obviously longed to meet Charlie and nothing ever happened. He made a suggestion: "Look here, I'll tell you what we'll do. One day when Mr. Chaplin is shooting, I'll take you round, just to show you the lot, like. And when we come to the set I'll say, as though in surprise: 'Why, there's Mr. Chaplin!'"

I was sorely tempted but I refused.

Cedric Belfrage had by now moved to Malibu and lived there in a sort of exile. I used often to go out for a swim in the Pacific. I was a strong though slow swimmer and I loved the immense breakers. In those days the beach was often pretty well deserted and you could go out beyond the point where they were crumbling into white, rest in the vast gently heaving swell, or come in a little and dive through or ride the top of each rhythmically passing wave. Cedric was isolated because he had somehow got under the skin of the publicity offices by the studio gossip he had sent to England and now found every door closed to him. His tiny exquisite starlet wife was literally frail. The towering waves I loved had twice knocked her over and broken bones with their mighty undertow.

I made new friends, most notably Nora Hellgren, a strong-minded liberal-tempered woman, with silver hair and a husband from Sweden, whither in later years they had to retreat when McCarthyism got going. Nora Hellgren had been in Russia during the early days after the October revolution. She used to tell how she had worked as a secretary in the Foreign Affairs Commissariat and it had been part of her duties to clip the "funnies" from the American papers whenever they came in and lay them on Chicherin's desk.

Fraenkel took me to meet members of the film colony from Central Europe. It had astonished me to learn that the principal Lawn Tennis club in Los Angeles, a city whose prosperity up to that time had been so closely linked to the film industry in whose foundation Jewish pioneers from the Eastern seaboard had played so important a part, banned Jewish membership. I knew that the New York Tennis and Racquets Club did, but had not expected such ways to be tolerated, even imitated out of snobbery, in the growing West. Many of the film incomers from Central Europe were Jews and, rather than contest this ban, Lubitsch, Korda and others, stimulated by Bachmann's young son, Larry, had got together to found a Hollywood Lawn Tennis Club with fast cement courts and, as resident professional, the aged but immensely knowledgeable and fine teacher Alexander, a U.S. doubles champion of the far-off years. He used to play in spectacles and cry out in a high voice at one's mistakes.

I was very eager to meet Lubitsch and this was arranged by a friend of Heinz Fraenkel, Paul Kohner, dark, elegant and young, who worked at Universal. He introduced me to a poker circle that met regularly and which Lubitsch — up to that time the only first class foreign-language European director who had ever come in to Hollywood and achieved in the end a permanent success — regularly frequented.

I can play poker. As a child I studied it in the Encyclopædia Britannica, but this gives you only the mathematics, not the psychology. The latter only comes with practice, so I would admit to being a tyro. But here the situation was worse. The game was stud-poker, where only part of the hand is hidden. As a result, there are certain stages in the game when you can know with absolute certainty that your hand must be the winning one. For example, you might hold four kings and know from the cards exposed that none of the few other players still left in could possibly hold four aces or a straight flush to beat you. Yet, even so, you still felt in deadly peril.

The trouble was the divergence between the salary scales of those sitting round the table. To some a loss of a few hundred dollars might mean necessary retrenchment in the next weeks ahead. Others would not notice a loss of thousands. I do not mean that the rich took advantage of this position deliberately. I am quite sure not. But as the evening advanced there were always a few drunk enough not to notice that the exposed cards proved they must have lost already, that is if the proper fifty-two cards and only these were in play at the time. As the bidding rose to thousands of dollars, I would be horrified at the idea that somehow, even by accident, fifty-three cards might be in play and there might be a fifth ace somewhere so that I might become involved in argument, debts, losses beyond my compass. If I had a weak hand, of course I would throw my cards in early and lose little. But if I had a strong hand, even a winning hand, and went on, there must come a stage when the drunks had carried on to the heights where I dared not follow and then I lost a lot.

So, although I played poker too in Paramount circles, I was an obscure, miserable, mean and steadily losing player. (Later I tried hard to get the Excise authorities to admit my poker losses as expenses when I applied for the certificate of payment of income tax necessary before an alien quits the country. The tax form defined expenses as "money spent in defence of income" and I argued that poker losses came under this heading because I had not wished to play poker, or enjoyed playing poker, but had had to accept invitations to poker parties or risk offending my employers. However, I did not get away with this either.)

At one poker party Paul Kohner took me aside. He had heard from Fraenkel of the Eisenstein interest in coming to Hollywood. Was Eisenstein really free, and would I be prepared to come to Universal next day and talk about it to its head, Carl Laemmle? Universal had just earned a huge revenue and just acclaim by their production of "All Quiet on the Western Front". Kohner was a bright favourite of the elder Laemmle in the front office, and it was evident he thought Universal's appetite might have been roused for a new spectacular production shaded slightly pink.

Carl Laemmle, Sr. was an elderly gnome-like man, bald, round-shouldered and very kindly. He blinked through his glasses and rather shyly asked me many questions about myself, my work, my past, Eisenstein's availability, the subjects we had thought of and so on.

I gathered that he was very eager to conclude the deal. We were just beginning to discuss possible conditions when the door opened and his son came in. Carl Laemmle, Jr. was the same height as his father but his total opposite. Smart, dapper, handsome, black-haired, clad in a white silk shirt and white kid riding breeches with gaiters, he sat on the edge of his father's enormous desk with one foot on the ground, switching his riding crop while his father pleaded with him. His greeting had been perfunctory and he said but little. From the way he shook his head as his father explained matters it was clear he would have no truck with it. My impression was that his opposition was less related to any feature of the proposed engagement of Eisenstein itself, as to the fact that the initiative for it had derived from Kohner, that he resented the latter's influence and was determined not to let him score a point if he was able to prevent it.

The scene became embarrassing. There was no point in wasting further time and I decided to leave. As I closed the door I could hear Carl Laemmle Sr. still pleading: "But Mr. Montagu comes of a very good family...."

Setback, but then at once success.

On the heels of this incident the news came through, almost simultaneously via telegram to head office, report in the daily press and Louella Parsons' gossip column. The long-awaited meeting in Paris had taken place. Lasky and Eisenstein had reached agreement. The whole unit would come to the West Coast, the contract would be signed in New York on the way. The reports added that among the subjects to be considered for production was *The War of the Worlds*.

This climax made no immediate difference to the position at Paramount. I was still helping to tidy up whatever stage "The General" had by then reached. It was agreed that as soon as the Eisenstein unit reached Hollywood I should become absorbed in that, but as Bachmann, to his and my delight, was to be our Associate Producer, much would still remain the same. A good deal remained to be arranged before they came out however. Of the details I heard part from Schulberg, part in letters from Hell.

Eisenstein would leave early, but the others would have to stay behind in Paris for a time. There were ties to sever, debts to settle, loose ends to be left neat. Hell joined them in Paris, where she found them in a modest hotel whose name had appealed to Eisenstein as propitious: *Les États Unis*. Other residents included Erna Ruttmann, Walther's wife, a short, handsome woman with a tight-black Eton crop, and that miraculous grotesque dancer of Berlin cabaret and player of sinister character parts in films, who has survived into our own day to bring it a breath of between-wars Kurfürstendamm decadence, Valeska Gert. My sister Joyce came out too for a time, but, being no Bohemian, stayed on the Avenue Georges Cinq.

At last the laggards left for the New World on the Île de France. At the last moment they were somehow joined by a newcomer, a brother of the great stage producer Granovsky, then touring Western Europe, named Boris Ingster. This young man was almost the double of Grisha in height and build and colour, but of less prepossessing features. It was evidently his ambition to reach the United States, where he has certainly lasted longer than we did. I see his name now on my television set as producer of "The Man from Uncle".

In New York Eisenstein met them and pressed into Hell's hand one hundred dollars, telling her it was her first week's expenses. This was the only money she or I ever received as members during all the collective's work together. He was busy being lionised and at a party, as the press reported at the time, he repeated a gag he had already brought off in Paris: In this period it was the legend that Russians were all gloomy, half-insane characters out of Dostoyevsky and some imbecile asked the famous question: "Do the Russians ever laugh?" — leaving himself wide open to Sergei Mikhailovich's equally famous answer: "They will when I tell them about this party."

Let it not be thought that Eisenstein was at any time, even for short periods, a playboy. He was a man of the utmost energy, of all-embracing and all-absorbing interests, who made the most of every new place and scene he visited to see all, learn all, meet everyone. If art is the reproduction of experience transmuted by passage

Our House in Cold Water Canyon.

Vulgar Boatmen: Alexandrov and Chaplin.

The Lady's Not for Drowning: Hell surfacing in Chaplin's pool.

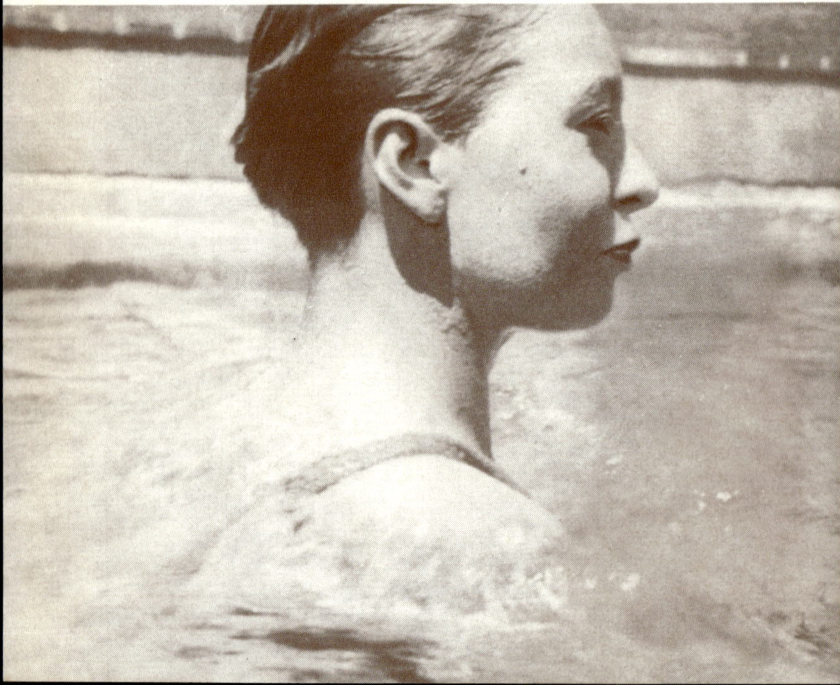

Homeward Bound: l. to r.: Georgia Hale, I. M., Eisenstein, Eduard Tisse and Charlie Chaplin.

Catalina ... Catalina ...: Eisenstein and Chaplin.

Gold Rush Baby: Ivor Montagu and Eisenstein with a veteran born in 1867.

through the artist's consciousness, Eisenstein everywhere and always acquired and stored the maximum of knowledge and experience to transmute. Hell found him on the threshold of yet another party, trying to fix up his unfamiliar tuxedo — a skill all three acquired outside their country — and worried lest his appearance might be ruined by the toothache that at the moment had swollen one side of his jaw and prevented him from shaving.

"It doesn't show, does it?" he asked her anxiously.

I regret to say that Hell, who has a reputation for candour, replied that it certainly did, and this perhaps won her leave to precede the others and fly out ahead of them to join me.

She stayed a few days with the Moskowitses, for at that period of air travel you had often to queue to get a passage.

I was waiting, eager for reunion, when suddenly the telephone rang.

"This is Mr. Chaplin's butler speaking. He would be glad if you would join him at his residence in Beverley Hills for tea tomorrow afternoon."

The voice was Japanese. It was, of course, that of Kono, the factotum, far more than any butler.

I burbled something about my wife just arriving in Hollywood and coming with me, was told to wait one moment and then assured:

"Everything will be quite all right."

Well, Hell did arrive all right. Douglas Fairbanks was at the airport, by chance, and greeted her. Heinz Fraenkel was there, too, and far too friendly to both of us for it to occur to him that he could be *de trop*. Would he never go? At last we got back to the hotel, and hastily unpacked enough for bath, dressing in un-travel clothes and preparation of party face, then rushed off to Beverley Hills.

In the Chaplin garden all was incredibly decorous and English county. People sat around. (Charlie afterwards confessed to us that this was an "occasional garden party" when enough people had piled up to whom he owed hospitality. From time to time he would nerve himself to hold one and rid himself of all the accumulated obligations in one fell swoop.)

Constance Bennett sipped her tea with little finger metaphorically raised as at any vicarage. Myron Selznick was there — the brother of the attractive, young and enthusiastic David Selznick, Schulberg's personal aide. Myron was feared and powerful, as head of the principal film agency in Hollywood. He was also a keen lawn tennis player and organiser of the film colony's annual tournament.

Someone, somehow, said — no doubt not in those words — "anyone for tennis?" Here luck struck. Los Angeles Lawn Tennis courts are, in general, iron-hard. Hence the ball bounces high. Hence such sloggers as Helen Wills and Ellsworth Vines. Hence, for the unwary, tennis elbow (I contracted it myself and suffered from it for years after). But it turned out that Charlie's court was the only one in Southern California that was not concrete. It was of a sort of clinging asphalt that took spin beautifully. I had thought there were no such courts nearer than San Francisco and it suited me to a T. (Spin was, in general, so useless on the concrete courts and so unused that it was known locally by the old poolroom jargon phrase "putting English on the ball".) I was in devastating form and in singles beat everyone else, including Myron Selznick, 6/o. Charlie I beat 6/3 and this was the foundation of a beautiful friendship lasting to this day.

Reader, do not think what you might think for you would be wrong. Charlie is — I suppose, considering our joint advanced years, *was* — an excellent player. He could run indefinitely, being superbly fit, and hit steadily, hard and accurately, forehand and backhand. (Indeed, he was so good an athlete, so perfectly supple and in command, that he would tease Douglas Fairbanks by beating him at everything the latter took up, be it running or lawn tennis. Only when his rival resorted to golf did Charlie throw up the competition, declaring that he would leave Douglas that refuge, here he would not follow.) At lawn tennis his steadiness counted, however, only at the back of the court. If you drew him to the net — which was not difficult with a drop on that spin-sensitive surface — he would become too excited to volley properly.

Anyway, it was a wonderful day. Back at the Beverley-Wilshire we had a lot to catch up with, and anyway sleep was out of the question for Ben Lyon and Bebe Daniels had chosen it for their wedding festivities and the rejoicings lasted far into the morning.

MEN AT WORK

Rooftree

As soon as the others arrived and as soon as we possibly could we got out of hotels and under a roof of our own.

J.G. Bachmann helped us to find a landlord. We found him at a party. His name was Ted Cook. He was a solid, quiet person, a man of taste. By profession he was a columnist, and ran a not very serious comment column syndicated up and down the country. He was about to leave for a sort of sabbatical year, and open to let.

His house was indeed a discovery. Can there have been a more easeful house, in more relaxing surroundings, in all the whole of Hollywood? The place? In Cold Water

Canyon, that is to say right at the end of a perfectly smooth road built into a remote and then unfrequented corner at the head of a valley in Beverley Hills. The house was a snow-white block up on the side of the mountain. The surrounding tops beneath which it nestled sheltered it from all but earthquakes, (which you must never mention, if you live in California). We had two that only shook the dishes.

The view led below, along the winding approach, with the nearest houses not too near and not too far. Once, when I left the car outside and forgot to put the handbrake on — I often forget such things — it ran straight down the hill and across the road below into someone else's field, nearer half than a quarter mile.

The house, of course, was Spanish-style. This was made mandatory by tradition and surroundings. Being new it could not have been real Spanish. But it was not in the least mock-Spanish. Ted Cook had employed Spanish workmen or rather, Mexican craftsmen, who had worked with love. The adobe and the plaster, the reds, blues, greens, yellows, the tiled patio between high-set bedrooms and the tall airy living room, all fitted in their place. The woodwork of staircases and pilasters, tables, chairs was all handshaped and solid, carefully rounded by the touch and pressure of man's hands. Cook had taken infinite pains and it was perfect, a joy to dwell in.

We could not live in such surroundings without servants. As soon as our intentions became known to friends, applications began to come. Choice was made more difficult by the fact that in addition to the more ordinary criteria, whoever entered our household must satisfy Eisenstein's sense of the exotic and the bizarre. We nearly chose a strong man, who sent us his photograph bald and with muscles bulging out his vest, declaring himself a rabid vegetarian.

In the end we chose a Negro couple, Rose and Lester — Rose for her beauty, which was considerable, as was her spread and weight. Her combination of qualities fascinated Sergei Mikhailovich, she was half Negro, one quarter Red Indian, one quarter Irish. Her post was cook and her only drawback that her cooking was limited. Lester, her husband, buttled in a short white coat. He was languid where she was gay, and much too capable, for when we discovered he took a commission in kind from every tradesman who visited the house, he convinced us that this was the custom in America.

Boris Ingster did not belong and soon he left us, to seek his own support. But not before he, too, had experienced the quality of this new country. This was the time of gangsters, "X marks the spot" and Al Capone. Out late at night Boris had been walking along a quiet road when a car pulled up beside him and he was ordered peremptorily to mount. The bandits took every cent he had, wrist watch as well and then informed him: "No hard feelings" but he would understand they must now beat him and leave him for senseless on the roadside in case he were too soon to shout for the police. Boris, who knew a few English words, pleaded for mercy, explaining that he had been on the way to a romantic appointment and that, if beaten unconscious, he would be unlikely to recover his strength sufficiently that night and so must inevitably disappoint his girl. The sentimental bandits thought this eminently reasonable, they released him unharmed and gave him back a dollar for carface.

Hell, who had to manage the household, ruled it with a rod of iron. This was essential, for little enough money came in and what Eisenstein allotted to the common expenses out of this was less. Our contract with Paramount, signed in New York by Sergei Mikhailich and Amkino — the Soviet film agents in America — on our joint behalf was not a contract of service, but simply an agreement of Paramount to allow expenses for a period of six months — $500 for Eisenstein, $100 each for the four of us (Grisha, Eduard, Hell and me), $900 a week in all — while we tried to find a subject for production on which both sides could agree. This sum was sparse backing to maintain a reputation on Out West even in those days. Perhaps I should explain how we managed, though even today it is not at all clear. The money was paid by Paramount to Eisenstein. (Incidentally, by a peculiar and ingenious accounting system — I have no idea whether it still obtains — all cheques from the company were made out on the Thursday and given out on the Friday *after* the payment fell due. Unless the recipient hurried to pay it into the bank the same day it would probably not be presented for collection by the bank it was paid into until the following Monday. No recipient was likely to quarrel with this system — why jeopardise a good job by claiming the petty interest on one weekly cheque — but by this system the company retained throughout the year one week's interest on its total wages bill which must have totalled a considerable amount.) Eisenstein held the cash. What did Grisha and Eduard need regular spending money for? They rarely went out alone. We had the remains of my original stake money and what I had saved from my first short earning period before they came. There were still the leftovers of debts in Europe to be paid off. The conditions of their Odyssey had made it necessary for the three to borrow in Germany to go to France, in France to go to England, in England to go to America and so forth.

Eisenstein was punctilious in regarding settlement of these a priority over expenditure in each new environment, and we two contributed to repayment of the backlog rather than received. The rest was for his spending. Not that there would not sometimes be a shopping spree, when the boys would get cameras, or, back East, overcoats. It was not in the least that Sergei Mikhailovich was greedy, but when he bought books, as he did continually and copiously, he would say: "The others know the books I read are on behalf of all." The place of household expenditure in the queue was very low. Sergei Mikhailich each week would himself pay the outgoing bills. How we accomplished the miracle I do not know, but we were never short of anything or had to refrain from any activity we wanted.

It was not because of money shortage or even principle that Hell and I insisted there must be no liquor in the house. It was sheer prudence. None of the three drank, but all were angry. Quite reasonably they felt we should be lacking in hospitality if our guests had to go dry. Everyone else kept liquor, prohibition or no prohibition. But I knew we should be vulnerable. Not only was there professional jealousy — von Sternberg helpfully gave an interview in which he belittled the arrival of Eisenstein, saying that he was an airy-fairy theoretician and no real film-maker — but, and we were later proved right, sooner or later politics was bound to rear its ugly head. The studio was influential, and a police raid would have been a scandal, yet . . . it remains true that one man can steal a horse, the other dares not look over the fence.

Now we were ensconced, comfortable and with no more bickering than may be found in any happy family. Lasky arrived Out West and we were immediately bidden to dinner. Paramount was going to look over its new pigs in a poke.

The party was intimate: Lasky, Mrs. Lasky, Schulberg, Mrs. Schulberg, Hell, another woman to keep the balance, Eisenstein and I.

After dinner men and women went into separate rooms. This seemed an odd practice to me. I know that in pukka English households the women must postprandially leave the menfolk to their cigars and to the brandy which females are not supposed to tipple and the rude stories which they are not supposed to like. But if both leave the table, why separate? Anyway Hell did her best to keep her end up in the lone hen party, laying down the law on paintings in the colony's private collections she had not seen but whose quality she guessed from having met their owners, and finished with a reputation as an art critic that lasted out our stay in Hollywood.

We four men, in our other room, leaned back in the depths of our impossibly padded, doze-inducing, deep armchairs.

It was then that we made our first and, I firmly believe, fatal mistake.

Lasky spoke:

"Mr. Eisenstein, Mr. Montagu, now that we are alone together — what *do* you think of our pictures?"

Neither Sergei Mikhailovich nor I was foolish enough for either to look at the other. But we both hesitated a fraction too long. A fraction of a second was enough.

It did not matter what we said after that.

The Fleshpots

From the start Sergei Mikhailich and I disagreed about one thing. I felt that we had no time to lose. I have seen it all many times. When you are signed on by the firm you are the white-headed boy. Publicity has been at its peak to convince the world that the company has just acquired a genius. Nobody could be so rude as to contradict the boss in that atmosphere. Then is your chance and you must strike while the iron is hot.

Later on, when familiarity has had time if not to breed contempt at least to take the edge off novelty, then it may be too late.

Everything, however, was against us acting on this precept.

Six months seems a long time when you are young. Our contract provided: expenses for six months pending agreement on a subject, when new terms would be substituted. Hollywood in the persons of our kind hosts kept urging us, as Hollywood always does to newcomers —

settle down, absorb atmosphere, find your feet first. Why hurry? When we thought of doing so, there was always the fascinating new world of a thousand facets all around us. And the relaxation of Cold Water Canyon.

To Sergei Mikhailich, everything was strange, exotic, examination-worthy. Not only was there America in all its variety, but corners of other civilisations to be tasted. Like other U.S. cities, Los Angeles contains colonies hardly touched by English speech. Eisenstein and the boys found a Russian unorthodox community whose church services and private affairs were all conducted in their native tongue.

Here again he was the lion. Invitations had to be accepted, parties attended, lectures to universities given. It was not the fleshpots that had to be tasted, so much as sights to be seen, people met, ideas pursued.

Though the expression had not yet been invented, "culture vultures" were a-wing in flocks.

I remember two old ladies coming to tea and confiding to us that, though Mr. Eisenstein's lecture the previous day at the University of Southern California had been "so interesting", it was a pity that it had not been given in English. Needless to say the lecture *had* been in English, and perfect linguistically. It was the technical jargon of aesthetics that had got them down and so perhaps their comment was not so far off the mark as it appeared.

It reminded me of the time when I had taken Sergei Mikhailovich to cash a cheque made out to him at a bank in Leicester Square. The teller had looked hard at that dome of brow and at the incredible squiggle — it was a sort of Japanese-style pattern he was very fond of — and said:

"Is that your signature, sir?"

Eisenstein could only answer: "Yes."

"Then, sir, would you mind kindly *drawing* your name."

There was a young couple called Seymour Stern and

Christel Gang, who were as worshipping as the young Herbert Marshall had been. They ran a paper called "Experimental Cinema" and asked us specially for a contribution. I translated for it a short article by Eisenstein: "The Cinematic Principle and Japanese Culture" in which occurs perhaps the clearest brief statement of Sergei Mikhailich's cardinal principle of the creation of a new, third effect, by the conflict, or collision of two others, the basis of his graphic and dramatic aesthetics. He was insistent that the syntax should be followed exactly. At that time, he disliked simple sentences in writing with subject, verb and object. He wanted them simpler, consisting sometimes of just a clause, a noun or verb alone.

Eisenstein specially admired the work of Disney. He had already declared in Europe that Walt Disney was the only man working in the United States who used sound film properly, associating the action in Mickey Mouse with sound chosen for its arbitrary effect. So of course we all visited his studio to meet him and came away with drawings autographed.

A meeting of the Hollywood Motion Picture Academy of Arts and Sciences was astonishing. Here Grandeur Film and other of the many attempts of the day to enlarge the screen sideways were being discussed. Eisenstein complained that a wide screen would deny access to all the aggressive male shapes like trees and factory chimneys. The discussion led to his famous article "The Dynamic Square" in which he called for a screen that could change shape according to the composition best suited to the nature and context of the image required to be shown.

In the course of the argument a Fox cameraman, who was making the first picture in the new wide shape, observed that it was true that, with the system used, a face could not be shown in close-up, but that this would not be felt as a limitation because the whole image would be so big that even the expression of features not in close-up would be clearly seen. Incredible as it sounds, had Eisenstein and the boys not been there, *no one* would have pointed out that the role of close-up in cinema is not so much simply to make something visible as to concentrate attention on it by excluding everything else.

Nothing could have indicated so clearly as did this meeting the degree to which Hollywood's art was a pragmatic art — its achievements (and nothing can diminish these, as a general standard they were far in advance of those of any other country) depended on trial and error learning. No one had stopped for a moment to consider what was really being done.

We made double car trips in the neighbourhood. The boys in one, Hell and I in another, keeping together.

One was to a show ranch, the home of millionaire William King Gillette, whose portrait and signature appeared on his every safety razor blade packet. The boys were determined, they said, to see the home of a man whose name at that time was more widely known throughout the world than Lenin's. The ranch was set in a ring of arid hills and was in no way distinguished except for some exquisite Chihuahuas in the garden. I thought I had stumped the guide when I asked him how William King Gillette got rid of his used razor blades, but he showed us a slot in the lapis lazuli bathroom wall, whence an oubliette-pipe led down into the foundations.

Another excursion was to the redwoods. We were all of us overwhelmed by the majesty of these great trees and the beauty of their surroundings. Eisenstein then and there must have resolved not to miss using them pictorially. (He includes them in their phallic glory to heighten the scene of erotic struggle in the script of "Sutter's Gold".) The Fox cameraman who had argued with us at the Academy meeting had promised us that, contradicting our fears about wide screen, we should actually see a very strong tree scene, and of a Big Tree at that, in the concluding sequence of the pioneer film on which he was engaged. When we attended the première and this scene came on it was set in the redwoods all right, but it proved to be a struggle to the death between hero and villain *wrestling on the recumbent bole*. Incidentally, at the souvenir kiosk I bought for my brother in England a pipe of reddish wood — he collects pipes. The bowl was carved in the shape of a feathered Indian's head, but when the stem came out the concealed part bore the legend "Made in Birmingham".

Our most ambitious journey was into the desert, then Yosemite and return. The desert road runs past Death Valley and the heat is considerable. It was a strange experience to open car windows to get air and have to close them again because it is hotter out than in. Sands surrounded us on every side. There was nothing else to be seen but prickly pear.

Suddenly our companion car far ahead on the ruler-straight road completely vanished. It was there and then not there. What could have happened? When we drew level we discovered that, with their mania for self-photography in romantic surroundings, on sudden impulse the three had swung their car 90 degrees around straight off the road to take a picture of themselves posed in front of a giant cactus. Fortunately we remained on the road. All went well until the picture was taken. Then, when the boys tried to remount and resume the journey, it turned out that, of course, the sand below the wheels was so dry the car was immobilised. There they were, not ten yards off a perfect motor surface, as hopelessly stuck as though they were on a greasy pole. The wheels revolved, the sand grains flew, nothing happened. There were no coats or blankets to put beneath the wheels. Grisha and Eduard were strong, but even they could not lift and carry the car a distance of ten yards. Fortunately they were also resourceful. Soon four golden streams were irrigating and binding the sand just in front of the rear wheels. This was enough. The wheels got their starting grip and the journey could be resumed.

The beauties of Yosemite have been described so often they require no space here, but an instructive incident occurred on the journey back. The road runs straight, mile after mile, and along one valley it runs through mile upon mile of peach orchards. Presently you come to a dingy township consisting of small board houses and surrounded on every side by orchards. Across the road was flying a tremendous streamer: *Welcome to Selma, the Home of the Peach.* We stopped for lunch. At the end of the meal, concerned to sample the local product, we asked for a peach. Consternation. No one in Selma had ever sold a single peach before, nor could one be found. A case of peaches, yes, though possibly the least they could sell was a gross of cases.

If this story seems strange, try to get any fish in the Scilly Isles, or even a Dover Sole in Dover, that has not come frozen in a box.

We made new friends. Eisenstein got on with King Vidor. Heinz introduced us all to the Viertels — Berthold, Viennese Socialist and humanist for whom I was afterwards to act as Associate Producer in Ealing on "The Passing of the Third Floor Back", and his wife Salka. One day when we were all talking round the coffee table, the bell rang at the door and Heinz got up to answer it. A tall young woman with bare legs, in a lightweight tan-coloured dress and sunglasses, stood outside.

"And who shall I say is calling?" enquired Heinz.

I suppose he is almost the only man in the world who could have failed to recognise Greta Garbo.

We only met her this once but we became confirmed as fans for life. She radiated warmth, serenity, good sense and solved a problem which had been bothering us, Hell especially. After the novelty wore off, none of us really liked Hollywood parties. Yet we felt it necessary to go, especially when the invitations came from studio bigwigs, in case they should think us high-hat when we refused. Only the previous night there had been a "Moonlight Beach Dance" at Malibu which seemed to have gone on and on. To make sure of his moon, the host had suspended an artificial one high in the air, and as the regular one had been normally on show as well that had given us two.

Garbo's advice was perfect. "It is true you must accept," she said. "They don't like you to refuse. Accept and then don't go. Nobody ever misses anybody."

From then on we followed her counsel.

Of course we met Upton Sinclair. This legendary world-hero, the Red David who had challenged Goliath with *The Jungle* and *The Brass Check,* had become pink by now. Settled in California, now white-haired and wearing glasses, he had grown domesticated, secure in the friendship of a noble elderly woman who spent a fortune on human causes. He made us welcome and gave us good moral support.

As a special honour — and I still appreciate the warm intention behind it — he invited us to a quiet dinner to celebrate his sixtieth birthday: Eisenstein, Hell and me, himself, his wife and the lady philanthropist.

Halfway through dinner Mrs. Sinclair turned to me and said:

"You know, Mr. Montagu, whatever happens now to the Russian revolution, it has been a wonderful help to Upton and me in our propaganda."

I found myself as speechless in reply as when we dined with Lasky. Nevertheless, as later time unravelled, the Sinclairs, despite all zigzags, still had much good work ahead.

Friends from Europe visited us. First my sister Joyce, then later Sidney Bernstein, came out to look over Hollywood while we were there. We took each in turn to see Charlie, for we were with him most of all.

Charlie's home and garden became our second home. We would always ring up and ask Kono before dropping in, but Kono, who, when he wished, could be an impenetrable wall, treated enquiry from us as a polite formality. Sometimes we would be rung up and asked over.

We were always on the tennis court, for Grisha and Eduard took lessons and attained an earnest minimum. Even Sergei Mikhailovich bought ducks and tried pursuing the ball with a sort of savage spite. He spoiled all by wearing braces and scarlet ones at that, as well as a belt for security. When I told him this was improper he was downcast, but reassured when I added that braces for tennis were a practice of the late Lord Birkenhead.

Charlie's court had lights for play by night. One night an aeroplane flew low over the twinkling lights spread over the blazing landscape, the pilot from time to time shutting off his engine and bellowing through a megaphone a call for everybody to go to the current next première. Seeing the blaze of our tennis court on the hillside he circled low, switched off and shouted tentatively: "Harold Lloyd?" Charlie was furious and yelled back at the top of his voice: "No! 'City Lights'!"

This was the name of his "Work in Progress" at the time.

I had met Harold Lloyd at a party. To us he was quiet and courteous but talked of nothing but real estate.

Charlie had an organ in the house and used to play it regularly, but the joy of his Beverley Hills home in those days was the swimming pool, built by an architect to an exact copy of the inside outline of his famous bowler hat. It was a sybaritic pleasure to plunge in after lawn tennis, to lounge by in the sun with ever and anon a cooling dip, to bathe in alone with Charlie in the after-dark warm with no lights but the far-off Hollywood sparkle. We would hold onto one side and tread water, exchanging confidences about our respective pasts and hopes.

One day when we were all there, with my sister, we set out to encourage Hell to swim from shallow end to shallow end across the deep. Hell can swim, slowly but adequately, if she plucks up resolve to, but she prefers to dwell in her own depth.

However, under encouragement of Charlie this time she ventured. Steadily, bit by bit, she approached the middle. Now she was across, nearing the shallows.

"Good. Good. Splendid. Come on. Now you're all right," urged Charlie.

I have never forgotten Charlie's face of astonishment as she took his last encouragement literally and tried to put her feet down, only to sink to the bottom like a stone. She was only out of view a few seconds, fortunately, and rose spluttering, to be fixed on a negative as she did so by Grisha with a Leica.

One night I bathed in the dark alone and turned the light on to enter the pool dressing room. As I was putting my clothes on I looked back and found that when I had felt for the light switch I had put my hand in the darkness within an inch of a large tarantula on the wall. I kept my eye on it carefully as I finished dressing, alarmed lest it should be offended, and gave it a wide berth as I sidled through the door and ran. There were plenty of these things — the big hairy ones, so-called bird-eating spiders — in the hills. We found a body of one, crushed by a slipper, on the verandah at Cold Water Canyon one morning, outside our bedroom. Its bite is, however, much less dangerous than that of the smaller and more furtive Black Widow, which is also found in California.

Once Charlie was caught in a situation despite Kono's best precautions. A young man-about-Hollywood of perfect exterior and elegant manners — here designated Count B. — one day brought to Charlie's two visiting Spaniards, men of infinite dignity and intelligence but who could not at that time muster one word of English between them. Only Sergei Mikhailovich was fluent in their language. The name of the older was Ugarte — a noble writer, I learned to know him in the Spanish war. That of the younger and darker with a flashing eye was Luis Buñuel. Charlie's two children by his second marriage were visiting us, Charles and Sidney (what an excellent actor the latter is now), two dark-curly-haired small boys with an accordion. Ugarte entertained them by making little horns with his forefingers and prancing light-footed before them as a bull while Buñuel helped to teach them passes with their handkerchiefs. That afternoon was a triumph, but less so two days later when Count B. arrived once more with his protegés, deposited them on the lawn, and dashed off to keep an appointment with a girl. Sergei Mikhailich happened not to be there that day, and we had a complicated four hours trying to converse with Charlie's few words and otherwise by signs, for although Buñuel spoke French excellently it never occurred to the rest of us to try him out in it.

Thanksgiving Day was a special day for the Hollywood English. Hell and I, alone in Hollywood for the moment while the others were in New York, went round to Charlie's. Lawn tennis in the sun, a swim, an English Christmas dinner. We were replete, Charlie was mellow. Feeling expansive, he started to tell and act for us the entire story and every gag of "City Lights", until then a pretty secure secret. This was the most dreadful experience of my life. I have a habit of going to sleep on the most embarrassing occasions: in the front row when a delegate-of-honour at conferences, particularly when an important speech is being made, as a number of unfortunate newsreel films and photographs testify, but then sometimes, perhaps, my unconscious *wants* to go to sleep. This was different. A unique privilege, a unique opportunity, a marvellous entertainment, something that I had longed for months to happen. But what with the exercise, the meal and the fire — yes, a roaring Xmas-style log fire — I could not keep my eyes open. I felt that I was not only missing treasures irreplaceable but that I should be disgraced forever. Hell loyally kept pinching me from time to time but, alas, every pinch roused me with a jerk only for a moment. I retain only scraps and how Charlie missed my nodding I shall never know.

This incident merits a comment and an addendum. The comment — it had long been my conviction, started by the scene with the peasant-boy's wounded hand in Pudovkin's "End of St. Petersburg" and sustained by working with Hitchcock, that a good director must have something of the sadist in him. I do not mean necessarily to a pathological degree, but that his way of looking at things and telling characters to do this, undergo that, is necessarily akin to dominating them, ordering them about. I noticed now, and indeed on other occasions, that Charlie speaking of films in which he himself plays as well as directs, identifies with the director, not the actor. He does not see himself as we see him, that is, as the Little Tramp. The Little Tramp is a third person, whom he, the director, makes receive the buffets of fortune and so, indeed, he speaks of him.

The pendant is that Charlie did at last show us some rough-cut scenes from the film itself, still later, when we were staying with him, and I am convinced that they were funnier then than when we saw them "perfected" at its première. I have thought since — it is only a guess of course — that at that stage, and in some cases later, his unique position among film-makers of being able to spend as long as he likes on a film paring it and paring it away has not always been good for the result. Quite often — and he has not escaped this either sometimes — a film at première turns out to have been left at too great length, and ten minutes or so removed turns out to be a great improvement on release. With some of Charlie's scenes, the reverse. For with comedy it must be excruciatingly difficult to get exactly the right length of a scene, you look at it yourself again and again and the more often you see it the more judgement must become jaded, so that you let the scene run too long or cut off the gag just before maximum effect. My impression, for instance, is that the scene in "City Lights" in which he steps forward and back outside the shop, each time missing the hole left by the descending lift, was more hysterically funny at this early stage than when its polishing was complete.

One of the telephone calls from Charlie's house earlier that year had taken us all down to Venice on Independence Day. The fun-fair was blaring as we shied at everything and walked along the front avoiding firecrackers. There is a habit in America of throwing firecrackers into parked cars on such occasions and it is not uncommon for total casualities in one twenty-four hour period to exceed those in the War of Independence.

Another took the five of us on Charlie's yacht to Catalina. I questioned him about the desertion of the studio this implied. Our trip meant cancellation of shooting for three days when all the technicians, cast and crowd called for that morning were already waiting on the set. His answer — unanswerable as are all reasons in Hollywood: "There are days when I wake up without an idea in my head. What would be the use of working on such a day? The result would be no good."

Our seventh passenger, who was often with us at the house and pool, was Georgia Hale. The career she should have had after "The Gold Rush" had failed to materialise. A studio quarrel which her independence and uprightness forbade her to compromise had brought about her blacklisting and, when we knew her, she was trying to cultivate her voice in the hope of opera. She was a fine person and, I firmly believe, one of the few women in Charlie's early life who cared for him frankly and unselfishly.

One evening, returning from the Hollywood Bowl with a girl friend she went for a late bite to Henry's, the restaurant run by the faithful actor of that name who graced so many of Charlie's later films for about fifteen years. Henry Bergman came over to their table and they grew sentimental together.

"Ah," said Georgia. "Three hearts that beat as one — yours and mine and Charlie's."

"Yes," replied Henry, "and they're all thinking of the same thing — Charlie."

When we retold the tale to Charlie in Georgia's presence, Charlie considered, then admitted: "Yes, it's true."

Charlie told Georgia, and told us, that a gipsy in San Francisco had warned him he would have three unhappy marriages before happiness. That was why, after his two divorces he must not think of a third wedding. Primitive myth, the Greek classics — for example *Oedipus* — and modern literature such as *Lord Arthur Savile's Crime* contain many examples of the prophecy that contributes to its own fulfilment. This is the best example I know of in real life.

What sort of man is Charlie? I cannot tell because — I declare my interest — for me he can do no wrong. Whatever he may be or do, ever, he has created so much delight for mankind his credit, by any right proportion or standards, must be infinite. One *likes* people *despite* their faults. But those one loves have no faults because one cherishes them as they are.

The crude stories told against him are nonsense. I remember a Hollywoodian, X, the "tramp writer", who had briefly been in Charlie's employ, inveighing against him at a party, sneering at him for intellectual pretension. "He has a library full of the books of the day, but he has never read any one of them from start to finish." This was very likely true, but to put it in proper proportion one should realise that there was probably not another star of his eminence in the Hollywood of that day, or any magnate, who had a serious library at all or had even looked at any of these books, whereas Charlie had looked into them all and had ideas about them he could present with point.

His enemies alleged that he was money-mad. They fed this fiction with the story of what happened when, on the arrival of talkies, M.G.M. made a grand synthesis of separate talking "bits" by all the biggest-drawing silent stars ("Hear the stars talk"), relying on star-appeal and novelty to make it a gold mine. "I was in a jam," said Charlie. "If I agreed to do it I should have made a fool of myself, because I had never spoken on the screen and it could harm the picture I was making. If I refused, everyone would have thought me crazy to turn down the offer of good money for a couple of minutes. So I agreed, and asked a million dollars. They went away muttering, but at least my reputation as a commercially-minded film man was intact."

If he repents good deeds, at least he does them. In "City Lights" he typecast a gunman. When the day came for the shot the gunman was in prison. Charlie pulled all the strings imaginable, and the authorities sent him to the studio under escort of two armed policemen. Charlie was embarrassed and terrified. The policemen sat in the studio while the gunman made up. Behind the curtain he told Charlie that he had been grilled for forty-eight hours and was at the end of his tether. He implored Charlie, somehow, to give him a chance to get some sleep before he sent him back. The shot already in the can Charlie made excuse after excuse for retakes, sending the poor devil behind the curtain for make-up each time, all the rest of the shooting day. When all was over, in his relief he sent him packing and hoped never to see him again.

Who is there who does not like to have his cake and eat it? After the U.S. Lawn Tennis Championships at Forest Hills, the great "amateur" stars usually come on to the Pacific coast, the Los Angeles Lawn Tennis Club managing to raise their "expenses" from the money received for courtside boxes from the stars and magnates; many of the latter, being Jewish, would not be allowed into the club as members. Just before the event Louis B. Mayer rang me up and invited me to his box. It was kind and courteous of him, but in those days I was impetuous and intolerant (I hope that, in such matters, I may ever remain so). I told Louis B. Mayer plainly why I would not go and, by plain implication, what I thought of people, especially Jewish people, who were prepared to support the tournament under such conditions.

When I told Charlie about this, he was torn in two. He swore he would never have taken a box had he realised the position. But he had so looked forward to it, and since he had paid already... He compromised by going and making loud remarks uncomplimentary to the club whenever anyone was listening. Later he brought the stars to Beverley Hills (the mountain to Mahomet in this case) and Berkeley Bell and I beat Charlie and George Lott, which caused me great delight, Charlie as usual playing his strokes too quickly at the net.

Charlie is not a Jew or of Jewish origin. He attributes his black curly hair in youth to a Spanish strain. But he has rigorously refused ever to deny publicly that he is a Jew. He says anyone who denies this in respect to himself plays into the hands of anti-Semites. From Germany in the thirties I sent him the filthy Nazi propaganda book of photographic portraits of Jews, *Juden sehen dich an* (Jews are looking at you). His portrait was included and the caption began: *Dieser ebenso langweilige wie widerwärtige kleine Zappeljude....* (This little Jewish tumbler, as disgusting as he is boring...). Charlie is no sort of correspondent and the present evoked one of the only three letters I have received from him in the course of thirty years' friendship. I like to think it had some part in stimulating "The Great Dictator".

Human beings are compact of opposites. Charlie's youth, as he has described it so well in his autobiography, made him a combination of toughness and sensitivity. Without the second, he could not have created with sympathy as he has. Without the first he could not have got through. Like many sensitive creative artists he experiences alternating moods of pride and self-doubt. At one time toward the end of "City Lights" he was on top of the world. There were passages about which at one moment he would be supremely delighted. They had come right, they would be remembered. They could be thought of in the same breath with moments of Shakespeare (who, by the way, is not one of his favourite authors either). At another the film had not come off. It was a certain failure. No one would pay to see it. At one such crisis we were travelling in his car, and he cried in despair: "I shall be ruined!" Georgia tried to reassure him: "It's not as bad as that, Charlie, you'll still have a million dollars left." But Charlie was not to be reassured. He groaned on without interruption: "What is a million dollars? What can you do with a million dollars." For a moment I was startled and might have thought, as so easily anyone might, that his anxiety was rather inordinate, but reflection made me realise what he was talking about. Charlie's whole being, at that stage of his creative career, depended on his freedom, the liberty he had won so hardly to be free of employers or the exigencies of a slave-driving distributor. With two million dollars, he was free to make what he wished, how he wished it and still be free to go on despite any failure. Down to his last million he would be back to being the servant of these masters once again. That second million was the minimum cushion an artist in the film world needed for freedom.

One day we gave an evening party (strictly dry) to people we knew and liked in the tall living room at Cold Water Canyon. We sat about on the wood chairs and the gaily coloured mats. At that time there was a vogue for a horrible, sadistic parlour game. You agreed a list of qualities, such as good temper, sense of humour, beauty, intelligence, etc. These were written down on two sheets of paper. The chosen victim went outside, carrying one list. This he marked with the number out of a ten maximum that he thought he deserved for each of the listed qualities. The poor devil was then called back into the room and asked to read out his self-awarded marks, while each was echoed by the corresponding mark a consensus of those remaining had meanwhile agreed on as the right one.

I know of no more cruel game.

Soon the lot fell upon Charlie. He went out and there ensued a discussion about his sense of humour. "4" was finally agreed upon. Charlie returned and was clearly taken aback when his would-be-modest "7" was undercut by our "4". But our "9" for "Charm" consoled him. Alas, when, later Eisenstein went out, Charlie endured the assembled company awarding Sergei Mikhailich "8" for "Sense of Humour" (the "Kindness" award for S.M. was pretty low), but it was too much for him when we wished to mark Eisenstein's "Charm" as "10". Only God himself could deserve "10" for "Charm", contested Charlie.

Nine or ten we had evidence of Charlie's charm a little later on. At that time Charlie would never sell any of his pictures to the Soviet Union. Amkino, from New York, kept pestering us with letters to find out why and try to do something about it. Charlie explained that it was not because he was in any way anti-Soviet, but business was business and the money they were offering was less than he would get for a film from one middling-size town in the United States.

"Look at the size of the place on the map," he would say, pointing to the U.S.S.R. stretching over Europe and Asia.

I used to explain all about the five-year-plan, the need of the Soviet Union to import machinery, the shortage of valuta. He would not budge.

"It is the principle of the thing," he said. "Pictures are worth something. They give Henry Ford valuta for tractors and my pictures must be worth at least as much as several tractors."

Again an unanswerable argument. Just about then came news of the sale of some of the Tsar's furniture, and I had the bright idea of suggesting to him that, instead of valuta, he should take a few of the Tsar's armchairs. It might have worked, but about this time we had a letter from Monosson, the grey-haired, grey-moustached old bureaucrat who ran Amkino and had signed, together with Eisenstein, the agreement on expenses with Paramount, to say that he was coming out to Hollywood to see things for himself.

He was not a bad old stick, was Monosson, but as soon as he arrived he insisted on meeting Chaplin immediately.

"Once and for all, I will determine Chaplin's attitude to the Revolution," he cried.

Charlie was shooting and we duly took Monosson round to the studio. On the floor he sat resolute but fascinated as Charlie continued with his shots, but between takes the latter came over and sat with Monosson, exerting the famous charm. Monosson ate it all up, open-eyed, thrilled to his very marrow.

Presently, at something Monosson said, Charlie commented:

"That does not sound very Communist to me.... Are you a Communist?"

"Not exactly," replied Monosson. "I think you might call me a Soviet conservative."

It was not Charlie's relation to the Revolution that had been established.

Fairy Gold

I pause here for breath. It must not be thought that this Life of Riley we were leading was a mere self-indulgent round of dissipation and wallowing in fleshpots.

We were working hard all the time, in our own way, although, as we shall see, the work was blighted in the bud. So far I have concentrated principally on the pleasant sides of life in that Hollywood epoch and it was right to show this because those sun-bathed days and star-studded nights were not unpleasant. But perhaps I have let myself be carried away. Never for one moment did any of us lose sight of our common purpose, and this was different from that of many of our co-adventurers who also made the pilgrimage to Hollywood. We did not seek career together or personal success. Our objective was — to make, with the nearly unique resources available there at that time, one picture that should be faithful to our principles of life and art. No more, no less. This is the story of how we failed.

I have spoken, for example, of Eisenstein's acceptance of lionising, not only here, on the West Coast, but all along the route. Of course he liked it, but not in the least from empty vanity, as a peacock would like it. He revelled in it as I have already in some degree tried to make clear, because of his immense, dominating appetite for experience, for the unrivalled chance it gave of direct contact with unfamiliar forms of society and personalities previously known to him only through literature and newspapers, the buzz and variety that make up the beehive of the world.

Everything, everybody, had to be inspected and tasted. Nothing was not grist to his mill, material that might be worked on — if not immediately then sometime in the unforeseen future — to be absorbed into his knowledge and bring nearer to universal truth the representations it might some day be his lot to create. I have noticed this all-absorptive energy in other creative personalities besides Eisenstein. It was marked in H.G. Wells, who when I first met him would talk avidly with anybody to measure his own ideas against their know-how in their own particular field. (Near the end of his life, things changed, and he only wanted to talk to people to confirm his own ideas. This evidence of the rigidity of old age served as a profound warning to me, and has given me a mistrust not only of my own ageing but of the limits of that state for everybody.)

I am quite certain that it was the same with Chaplin. Denigrators have seen in the middle section of his autobiography a mere catalogue of name-dropping. It is true this part is not so well written as the first, perhaps because it was not felt so deeply, but those who read it in this condemnatory sense quite misunderstand Charlie's character. He is as far from being a snob, intellectual or of any other kind, as any man can be. The clue is his avidity for knowledge and experience. Human nature he knew from those who shared his life in youth but his fate at that time kept him inevitably outside the periphery of world affairs. When success and the lionising that went with it gave him the chance, he seized with both hands and without illusions the opportunity to see everything, inspect everyone — study from outside those who seem subjects in the syntactic relationship of which the common man is object — to find out, as far as possible and quite undazzled, how the world ticks.

Eisenstein was a man of the same stamp. And because his learning and his interests were so all-embracing — I have already called him a Leonardo and he certainly united in his grasp the two cultures whose growing separation has roused the alarm of C.P. Snow — so nothing he experienced was not gain for his creative work.

There is, also, perhaps in all show business, inseparably in large-scale show business where money dominates and art is commodity, the world that Hollywood was and

T.V. is today, a hard-headed business aspect to what in other atmospheres might rank as playboy idleness. The more people you know, the readier you are to share their life uncritically, the stronger the insurance against suspicion and eventual isolation. This was an especially important factor in such circumstances as ours, poised precariously in an alien land of alien thought. For me, the enforced state of suspended animation when a blare of music you would never willingly be subjected to for its own sake mars or even precludes all intimacy with those accompanying you, is a foretaste of the tortures of the damned. But he who cannot go willingly to a party where others see no boredom, he who cannot sit in a nightclub and share the relaxation of others, is inevitably construed as implying criticism of their standards. I do not mean, of course, that there was any Machiavellian scheming to win victory by a hypocritical masquerade; just that, abroad, Eisenstein had superbly that essential ability to *mix*. He did it naturally, but it was done for all our sakes and that of our task, and I certainly do not know any other Soviet film director who could even have approached him in this vital talent, without which our enterprise could not even have begun, let alone come near fulfilment.

None of us ever doubted each other's part in this common aim for a moment. I have written of the unity and dovetailing of the three at work. In Hollywood this same unity embraced all five. Three of us — Sergei Mikhailovich, Hell and I — had occasionally acid tongues. (I do not include the other two here, for Grisha, in English at least, was somewhat restricted by the language barrier and Eduard taciturn.) But this notwithstanding and despite a tactical difference I had with Eisenstein at this period and our dispute at the end, despite the wholly different temperaments and characters of our peculiar group, those were indeed halcyon days.

The tactical difference was on this matter of a choice

of subject, for we did work hard at it, much earlier and more attentively than may be suggested by the last section of my narrative. *The War of the Worlds* was, by tacit consent, soon dropped. *The Devil's Disciple* was never a starter. Eisenstein had brought several possibilities with him in his mind's kitbag from Europe. Some that have been mentioned since in various accounts did not come into the running. The Haiti idea, for instance — *Black Majesty*, the story of Christophe and Dessalines to feature Paul Robeson — never came up at all as a proposition for Paramount and was only spoken of when the Paramount deal was over and straws were being clutched at.*

One serious piece of baggage Sergei Mikhailovich had brought with him, however. This was Blaise Cendrars' *L'Or*, an historical novel called in English translation *Sutter's Gold*, a story as rich in sociological implication as in personal and melodramatic romance, based on real events and characters from the early history of California.

Imagine a Swiss who abandons his wife and children to pioneer in the New World and who becomes one of the richest men in America — the type of the one-time American ideal, the cosmopolitan poor boy who "makes good". In ripe age he decides to send for his family, but they arrive to find him ruined and penniless, impoverished by what? The discovery of gold on his estate.

Should not this make him richer yet? But no. From all over the world crowds gather to dig, to exploit the new discovery, to create San Francisco. But first in the great rush are also all the peons and servants on his — Sutter's — great estate. His barns and byres are filled to overflowing, the land is bursting with fruitfulness, but there is no one to move and reap the grain, pick the fruit, milk the cows. On one plane, a poem of romantic irony, on another a parable of the nature of real wealth. And it actually happened.

* See note, page 345

What dished the project — as I saw it at the time — was what seemed to me an unreasoning obsession on the part of Sergei Mikhailovich for "The Glass House".

There were only these two in it. Paramount seemed ready to accept "Sutter's Gold". But Eisenstein preferred "The Glass House", which was only an idea.

The idea was this, as Sergei Mikhailovich explained it. People live, work and have their being in a glass house. In this great building it is possible to see all around you: above, below, sideways, slanting, in any direction unless, of course, a carpet, a desk, a picture or something like that should interrupt your line of sight.

Possible, I have said — but in fact people do not so see, because it never occurs to them to look. The camera can show them to us, at any angle, and the richness and multiplicity of possible angles in such a setting can instantly be imagined. Then, suddenly, something occurs to make them look, to make them conscious of their exposure. They become furtive, suspicious, inquisitive, terrified.

Fantastic, you would say? Even silly? But it was not at all in this manner that Eisenstein saw it. He did not see it as fantasy. He wanted to embody his idea on the most mundane possible plane. A serious, down-to-earth, ordinary story. He would patiently explain that such houses did exist, already (or "nearly already"), in our present-day civilisation. He would point, for example, to the system of American origin and then coming more and more into vogue, where in great concerns — banks, newspapers, counting houses, drawing offices and the like — everyone has his desk in a single huge hall, the manager and the clerk, with the only difference between them their names in gilt on a little three-sided rod resting beside the pen-tray. And where everyone works away, not bothering with anyone else, until perhaps some unexpected disturbance, such as the incursion of a robber, makes them conscious of their fellows.

It was of course quite true. Structurally, architecturally, his analogy did indeed exist. (Almost such a glass house was built soon after my return to England for the *Daily Express* off Fleet Street.) But nobody could see it. Nobody could see that this was happening or could happen.

I was no help to Sergei Mikhailovich in this situation. All I could see at the time and, indeed, right up to the writing of this book, was that in "Sutter's Gold" we had a perfectly good subject. If we agreed upon it with Paramount — so I thought — we should at once be able to clinch our deal. (I certainly underestimated the rocks ahead.) I could not see "The Glass House". It seemed to me simply an obstinate crotchet, a whim.

Now I am not quite so sure.

Is it conceivable that Sergei Mikhailovich saw more deeply than any of us supposed and that his conception, though he could not expound it to anyone for he was not clearly conscious of it himself, did reflect something that his "antennae" felt specifically in America and even, in relation to the general human condition, we can now see had a prophetic ring? In America, much ahead of Europe, the urban conglomeration was leading to an indifference of man to the interests of his close-packed fellows and a savagery of mutual mistrust when crisis made him conscious of the crowd. Now most mechanised civilisations are following this path, purblind toward the population explosion, and we know more now than we did then of the nervous aggression toward one another of rats and other part-social animals enclosed in a confined space.

Sergei Mikhailich was penetrating, in his political insights as in other fields. In later years he related to me vivid cameos of Soviet life that helped me much in understanding of developments there. And I remember that about this time he gave me to translate an essay he had written on the probability of a monolithic state system entailing a "monotypy" of form in art to correspond. I do not think it was ever published, either in Russian or English, but it comes back to me as a similar example of "antennal" prevision. He may have found warrant for the prognosis in past history, and with hindsight the connection looks simple enough, but up to that time there had been little in his own or others' direct experience of Soviet cinema to account for it.

Anyway, at that time he had, or at least vouchsafed, no explanation of his addiction to "The Glass House" and received no help from anyone. Indeed, his persistence made me angry.

Not that Paramount obstructed. Any writer we chose was at our disposal. The response of the American writers was uniformly barren. No matter how firmly we tried to convey to them Eisenstein's idea, that is, that the story we wanted must have nothing whatsoever fantastic about it, that it must be a perfectly normal and recognisable contemporary story but — just — set in a glass house — one and all could see it only as whimsy and started off, if with anything, with a sort of fairy tale beginning: "Once upon a time".

We tried to find writers more and more hard-bitten. Oliver Garret, for instance, author of scripts for current gangster films whose realism we much admired, just shrank as though deflated when the idea was explained to him, and became as whimsy as the rest.

I would not play. Grisha tried his hand and came up with something centred on a nudist club. But even that bright idea failed to jell.

At this stage something very unfortunate happened. We had met at Charlie's a psychiatrist, a certain Dr. Reynolds. I know the popular idea of a Mad Doctor is not that he is a healer of the insane but one who himself is eccentric. Dr. Reynolds really was eccentric — at least he was stage-mad. He helped promote the only (at that time) serious Hollywood theatrical circle, then an amateur occasional affair though it grew to repertory later on, and even played in it himself. His cadaverous unwinking earnestness appealed to something mischievous in Charlie, and you may see him for a moment walking on in "City Lights". Alas, it appealed to something in Eisenstein, too. He began to spend hours — and cash — sitting with Dr. Reynolds on our balcony being analysed to find out the obstruction that prevented *him*, himself, from thinking of a "Glass House" story.

Fortunately this could not go on. We lost weeks but at last the day came when Eisenstein gave way. "Sutter's Gold" it should be.*

At once all was action.

Eisenstein was ready for the switch. I have described in a short memoir how it was his habit always to mark the books he read. He would underscore passages, write in the margin, all indications of the possible visual treatments he could see in the subjects as he went along. (This did not always profit him, for his habit was always to buy every book that attracted him, retaining it for future consultation. His one-huge-room flat in Moscow had all its flooring covered. You could hardly take a step in it, there were piles on every hand — it was a veritable sea of books. As every book addict knows, it is impossible to find the book you want when you want it, under such conditions. If Eisenstein really did need to consult one, he had to go out and buy another copy.)

On this occasion, however, the marked copy was ready to hand and his thoughts in order. He also had a précis from me, notes of incidents and characters, grouped and sorted out in concert with him, which still exist.

We instantly planned a visit to Sacramento valley, to the old, deserted gold diggings, to absorb the atmosphere and soak up the scene, before the writing started.

For some reason we left Eduard behind, with Hell. I cannot think that it was only cruelty. Perhaps it had

* See note, page 345

something to do with travelling light and swift and not wanting to use two cars, but this could not have been a reason holding water. Anyway, it was sad. Eduard was in a low state. He had been suffering from serious headaches. I had taken him to an oculist who declared in astonishment that Eduard had the longest-sighted vision of any man he had ever seen — could this have had anything to do with the wonderful Tisse depth-of-focus compositions? If he had not had the strength of an ox, said the oculist, he would long ago have broken down. Now the muscles with which he had unconsciously adjusted his sight to nearer objects were failing him. He must wear glasses. Eduard was not a fool, he obeyed, but one could see that he felt his spectacles as an affront, an advertisement of physical blemish or decline. Then all the tension of waiting, the obvious need at some stage, for the cameraman, above all others, to see the setting and the scene, and now to be left behind. Eduard was hurt.

Our dash north was swift. A glimpse of the empty valley, the streams that had been panned, the once-teeming gold-digging villages now empty save for spare, almost troglodyte figures of oldest inhabitants waiting to spin yarns to tourists about events they could certainly not have witnessed eighty years before. A visit to the San Francisco waterfront, more notes by me of everything that struck us as odd or pertinent, Leica snapshots by Grisha, and then dash back again. But the broad outlines of treatment were ready in Eisenstein's mind.

The team was ready, too, to work at pressure. The three were accustomed to this, indeed preferred it. Finishing "October" in Moscow in 1927 the pressure had been so great they had had to receive injections to keep awake.

We worked like a conveyor belt, round the clock. Paramount provided typists in relays, translators, reams of paper. Cold Water Canyon became a factory. The pattern of work was so:

Eisenstein would be closeted with Grisha, narrating verbally the treatment he had planned. Grisha would go off and write it. As soon as it was written it would be typed and translated. I would take an English text, read it and go to Eisenstein. Now he and I would go through it, discussing and making emendations. Then I would go off and rewrite it. Hell would receive my manuscript — my handwriting is so erratic that few, if any, can cope with it but she, and I have never learned to master a typewriter, so she would have to type fair copies. The Paramount staff would then make more copies of this final state.

This process meant, of course, that Grisha would always be two or three reels ahead of me. While he was on, say, the draft of reel four, I would still be discussing with Eisenstein the revision of reel two. Eisenstein would have to keep the whole thing in his head and switch from one to the other, like a chessmaster giving a simultaneous display.

It did not take very long overall. Then, like all scenarios, the script in its various copies had to undergo scrutiny of those whose pronouncements would decide its fate.

I do not propose to discuss the work at length. The purpose of this narrative itself is, largely, to act as introduction and, though copies deposited by Eisenstein at the Museum of Modern Art have long been available for study by the few, it is here included and published to a wider readership. It is a romantic poem, based on historical fact, embodying a social theme. Although Grisha and I shared credit and, indeed, contributed to its authorship it is of course, like its successor, a true Eisenstein creation. Eisenstein always devised his scenarios as, in a measure, prose poems, works capable of being read, the prosody and punctuation carefully laid out and timed to enable a reader to visualise the succession of images that the film was to comprise. Some unnecessary weaknesses were due to speed or circumstances — for example: incendiarism used as climax in *both* Reels 6 and 7; and the dog left behind to die heroically in the grim scene at the end of Reel 2 reappears later at his side as a convenient reminder of lost love smouldering beneath Sutter's stern exterior. I imagine that this latter error was simply because Eisenstein had not yet considered in which guise the animal could be more useful and I, in hurry, overlooked the flaw.

But by and large it is necessary to see these scripts in the setting of the period and the stage of development attained by sound film at the time that they were written. Except for a very few innovators, like Hitchcock, film-makers were still bogged down in the all-talkie, the exact correspondence of image and its natural causally associated sound. Now, of course, the use of imaginative sound in other associations, transcending literal naturalism, its elevation to new planes of realism, emotion, satire, or psychological and social comment is quite familiar.

Only Eisenstein at that time visualised the full possibilities of film where music is not an accompaniment or an interruption but an integral part of the whole creation. And it is noteworthy that one composer (Alexander Goehr in his cantata*) has used the scenario as inspiration.

Now and in the future these scenarios will inevitably be principally judged by readers on their merits as narrative and the speculative merit of the effect of their images had they been achieved as films. But it is right also to remember that, had either been made when it was written, the subsequent development of cinema might have been speeded by a decade.

The reaction? At once: "Sutter's Gold" was splendid,

* Performed at the Leeds Triennial in 1961 (pub. Schott, London & Mainz; Esching, Rome; Associated Music Publishers, N. Y.).

just what one would have expected of Mr. Eisenstein. Paramount would have it costed at once. Next: it would cost too much.

We were up against a blank wall that nothing would shake.

In vain we used every argument.

I pointed out that Sergei Mikhailich was known as a master of spectacle. When Paramount signed with Mr. Eisenstein they must have known his style was not cheap drawing-room comedy.

No, it would cost too much.

How much would it cost? We demanded, and obtained, an interview with the costing department. The chief of the department was charming, amiability itself. But he refused to itemise. Which particular sequence do you regard as expensive, we asked. We will see what we can alter. Are you thinking, for example, of the rush of the gold seekers across the continent by train (Reel 5)? This does not need any great expenditure, we have planned to create the impression with only two or three shots with a backing painted upon glass.

But to everything, just a shake of the head.

All the chief of the costing department would say was:

"I know these things. I know the cost of production in this studio and I am not wrong. It would do no good to itemise. This is a three million dollar picture."

Three million dollars for a picture was not a triviality in those days, when a British production would rarely cost more than sixty or seventy thousand pounds. On the other hand, by Hollywood standards, it was even then not all that much, certainly for anything at all spectacular. However, whatever we advanced, all we could obtain was the answer:

"I know this studio. It is a three million dollar picture."

There were dynasties in Hollywood in those days and they intermarried. The chief of the casting department was the double brother-in-law of B.P. Schulberg. That is to say, he was the brother of Mrs. Schulberg and his wife was Schulberg's sister. There was a story of a studio where a relationship something like that existed and the boss one night won thousands of dollars from his relative playing poker and then next day raised the latter's wages so that he could settle it. No doubt the story was apocryphal. But such solidarity was not. Up against it, what could you do?

Schulberg tried to console us. Although the script was so good, and although they had agreed we should work on the story, it must be admitted — he said — that it was not really the type of subject that would interest Americans. Foreigners might come along and think so in their endeavour to find something indigenous, but real natives, no. It was their history, past and dead now. To try to interest Americans in it would be, say, like making a film in England about Richard Coeur de Lion or Henry VIII. The British — and the Americans too — are constantly making successful films about Richard and such characters but there might be some point in Schulberg's theory that we had missed. We remained unconvinced.

However, Lasky was away in the East and would soon be back. There was nothing we could do but await his return.

DENOUEMENT

Sudden Death

When Lasky came back he surrendered the fortress without a struggle. He had a new import from the East in tow, Horace Liveright, and a new excitement, Theodore Dreiser's *An American Tragedy*.

If any reader has worked in one of the really big concerns that is managed by a group, I do not need to explain to him the position. For experience has taught me it is always the same. To others, perhaps I do.

A big organisation, even if controlled by a board, needs top management. At the top there is always a jostling for position. Efficient management necessitates the devolving of responsibility for separate tasks and undertakings. Each man around the top is out to show his initiative and capacity to carry an undertaking to success. Each other there is out to thwart him and prove his rival unlucky with his enterprises, himself by contrast the more sober and efficient. The "little men", the weekly pay-check level company employees, are unaffected by these battles. They are the lower depths, barely shuddering as the tempests toss the surface of the ocean. The upper waters are very much involved. So it was at Paramount. We were, for better or for worse, Lasky men — it had been Lasky's idea to engage us. This meant that it was in Schulberg's interest that we should not succeed. And the execution was carried out neatly and efficiently.

It could not matter that we very much liked Schulberg and, I think, he liked us well enough. We often visited his family. His wife, clever as he, carried on a successful agent's business in rivalry to Myron Selznick after her husband died. There were several bright children of whom one, Budd, was to become a brilliant novelist — portrayer of the seamy America of his day. Jesse Lasky I knew very little of. I saw him only at far intervals and on formal occasions. He was only made human to me by a charming story of the early Hollywood days told me by Bert Levino. Fate had brought them together on a Western, Levino as the title-writer. Bert thought he had found a fine one, the perfect "splurge" or introduction setting the keynote of the film:

SO-AND-SO CITY — ONE HUNDRED MILES FROM WATER AND ONE MILLION MILES FROM GOD.

"That won't do, you know," said Lasky, fixing Levino

with a deadpan eye. "God is everywhere, how can he be a million miles from anywhere?"

Levino pleaded, he urged the succinctness, the expressiveness, the epigrammatic quality of his title. In vain. However, Lasky made a concession.

"How about," he asked, " 'So-and-so city — one hundred miles from water and *almost* a million miles from God'?"

This upset Levino almost more than the flat negative.

"Do you not see that it destroys the whole rhythm of the thing? After all, Mr. Lasky, you started as a musician," Levino tried one last appeal. (Unlike most of the Hollywood bigwigs of the day, who had been furriers or clothiers, Lasky had started in a band.)

"No, Bert," corrected Lasky modestly. "I was a cornettist." And *almost* it had to stay.

This story, to my mind, has completely the ring of truth. Lasky was a kind man, a just man, he was capable of decision and ruthless decision when this was unavoidable, but he wished to temper the wind to the shorn lamb.

Even so he dealt with us now.

In New York he had been faced with the démarche from the West coast reporting that his risky highbrow protégés had put in a script of doubtful public appeal that was going to cost too much. Could he support us? That, regardless of the possibilities of the script, would now involve sticking his neck out in a head-on clash with Schulberg. Could it be worth it? Certainly not. On the other hand, to let us down would be unfair. Here was this other, glittering, new toy that had come along. Two birds would be settled with one stone.

The fateful meeting was again a family dinner.

This time, besides Mrs. Lasky, was present Jesse Lasky Jr., a personable and fresh-faced young man. Eisenstein was sure he had seen him before — at a Paris night club — but as they had not been introduced then he did not mention it. Also present was Liveright, a thin yellow man with a hatchet face and grey hair. It transpired that Liveright, who was a famous and successful publisher, had long known the Laskys. He had issued, in slim volumes, a book of poems by Mrs. Lasky and another by Jesse Jr. entitled *Poems from the Heart of a Boy*. It had occurred to Lasky that Liveright, with his flair for choice of manuscripts, might prove useful to a big company like Paramount, with its huge picture output and consequent all-devouring appetite for stories. He had been persuaded to sell his publishing interests and had come to Hollywood with one valuable property as, so to speak, his severance pay from Literature, an interest in the film rights of *An American Tragedy* that had been lying fallow since he sold it to Paramount several years before.

There was no discussion. Sergei Mikhailich had painstakingly worked out modest means of shooting "Sutter's Gold" but it was not to be. Liveright, a cobbler to whom there was nothing like leather, passingly agreed that "Sutter's Gold" was indeed old hat, dead, past history, and the subject lapsed. What was needed was something modern, *An American Tragedy* for instance. How lucky that, at this moment, etc. . . .

The atmosphere was entirely warm, friendly, unconstrained but, without bruising it in any way, Lasky managed dexterously to convey that the Eisenstein group might have the wonderful privilege and unique opportunity of assignment to *An American Tragedy* — that is, if they would like it, of course. If not . . . .

We asked for twenty-four hours.

"No hurry, boys. Take your time."

We discussed the situation far into the night. There was not the slightest doubt in the mind of any of us. This was a sentence of final doom on the Eisenstein expedition at Paramount. We would never be allowed to make *An American Tragedy*. It would never be permitted to foreigners, some even Russians, to make *An American Trag-*

edy in the way we were bound to make it, the only way that persons of integrity with respect for literature could possibly make it. Sooner or later, someone in authority was bound, before it reached the screen, to wake up to what was happening.

It was not a matter of politics, so much as of self-respect. *An American Tragedy* is one of the stodgiest great books of literature. Stodgy it is — it would not be true or right to call it dull — because its virtues arise from the steady and concentrated accumulation of authentic detail. This detail, if he keeps at it, gives the reader an entirely convincing picture of the America of that time, its social distinctions, its ambition, its grinding machinery. It is the story of a crime, or not-quite-crime — which, is never quite determined. A boy, poor in circumstance, his petty ambition shaped by corrupt and menial beginnings, forms the resolve to get rid of his first sweetheart when the opportunity of a more glittering match presents itself. The rest of the long account turns on the event — murder or designed murder turned by chance to accident — and its inevitable sequel up to execution. The power and majesty of it — because it has this immense power — turns on the fact that it is not a mere crime story or thriller, not primarily even a study of personal guilt or innocence — this is purely incidental — but an indictment of a whole society. The criminal that brought about these events is not an individual, but all America of that period, acting on weak humanity.

How could we — not because we were all believers in Socialism to one degree or another, but because we were human and owed our integrity a minimum of loyalty — how could we, recognising these virtues in a literary masterpiece, pervert its content? And for us to make it straight, once this content was recognised, could never be allowed by a firm with responsibilities to the social setup such as are owed by an organisation of the magnitude of Paramount.

This was crystal clear. Doom lay ahead. We could develop the subject in no other way than with fidelity to its core. Sooner or later it would be stopped. Should we quit now, or march on to meet our fate?

It was my opinion, and I adhere to this guess, that Lasky had never read the book. If he had, he must have known the fire that he was playing with. But I am sure that was not his intention, nor did he wish to break up our association. Busy tycoons simply do not have time to read books of such length which require, to understand them, such a degree of application. What he knew was its fame. And he had certainly seen its stage adaptation in New York which, to meet the dictates of stage convention and the limitations of after-dinner entertainment, necessarily concentrated on the personal adventures of the novel and let the background slip away. As such it had been a success, and this is how Paramount, if they thought about it at all, expected it to be treated for the screen.

That we were right to suppose this was shown by the later vicissitudes of the novel as film subject, for it has been filmed more than once. The first time was by Josef von Sternberg, for Paramount, just after we left. It was hopelessly compressed and led to a suit for travesty by Dreiser. The second, better balanced as a film, was made twenty years later by George Stevens and renamed "A Place in the Sun". The names of the characters were changed too, the play adaptation was part credited and the relationships subtly altered with novelettish effect.* But such paths were not for us. A minor work has no claim to act as more than springboard when adapted for another medium, but a major deserves that any approach is made with respect for its essence.

* Sylvia Sidney was a fine Roberta in the first version, Elizabeth Taylor a fair Sondra in the second. Incidentally, the year 1936 saw both a "Sutter's Gold" made by James Cruze for Universal and a German version by Luis Trenkers "Der Kaiser von Kalifornien".

So our unanimous conclusion not to drop out at this stage, but to go on, doing what we had been asked to do but which we knew was not expected or understood, was taken with eyes wide-open. We were ready for what we got and although in the end the blow came when the attendant circumstances made its incidence least foreseen, it appears in perspective as one prescribed by the fates from the beginning, a truly Greek rather than just an American tragedy.

Having taken our decision we threw ourselves into our task with ferocious energy. The job should be done as well as it possibly could be done. The scenario must express, to the acme of the means that had been thought of at that time and resources as far ahead as Eisenstein could invent from his imagination or might emerge from our collective arguments, the quintessence of the book. It must emerge as clearly as possible, an honour to the original, to our powers of transposition and to cinematic art. It must add nothing, subtract nothing, but be faithful. We would go down, if down we must go, with flags flying.

How far we succeeded may partly be inferred from subsequent events, but in any case the scenario has survived to make it possible to judge.

At the time we saw nothing in the least heroic in what we did, but only what was natural and necessary. Now, with hindsight, I see a sort of comic precursor of Eisenstein's "Ivan the Terrible", when, with his daemonic creative determination, he put everything he knew into a graphic rendering of the clash of social forces of the period. I have written elsewhere* how others, guessing *post facto*, have supposed that in this film he had modern and contemporary parallels with the latter days of Stalin in mind. This is absolutely incorrect, the dates alone — the making of it in the depths of the war suffice decisively

* See my introduction to the "Ivan" scenario, pp. 11–17 (Bibliography item No. 7).

to disprove this. He thought of nothing but the correct solution of the task undertaken and its embodiment in the most perfect and expressive images. (This is confirmed by those who were close to him when he conceived and was making the picture — he intended no criticism and was solely intent on fathoming and vividly representing the true essence of a past patriotic glory, spots and all*). Parallels suggested themselves only when the film was nearing completion and its finished lineaments came into view.** To one intimate who then warned him that the final sections of his picture were liable to run into trouble he replied inflexibly, with the savage obstinacy of his integrity as an artist — I can see him with the spoiled-schoolboy pout so characteristic in such moments: "This will be the first time in history a man has committed suicide by cinema!" (In the event, the fate he foresaw did not befall him, it partly befell the picture.)

Eisenstein knew the book well. He also knew Dreiser, having met him in New York. The two respected each other and Dreiser was well content to have us working on it. There began a short period of study, while Sergei Mikhailich made on the margins of his copy the usual annotations, I read diligently, and by conversations and discussions we all familiarised ourselves with its contents. The atmosphere remained gay. With his immense facilities for draughtsmanship and ribald imagination Eisenstein produced many caricatures of the personalities of the "Tragedy" that belong to this period.

We had little time for Horace Liveright. Perhaps for no reason we did not take to him. He, not unnaturally, was anxious for the fate of his ewe-lamb and, not yet having found his feet and congenial company in his new surroundings, used often to call upon us.

I remember the first of such visits, only a day or two

* But Professor Veselovsky in a recent study quite disagrees with this interpretation of the historical Ivan.
** How and why is also discussed *loc. cit.* (No. 7).

after the dinner, which gave us the only contact any of us had, and that at second-hand, with the orgy side of Hollywood, so famous at that time yet wholly passing us by. Liveright arrived, composed in manner but obviously shaken to the core, having spent the previous evening with some writers. Immediately after dinner, when host and guests were sitting on the verandah and apropos nothing in particular, one of the starlets had taken off her clothes and so seated herself astride on the neighbour's lap with the natural consequences. "Was this usual?" enquired Liveright. Our own experience was inadequate to enlighten him, but I did recall that a visiting friend, when he first arrived, had been startled at being presented by the hospitable tycoon who was his host with the office copy of the casting directory and invited to choose a companion for the evening from its pages.

As can be seen from the scenario itself, with its fourteen reels outlined instead of seven, and its very different character and treatment, no less poetic perhaps but epic realism instead of epic myth, preparation needed much more industry than in the case of "Sutter's Gold". This intense work, though, was done mostly by Eisenstein alone. Certainly there must have been conversations with Grisha, but the first draft of his imagining sprang, as always, ready-armed from Sergei Mikhailich's head.

I think this script is especially interesting from a particular point of view. There is nothing like it in any other known work of Eisenstein — apart from the very differently treated, historically stylised and "conventionalised" film of "Ivan the Terrible" — in its adoption of the task of expressing plot and character. The "Sutter's Gold" script nobody but Sergei Mikhailovich could have shot, for the qualities are primarily *pictorial* and would have been elusive if eventually composed as a film without his special powers of visual imagination and realisation. But the Dreiser script is unique in his own *oeuvre* in that it reads much more like one of those exercises to his students in which he inculcated the laws of film representation by setting them to extract — in cinema terms — the utmost thematic essence of *another's* written creation. It is more anonymous, and although there was certainly no one else who might have seen the subject like this at the time, one can think of many another skilled director who today could take it as it stands and film it effectively.

He made no secret of his approach and taught lessons that I have ever since borne in mind and tried to apply. When you are trying to develop a film subject, he used to say, you should first try to sum up its theme in a single sentence. If you cannot sum it up briefly it is no good or you are approaching it wrong. When you have your theme expressed in a single sentence this must be borne in mind and dictate everything else. You then work out the development of the action in successive episodes; their content must each express the quintessence of a single aspect of the theme, and the content of the totality of these episodes — call them for convenience "reels" for that had best be their approximate length — must amount to the whole theme; their form must be such that each grows naturally out of the other and represents an increasing stage of dramatic tension. (I am not using his terminology nor am I attempting here to reproduce his words.)

The outline I have given here of each of the subjects we developed as scenarios shows sufficiently what we understood in each case the theme to be, and the reader who is interested can study reel by reel in the respective scenario texts how we understood the relation to it of the episodes.

Soon, much sooner this time, the conveyor belt process began to roll again. The translators, supplementary typists, sheaves of stationery descended once more on Cold Water Canyon, Grisha and I each took our turn in the room of Sergei Mikhailovich, Eduard when he could get them examined the sheets as they came from Grisha and grunted his observations, Hell typed my MS. all day and night for days on end.

Very quickly it was finished.

The result was electrifying. Lasky was still in Hollywood. There was no difference between his reactions and those of Schulberg. The same for Selznick, everyone who read a copy.

We were called to the studio and told that it was wonderful. Schulberg said roundly that it was the best scenario that Paramount had ever had.

Lasky said:

"We must proceed without delay. You should leave at once for the East to see at first hand the actual settings of the novel."

It is in upper New York State that many of the vital scenes, including the drowning of Roberta, are set by Dreiser.

He continued:

"I am going to New York. Are you ready to leave with me at once this very day?"

We hurried to pack our handbags. It was decided that the four of us should go this time. Hell was to stay alone in Cold Water Canyon and look after the house.

A day or two after we arrived in New York we were shown into Jesse Lasky's office.

On his desk was a pile of papers. He said:

"Gentlemen, it is over. Our agreement is at an end."

Tidying-up

There is not a great deal more to tell of this adventure, so what there is may as well be put down in black and white.

We were shocked, but not surprised.

Lasky pointed to the pile of papers on his desk, read some aloud and passed others to us to examine.

They were all letters denouncing Paramount for treason to the United States in having imported the "accursed Red dog, Eisenstein" — yes, there were such words — to defile its purity.

We had been aware that there were such letters. Indeed there had been something of a campaign from the very first hour that Eisenstein had arrived in Hollywood. It had been promoted vigorously by a Major Frank Pease, but with such intemperate abuse and not a little tinge of anti-Semitism that he had been regarded as a crackpot and it had been given prominence only by lesser scandal sheets. Later it had been taken up by a member of the House of Representatives. Hamilton Fish was his name. This man, an Eastern aristocrat in his background, had wanted to be a sort of precursor of Senator McCarthy, and had got House leave to form an investigation committee, eventual ancestor of the Un-American Activities Committee. But the times were not propitious. There was less intolerance, or more indifference, no doubt because of less anxiety or fear of the Soviet Union. No breath of disquiet or insult had ever been carried to us personally and it had made no difference to our lives. Bachmann used to show us letters and cuttings. Once the police called with copies, but as a pure formality; they were polite and brief. Otherwise — overtly — everyone ignored them.

Here they were, collected and carried east, and they served a purpose.

Everything was discussed, arranged, with the utmost courtesy on either side.

There was still a short time of our six months to run. We must not hurry, we must regard ourselves still as guests, with the free run of the studios and always friends. But still, what with all these criticisms and the difficulties that could be foreseen, it was wise to decide now, cleanly.

This would give us time to look around and make other arrangements. The scenario had indeed been so good, it was a pity, but....

The affair made its public stir at the time, it was bound to, but it was of course a less than nine days wonder.

However, there was time for Eisenstein to deliver one dig. Running in New York at that moment was a farce "Once in a Lifetime". The theme — quite standard in comedies about Hollywood — a young man involved almost unintentionally in the crazy world of cinema, suddenly lifted to undeserved success and as unreasonably smashed down again. It was a hit — everyone was talking about it. We all four went ostentatiously to see it and, when the press asked what we thought, Sergei Mikhailich replied that he was negotiating for the rights to produce it on the Soviet stage.

I flew back ahead, to rejoin Hell. When the others arrived a few days later, we considered possibilities. A Japanese firm offered an immediate contract for Eisenstein to stop and make a film on the way home. Sergei Mikhailich was eager not to leave Hollywood without exploring every avenue. We let it be known that he was available and fished for nibbles. Third parties raised hopes which came to nothing.

It was after Sam Goldwyn asked us to come round to see him that I put my foot down.

The scene is indelibly engraved upon my memory. When we went around to do business it was Eisenstein's custom to leave the formalities to me. We sat down around the office and I introduced everybody. Then Sam addressed us — he spoke to me, seeming to be under the misapprehension that Eisenstein needed an interpreter.

"Please tell Mr. Eisenstein," he said, "that I have seen his film 'Potemkin' and admire it very much. What we should like would be for him to do something of the same kind, but rather cheaper, for Ronald Colman."

Yes, every word. Evidently Goldwyn was real and not a legend.

At this stage I quarrelled with Sergei Mikhailovich. I was of the opinion that by thus offering himself he was becoming cheapened. We should attain no result and he would be devalued. I wanted to stop it.

Our financial situation was near the border line. Of the last resources that remained to the unit, Eisenstein, always generous if impractical, insisted on telegraphing one hundred dollars to Dovzhenko, who had just arrived in Germany on holiday. He remembered the shifts the three had been driven to when they had started their trip outside the border a year earlier and Dovzhenko was one of the few Soviet film-makers he admired and recognised as a peer. (Pudovkin too he respected as a director.) But what did that leave us with? How long could we hold out?

Two windfalls that now befell us showed a possibility of clearing everything up and coming out all square. I must describe them because they are as ridiculous as anything else that happened.

The first thing that saved us was my writing. Not anything that was published, quite the contrary.

Publishing houses did approach me for an account of our experiences. Till now, when a generation has passed, I always found good reason to refuse. "Once in a Lifetime", was a *succès fou* because everyone took it as an exaggeration. Characters running through the play were the seven Slapkin brothers (this or some similar surname). This was an obvious take-off of the Warner Brothers and, as a running gag, their every on-stage entry was absurd. My first introduction to the Warner brothers in actuality was when several large men, like so many sea-monsters, emerged from the surf at Malibu Beach with their names picked out in Hebrew characters in the peeling skin of their sunburnt chests. How write true history and be believed when nature in absurdity so transcends art?

What, indeed, brought us money was what was not published. Suddenly the two publishers with whom I had contracted respectively for an article and a book on ping-pong, each received a letter from the American firm of sports goods manufacturers, Parker Brothers. They demanded to see and approve in advance the text of what I wrote. If I refused (and of course I did flatly refuse) they threatened an injunction.

It is not generally known, except to specialists, that the justly popular name "Ping-Pong" is a trade name, like "Kodak" or "Gramophone", in this case registered by John Jaques of London, who retain their world rights in this word, except for the United States where they surrendered it to Parker Brothers. It was because those reviving the game in Britain in 1921, and later with an international governing body in 1926, wished to be free from any restriction in their organisation — not from any snobbish disdain for an excellent onomatopoeic word — that they had done so under its earlier designation "Table Tennis". Now Parker Brothers proposed to use their name-registration rights for censorship.

An incident to which I had attached no importance at the time came back to me. On passing through New York I had, as President of the then young International Table Tennis Federation, been entertained to a banquet by the firm of Parker Brothers. In conversation the name of an ancient Chinese board-game, Wei-Chi, akin to Japanese Go, came up. The representative of Parker Brothers, sitting next to me, observed:

"That is one of our games."

Astonished, I enquired how that could be, since the game is reputed to have been known in China for at least three thousand years.

"Oh," he replied lightly, "we saw the game described in several magazines, so we registered it in case it ever became popular."

Benjamin Stern explained to me that in the United

States a great firm with big resources could effectively control anything if it had even a shadow of a title, since the nuisance it could present with litigation must operate to discourage any would-be rival. In this case, of my book and article, he said, Parker Brothers would unquestionably lose their claim, since the Constitution would not allow literary censorship, but could it possibly be in the interest of the *Saturday Evening Post* and *Simon & Schuster* to be driven, on such a triviality, as far, possibly, as the Supreme Court?

This was evidently the opinion also of the two publishers, who paid me, the one $1,000, the other $500, for *not* publishing what I had not yet finished writing.

The second success was still more queer. One of my original letters of introduction — from the renter in England who had distributed the Wells comedies — had been to a firm that was about to produce another in the unending series of revivals on film or stage of "Charley's Aunt".

The heads of the firm, the Christie Brothers, had received me as manna from heaven.

"You have been to a British university," they said. "You are just what we need to advise us on details."

I had demurred, explaining that I had been to Cambridge and "Charley's Aunt" is about Oxford. No matter. With consent of Paramount I was instantly signed up as University expert, read the script, inspected the sets.

There were some obvious things to say. For example:

"That telephone is wrong. In a British university a don — teacher — may have a telephone, or there may be one in the porter's lodge, but not in the rooms of an undergraduate." The Christies pondered.

"We cannot alter that," they explained, "messages by telephone will save so much time and footage in the script."

Again I cavilled: "Look, that won't do — that cricket bat and the football on the sideboard. It is true that

English undergraduates play cricket and football, but not at the same time of the year, and they do not keep the implements on the sideboard. Besides a man may have a bat, he does not have a ball, eleven men have a ball." There was a good answer to this one too — I have already said several times that the most unreasonable in Hollywood is always reasonable.

"But only Englishmen will know this and not so very many English people will see this picture. Far more Americans will see it and they know that bats and balls of that peculiar shape are used in England. For them, it will help the atmosphere."

A few weeks passed and Eisenstein came out. One day we ran into a postboy delivering letters in the Paramount offices who spoke British English. We asked him home and found him a delightful person. He turned out to be Paddy Carstairs, a son of Nelson Keys, one of the most entertaining popular comedians of some years ago. His father dead, Paddy bethought him of a promise made to his father by a bosom friend, now a Paramount executive, and determined to try his luck by the same pilgrimage that we had undertaken. The executive had received him effusively. "Of course we must have Nelson's son working for us," he declared. "I owe that to his memory." But Paddy's dice had not fallen so luckily as mine, or the debt — in the executive's estimation — was minimal for in this dull purgatory he had been forced to start.

I bethought me and suggested to the Christie Brothers that, as I was so busy, it might be an advantage to have as extra adviser someone who could be "on stage" throughout and see everything on the spot. They agreed, and Paddy attended the studio every day but with no more effect. For example, he pointed out that in Oxford (or Cambridge, for that matter) undergraduates do not wear gowns as these extras were wearing them, gravely and with respect, but perfunctorily, wrinkled, over one shoulder, or carried bunched up in the hand. "That would not look right," he was told. However, at least he had progressed several squares on the Ludo board. Frustration, but now on the floor.

At this juncture the picture was finished and the Christie Brothers invited me to call round and receive my cheque. There were two of them, both immense, beaming from about six feet, six inches in height. Embarrassed, I protested:

"I do not like to take this money. I have done nothing for it. For very good reasons, as I admit, you have not found it possible to use one of my suggestions."

"Don't say that, Mr. Montagu," chorused the brothers. "Please don't say that. You do not know what confidence it has given the company to have you take exception to so few things."

The cheque was for three thousand dollars.

With this in the kitty we were in a position to clear up all bills. The Paramount contract secured our trip homeward for all. We two could leave eastward now, and the others would be safe away, with a production assured en route westward, if they accepted the offer from Japan. I was against further threshing about, which I saw as meaning further expenses and jeopardy.

But Eisenstein hung on. We had words. Hell and I left Cold Water Canyon and became refugees with Charlie.

Charlie was a friend in need and put us up while we said good-bye to all our friends. He even gave Hell an English haircut — his manual dexterity is unlimited and the barber expertise was no improvisation for "The Great Dictator".

He also offered me a job. When I came to Hollywood I would have given my eyes for that moment. But I refused it. I preferred to leave our relations as they were and have never regretted it.

One morning Kono came to say I was wanted on the telephone.

It was Upton Sinclair. He had been talking to Eisenstein about a picture in Mexico. It would be an eternal disgrace if Eisenstein were allowed to leave America without making a picture. He thought he could perhaps raise the funds, but it would take time. Meanwhile the visas of all three must be prolonged. Could I suggest any ways of pulling strings in Washington?

I knew Eisenstein had a hankering for Mexico, but I did not believe that any good would come of Upton Sinclair's endeavours. Meanwhile, I feared, the Japanese project — awaiting only the signature — might fall down and the three become stranded. I refused to help and tried to discourage the venture.

Two days later Hell and I left by train. The Bachmann family overwhelmed us by their kindness at the station. Our railway compartment, prepared by Mrs. Bachmann, was one mass of flowers.

Within a week, the formalities completed, we were on shipboard. It was the Majestic again.

Sidney Bernstein was travelling at the same time. On the first day I succeeded in shutting his fingers in the cabin door. We played bridge all the way across — at my limit, sixpence a hundred. Sidney, arm in sling, could not hold his hand, which had to be played spread out on a chair close to the table. He is not a good player — he was by far the weakest of the four taking part — and although we each partnered him in turn, he was embarrassed to win every rubber. He need not have been, of course. If anyone took advantage of the circumstances to look over his cards it must have been the rest of us.

We returned home with cupboard bare and minus Uncle Lionel's ante. I did not wish him to know this, and Sidney lent us the sum to repay it. Within a year we had scraped together enough to repay Sidney. What we had gained was beyond price.

That, save for the pendants, is the whole story.

After Hollywood

MEXICAN POSTSCRIPT

Upton Sinclair did succeed in setting up the Mexican film.

The sequel is well-known and it would be out of place to rehearse it in detail. I shall confine myself to a bare summary.

The three did not go to Japan but to the land of Sergei Mikhailich's dreams. There Eisenstein, Alexandrov and Tisse strove mightily. Metaphorically, they worked their guts out. Tisse shot wonderful scenes, without peer for beauty and significance of composition in all the canon of exterior cinematography. But as they worked, Sinclair back in Hollywood grew uneasy. As their rushes mounted up, so grew his disquiet. He cried "Halt!". Eisenstein never came back to Hollywood, saw only momentarily in New York the material he had created. He returned to Moscow crushed and broken. His stuff was mauled by other hands. It can never be reassembled as he intended it.

That is the outline. At the time, and since, a great deal has been said in anger. Sinclair said much against Eisenstein. Sergei Mikhailich did not lack friends to denounce Sinclair. He himself remained silent. He was too much injured.

I do not write about it now to rehash old battles, but to do justice to all. Sergei Mikhailich is gone, Sinclair is a very old man now — passion must be spent. I know the principals. I talked with others, I received letters; to understand the situation is to have compassion.

Sinclair dealt harshly with Eisenstein, but he thought that Eisenstein had wronged him.

Sinclair accused Eisenstein of impracticality, megalomania, deceit. None of these charges was justified, but Sinclair's motives had been pure and it was inevitable that he should mistakenly think they were.

The key lies in the two errors Sinclair made at the start, which will be recognised as such by any technician with experience of the film business.

Sinclair's motives were: a genuine desire to benefit Eisenstein and help him to achieve his purpose; concern for the good name of the U.S. which he saw endangered by its failure to give Eisenstein an opportunity; a not ignoble desire to become patron of a notable development in film art.

Sinclair wondered whether it might not be possible, if such a picture as Eisenstein had in mind were made in Mexico, for the cost to be met, as an investment, by friends such as his own (Sinclair's) benefactress. To find this out he asked Eisenstein how much his film project would cost.

To the person who is quite outside the film business, this must seem a natural thing to have done. Nevertheless it was the wrong thing. J.B.S. Haldane used to say that science is not a matter of providing answers but of finding out what questions are capable of being asked. Sinclair's question was certainly not one that could or should have been put to Eisenstein.

How could Eisenstein conceivably know the answer to such a question? He was not a producer, he was a director. Nowadays, when the shape of industry has turned so much toward "independent" productions, it is not at all uncommon for a director to know something about the business end, organisation, costs and the like. Indeed circumstances make it pretty much the rule. In those days, when the rule was for the director to be the paid employee of some production corporation, he need know nothing of administration, costs were not his affair. As I have already explained in another connection, the director *per se* is the natural opponent of the producer. The director then could only make his plans, embody them as demands, the producer must provide the skilled organisers to work out costs and on their basis he would say yea or nay and cut down the director. How could Eisenstein, who had never had responsibility for working out costs or spending a single penny in film production outside the Soviet Union — or within it for that matter — and who had never spent a single day inside Mexico, possibly give a sensible or meaningful answer? He did his best. He approached the only source he knew. There was an excellent bookshop in Hollywood, the Hollywood Bookstore, where we bought all our books, and which was presided over by an exceptionally intelligent and interesting man who in his youth had fought with Villa. This bookseller used to hold us spellbound with his stories and recommend us magnificent published narratives of those days. Eisenstein asked him: "How much would it cost to make a reasonably economical film in Mexico? Mostly documentary, no professional actors — could it be done for — say — twenty-five thousand dollars?" The bookseller naturally replied: "Possibly," and this degree of information, thus obtained, Eisenstein optimistically relayed to Sinclair.

Of course Sinclair should not only have known that anything Eisenstein told him on the subject could not but be hearsay. He should have known that to get a meaningful answer would have required highly powered (and highly paid) experts, cross-examining Eisenstein to find out exactly what was in his mind, visiting Mexico to ascertain beforehand conditions of work and transportation, cost of labour, etc., able to make calculations on the quantities and cost of film stock, etc. All this expertise is required before anybody can possibly answer what Sinclair — or any other prospective investor —

needs to know about a film project. Which is only one of the reasons why filming is expensive.

The second mistake that Sinclair made was that he decided to appoint a relative, not an expert, as eventual watchdog, with virtually the role of a producer manager. He needed, he felt again, you would think if you are non-technical, quite naturally, someone outside this dread film world, somebody on whom therefore he could rely. The responsibility was given to Mrs. Sinclair's brother, Hunter Kimbrough.

But again, anyone with film experience or knowledge knows, a choice on this basis will not work. As again I have indicated earlier, a producer or associate producer, to do his job, must know at least as much about every aspect of film creation as his director. He need not be a creator himself — if he were he would probably be directing — but does need to have criteria by which to judge properly whatever solutions the director proposes to each problem that arises. For the director — of his nature as such a being — must strive ever for perfection in the solution. Honesty in the director is his conscientious effort to do so to the utmost of his capacity. The producer must know enough to be able to weigh the merits of the proposed degrees of perfection against the costs they will incur to achieve. Otherwise he will be as putty in the hands of the director. He cannot know when to say yea or nay. He will say yea, blindly, until he chokes for air and strikes out as blindly with a nay. It does not matter what his ability or character. I have seen city magnates in such situations helpless as babies, arbitrary and wasteful in their yesses, penurious and unpredictable in their noes, simply because they lacked the equipment wherewith to judge.

These two errors made the catastrophe certain.

Eisenstein in Mexico did *not* shoot wastefully or impracticably or unnecessarily. This was an entirely false impression of Sinclair's based on his own innocence and lack of experience. In fact Eisenstein shot economically, as the surviving material shows.

But it had been arranged that the film should not be processed in Mexico. The negative had to be returned to Hollywood for printing and development. When this happens, the cameraman must overshoot — because he will not know whether his shots have been successful until days later when he cannot retake, having left the location — and must order more shots to be printed than he would otherwise, for the same reason. Sinclair did not know this, nor had he any experience of how many takes often are made, and printed, in normal studio production.

I have heard from eyewitnesses of how, as he sat in the Hollywood projection theatre looking at the rushes, and saw take after take of the same shot repeating exactly the same action come up on the screen, he would mutter audibly: "Is the man mad?"

Eisenstein was not mad. The only respect in which he overshot — or rather extrashot — was that, besides the material for his planned feature film "Que Viva Mexico", when occasion arose and he happened to be present at some rarely colourful exotic ceremony unforeseen by the plan, a fiesta or a funeral, he would shoot it on the side. This, too, is an economy, and carried out by every competent film expedition to a rare location, because the material costs so little extra — the technicians are already there and no extra transportation is involved — that it is worth it to be held as "library material" or made up into separate shorts. But as nobody on the Sinclair side knew very clearly what exactly Eisenstein planned to do in his main film — of its nature he could not know before he got there and worked from a very sketchy outline in the manner of the best modern improvisation and holding most of his possibilities, like a chessplayer, in his head — what was for the feature and what for side-projects was not apparent at the time.

(Or later, incidentally. Parts of the invaluable reassembly of "rushes", put together many years after his death by his pupil Jay Leyda, a real labour of scholarship and love, were later identified as intended for "news" or "travel" use, not as part of the main film, by Eduard Tisse as soon as Jay showed them to him.)

But none of this did, could, Sinclair understand. As the too speculative originally allotted estimate was exceeded, as more and more money was called for — though to a total extremely reasonable for what was being done — as more and more shots kept coming through, the project began to take on the appearance of a bottomless pit, in which — and he would be morally responsible — more and more investment would be engulfed and with no prospect of reasonable return.

He grew frantic. Later, in a prologue to one of the films eventually made out of the rushes, he spoke of Eisenstein in his megalomania having spent a fortune and shot 35 miles of film. He said also, and obviously believed, that Eisenstein intended to make a film that could not possibly be consumed, as is normal, at one sitting, but would take a week to sit through, like a cycle of the Wagnerian "Ring".

The fact is that the total cost of the enterprise was less than Gaumont-British — the firm I was working for at about this time — spent on the Flaherty documentary "Man of Aran" and, although 1½ to 2 miles is the final length of a normal feature film and exterior shooting usually requires exposure of much more footage than a subject wholly shot in interior, the film we had just completed at Shepherd's Bush, an ordinary simple programme thriller made in the studio, exposed — as I checked — 40 miles.*

In reality Eisenstein intended his main material as one film in several episodes, totalling 1½ hours or 1¾ hours. Each episode would have been rigorously reduced, in his

* See note, page 347

intention, to balance it into a single unit reflecting Mexico's geographical, ethnological, cultural and historical diversity. What Sinclair took for a single film — later inflated to a whole feature by itself in one of the versions — should have been but one episode.

Misunderstanding as he did, can Sinclair be blamed for his resentment and his worries?

The sequel was brutal. When Sinclair said "halt", the film was in Hollywood, the boys still in Mexico. Eisenstein urged, pleaded that he be allowed to return to cut it. But Sinclair wanted to make a clean break. Eisenstein was given to understand there were visa difficulties. In actuality, at this time the luggage he had sent on was opened and searched and malicious play made by the authorities with the ribald caricatures (a sort of draughtsman's highbrow equivalent to the lowbrow's smoking-room story) that Eisenstein used to doodle to liven difficult moments and amuse his friends.

Even when he returned to the Soviet Union, he was allowed to believe the precious rushes would follow him. But they never came.

Nor did the Soviet authorities help at this stage. Was Eisenstein worth quarrelling with friends about? They were reluctant to believe that Sinclair, famed hero of the fight for progress and the people, could possibly have erred.

Pelion was piled on Ossa, when certain youthful admirers in America, thinking to benefit their idol by proving the imbecility and exaggeration of his opponents, made a careful collection of all the cuttings denouncing Eisenstein — the effusions of Hamilton Fish, the insinuations of gossip writers, the accusations of Sinclair — and sent them in a folder to Amkino with an indignant covering note (of course carrying less weight than its contents when the folder went on to Moscow).

It should be remembered that the original leave granted to the three pilgrims had been for twelve months only. The

Paramount episode was sanctified by an agreement concluded quite officially for the Soviet authorities by Amkino. Mexico was authorised too, in the beginning. But it was not only Sinclair who had been disquieted as the months went on, far beyond the total period originally planned. Rumour had it in Moscow that Eisenstein did not intend to return. This was rubbish, as anyone close to him abroad could testify full well. But that Stalin believed this at the time appears from an exchange of letters and telegrams between him and Sinclair preserved among material which Sinclair presented to the University of Indiana and which has since been published. Sinclair did, it seems, make an offer to sell the material to the U.S.S.R. but Stalin replied brusquely that no one was interested, Sergei Mikhailich was looked on "as a deserter".

Sinclair deserves every credit in that, despite his anger with Eisenstein, his almost frenzied indignation, he replied categorically repudiating the charge as slanderous and unfounded, and it is apparent, from the fact that it never reappeared after the boys' eventual return, that Stalin must have accepted this exculpation.

Left with it on his hands, Sinclair made what he could of the material, to cut his losses. Sol Lesser inflated an episode as "Thunder over Mexico". Shorts were carved out of it (e.g. "Death Day"). Later Marie Seton, who knew Eisenstein and had received an idea of the original plan directly from him, bought and rescued more of the material and put it together as "Time in the Sun". The balance was handed over to the Museum of Modern Art in New York, which also holds, received from Sergei Mikhailich, those copies of his American scripts and papers that we of the unit did not retain for ourselves, and various of his original notes. The stored remainder is, it has been understood, subject to strict injunctions from Sinclair that it be never sent to Moscow. So there in New York it reposes in its glory, like the mouldering ruins of some once splendid Gothic cathedral, with this difference, that the rubble was never finished to a fane.

Here eventually Leyda worked on them for his partial restoration of rushes. Here they wait vainly, for Sinclair's ban to be relaxed and Grisha to be allowed to have a try at them. Here they decay, as all films must, waiting for their existence to be prolonged by copying, and their survival better secured, as it should be, by distribution of copies to film archives eager to receive them about the world.

When I look back on this postscript I do not take any credit for my foresight in refusing to take any part in the Mexican adventure. What happened was what could not but happen. I confess I did not know then, as I do now, how much Sergei Mikhailich longed to make a picture of Mexico. Mexico was as personal and romantic a land for him as, later, Mongolia was to be to me. Some years earlier, when Pudovkin had been in London, he too had spoken of wanting to make a film there and when I heard Eisenstein speak of it I had foolishly concluded that Mexico must be something of a modish catchword among the Soviet film élite. I did not know then that the real dream was always Eisenstein's and that the subject had only come into Pudovkin's mind because he had heard Eisenstein mention it and, as so often with similar enthusiasms, caught the infection off him. When I was younger I saw only folly and failure in the stubborn effort and adventure, and the consequent disaster that struck Eisenstein to despair.

But now I see things differently. The ruins may be ruins, but they are still beautiful, and the attempts at restoration — however inadequate — will forever remain an inspiration in the corpus of the highest film achievement. If genius were not ready to face the risk of such disasters, mankind would be less rich.

CONCLUSION

What happened to all these people afterwards?

Schulberg and Lasky are gone. David Selznick soon set up his own producing company but died in early middle age. Sinclair still lives, an old man.

Eisenstein came back sad and at first could not work. He resumed his teaching, then a film: "Bezhin Meadow". It was stopped, begun again, stopped again, there was a row. (The negative of this picture was destroyed by water during a fire in the Moscow film store started by German incendiary bombs. Its ghost has recently been recovered by making a film out of short lengths of each shot that Eisenstein had laid aside for record, as was his habit.)

Then he made a new film, with music and singing, rousing patriotic fervour against the coming German invasion: "Alexander Nevsky". It was a success, won him medals, bonuses and honours. Just before the war he produced a real opera, Wagner, on the stage. This was at the Bolshoi Theatre.

Soon after the war broke out an extraordinary thing happened. He was assigned to start on his cycle of films: "Ivan the Terrible", in Alma Ata. How could a country, in the throes of so monstrous a destructive war, devote resources to reconstructing sixteenth century Moscow and the Baltic provinces in Central Asia? Part One was a success. Parts Two and Three — of which latter several reels were completed — struck too near the knuckle for Stalin and were stopped. Part Two has been recovered and shown since. Part Three is lost.

A heart attack hit Eisenstein and he was nursed back to convalescence in the Kremlin hospital. The war was over, his lectures at the school resumed and he was planning a revision of Part Three when a second attack finished him in 1948 at the age of fifty.

It was discovered after Sergei Mikhailich's death that already as early as 1937 he had married Pera Attasheva. Under Soviet law all his papers, books and pictures were thus safe in her hands. She catalogued them and cared for them. They now form the Eisenstein Archive and his writings are being published in a seven-volume edition by a State Committee on his Literary Heritage.

Grisha Alexandrov still lives and flourishes. The young athlete and Adonis I knew is now stouter, bushy-browed and respectable but has much the same grin. He made a separate career directing a genre new for Soviet cinema, singing comedy, and then married his leading lady, the beautiful and intelligent star Lyubov Orlova. Now they live happily, he still makes pictures and she has taken to straight parts in the theatre — Ibsen, Sartre and as Mrs. Patrick Campbell in "Dear Liar".

Eduard Tisse, perhaps the most unselfish of us all and the most deserving, was the most unlucky. While Eisenstein was discouraged and inactive, Eduard showed his capacity by directing more pictures. When Eisenstein himself returned to direction, Eduard was still faithful and returned to the camera. He was yet cameraman for Eisenstein, if only on exterior, to the last, on "Ivan". Fate dealt him two heavy blows. He married a beautiful Rumanian girl, Bianca, and they tragically lost their first-born, a son, in the cold of winter. Then he suffered a stroke and the once strong man was forced to sit, paralysed. He did not survive long. Their daughter Eleonora inherits the good looks of both her parents. When I last saw her she was off as a freshman to start her first-year course in the camera at the film school where Sergei Mikhailich used to teach. Now she is already in her father's old job in her first production.

The Hollywood quarrel between Eisenstein and myself never disturbed the intimacy of our friendship. The disagreement was ignored and forgotten. Letters never ceased to flow and of course we never failed to meet when I went to Moscow. Whenever we met we laughed and exchanged confidences as though we had never been apart.

He knew that if he called on me for anything it would be willingly performed, I knew that he would do anything I asked. In 1936 I came to Moscow to ask his help in planning the battle in "King Solomon's Mines" which I was scheduled to make at Shepherd's Bush. (Nothing came of this for I fell ill and, when I got well, went off to Spain.) The last message I had from him was brought by the rugged sailor-writer Vishnevsky to the Nuremberg Trial we were both covering as war correspondents in 1946. It asked me to translate the scenarios of "Ivan the Terrible" and this I began in the American Military Hospital there while getting better from double pneumonia.

I will end with conclusions on two questions.

Why did we fail in Hollywood?

It would be easy to answer, as I was for many years inclined to: because of our delays which gave the opportunity for the leadership conflict in Paramount to come into play. When I got back to Hollywood from New York immediately after the sacking I went to the studio and saw Selznick. The young man had only heard the bare facts by telephone and wanted to hear the details. When I had finished he said, his eyes glistening:

"Isn't Mr. Schulberg wonderful? He waits and waits and chooses the right moment to strike, and always gets his own way."

Easy, but it would be incomplete. It would be equally incomplete to conclude we never had a chance, recalling the profound mistrust of highbrows that existed then — incredible in these days when highbrows have proved themselves as capable of the commercial approach as the frankly real tradesmen — and which we aroused, as I have described, at our opening dinner. In the end politics certainly provided the finishing touch, but it would be equally incomplete, and very much an oversimplification, to imagine, as some leftists do, that it was simply a matter of politics and leave the matter at that. It must be remembered, as I have already pointed out, that real fear of the Soviet Union and the Cold War that it gave rise to were not as they are now.

There is a fine folk jingle that goes like this: "For want of a nail the shoe was lost, for want of the shoe the horse was lost, for want of the horse the battle was lost, for want of the battle the kingdom was lost, all for the loss of a horseshoe nail."

What is causative here? Which operated to lose the kingdom? None could be effective without the others. History can never be sure about "ifs". The only thing that is certain is that all these factors operated: mistrust of "intellectuals" (especially "foreigners"), tribal rivalry within the company, our own tactical mistakes, and political fears. It cannot be known which defeated us, which — if any — would not have been decisive without the others.

The final question is a compound one and needs answering more fully.

What sort of a man was Eisenstein, what was his achievement, what was his relation to the great social and philosophic problems of our day?

This can partly, but only partly, emerge from the incidents narrated in this book. I have deliberately refrained from detailing and discussing events of his life and work before and after the American adventure, for they spread too far outside its subject. Nevertheless, since it will illuminate this story some generalisation is not out of place.

He was above all many-sided, interested in everything, a sort of Renaissance man. Life is too complicated, knowledge too wide, for there to be many of these about nowadays. They are all exceptional people.

As a teacher he was outstanding. He was thorough and painstaking and prepared everything so that it seemed spontaneous, thought-of at the moment. He could be sarcastic, even waspish, but his pupils mostly adored him. He drew out the independence of mind of any capable of independence, taught them to argue, opened their awareness, by analogies, to all pathways of experience and thought.

As a film theoretician he was an analyst and materialist. His approach to aesthetics was almost purely scientific. The laws and methods he teased out of experience and speculation have wide application beyond cinema, to many other arts, in some aspects to all. To cinema they are basic, and like the laws formulated for all classic scientific innovators, they will never be superseded, only extended. His best writing is difficult. The more easy, the more superficial. When he was most profound, he lost all syntax, pretending that this was by design and that he was seeking to communicate by rhythmic arrangement, in which grammar and punctuation were handled as freely as scissors in film editing. To extract what is there requires application, so that the idle apprentices and merely film-struck among students delight to dismiss it as old hat. They do so at their peril, for to the industrious there are many illuminating passes to the heights.

As a graphic artist he was a draughtsman of extraordinary facility and talent, as exhibitions and collections of his work have recently shown. He could instantly sketch in a screen shape exactly what he had in mind for any film-shot, more lucidly than it could be explained in words, and tried to impress on his film pupils the advantages of cultivating at least a minimum ability to do this, not only to communicate, but to clarify and render precise their own ideas. In youth he used this gift to fix all kinds of movements and characteristics that amused him. Later he used it, as I have said, for ribaldry to relieve tense and difficult moments or caricature to amuse his friends.

As a film creator his product has a pictorial beauty that is never an empty harmony but always a harmony designed and packed with meaning, and a rhythmic composition that binds the most unwilling. Every foot is stamped recognisably with his personality.

It also presents many paradoxes. As a young man he left stage for cinema because he wanted realism and sought to stage a strike in an actual factory, but his "Strike" turned out not naturalistic but surrealist. "Potemkin" fathered the whole school of documentary but "Ivan" is one of the most mannered and stylised films ever made. "The General Line", designed as a Party political tract, is the most formalistic, "October" a fierce intellectual polemic, "Nevsky" a patriotic opera. "Ivan", profoundly studied to be true to the social implications of its period, turned out topical to a perilous degree. By precept and practice he taught the need for prior, meticulous preparation of every last particle and button, yet in "Potemkin" and the Mexican film he showed supreme readiness to catch and improvise from every passing opportunity. The uniting factor was his style, which was the extension ever wider of embrace and mastery of every resource, whether of art or nature, and its plastic incorporation into the arsenal of creative means.

His reputation rests upon a smaller completed *oeuvre* than that of any other major film-maker, except perhaps Dovzhenko and, certainly, Vigo. He began only eight films and finished only two, "Nevsky" and — probably — "Strike", exactly as he originally intended. "Potemkin" is an overgrown episode from what was first planned as a greater whole (hence, perhaps, its simplicity and unity, rare in Eisenstein); "October" was slashed to ribbons in response to political changes; "General Line" was increased by an extra — unforeseen and interrupting — episode added to illustrate a new development in the

Party's line on collective agriculture (Eisenstein told me about the meeting with the Party leadership at which this was decided on, and the impression made upon him by Stalin's "honey-coloured eyes"); the trilogy to which "Ivan the Terrible" grew was never finished; "Bezhin Meadow" was stopped twice and the Mexican film was taken away from him, the one survives only as stills, the other as unseen rushes and bits and pieces cobbled together by other hands.

It would be absurd to think of so small a range as compassing all or even more than a tiny sector of the range of cinema. The point is that what he taught was that all means are available; for each theme must be found, and used, those most appropriate to solve the specific problem. Other film-makers have been and will be confronted with other enterprises to which quite different solutions are apt. Those he sought and found resulted in pictures which will certainly not live for ever, for silver-nitrate images on celluloid cannot be preserved indefinitely and lose a little in quality at every duplication, but which will live as long as they last.

The frustrations he met, the rows in which he became involved, were legion. The most famous of these was the week-long argument with his assembled colleagues and the bureaucrats of the industry over "Bezhin Meadow", at the end of which he capitulated and renounced his theories, like Galileo, and then — still more like Galileo — *Eppur si muove* — bounced back with an article in which he extended them by explaining that his fault had been hypertrophy of only one aspect of *montage* whereas it was to all aspects of film creation — not only editing, but story construction, dialogue, intra-frame composition, etc., everything — that his aesthetic principles of "conflict" and montage should apply.

He was not a member of any Communist Party — at the time of Hollywood none of us were. This was because his *métier* was not direct political activity, not because he was not a Soviet citizen through and through. His whole art was steeped in the social and philosophical approaches of Marxism and his personality could have been produced by no other time or place. As a boy he tasted the cultural multiplicity of bourgeois Riga, as a young man the infinite variety of daring cultural experiment of the early Revolution days. Nothing else could have engendered his exuberant imagination, his energy of performance, his sense of social responsibility, the stubborn courage of his refusal to compromise as an artist with a duty of integrity to society and himself. Cold War crocodile tears at his difficulties and anguish founder on the facts. The artist will always meet anguish in creation everywhere, as well as joys, and the greater his innovatory passion the greater the obstacles and the pain. *Ifs* in human affairs are but speculation, yet the objective historian has only to contrast the measureless opportunities accorded to him in the Soviet Union each time he did reach the floor, the fresh starts again and again, with what happened in Hollywood and Mexico, to realise the impossibility of an Eisenstein in the cinema of the West.

As a man Eisenstein was delightful company. He had humour, wit, brilliance of conversation. He could be malicious and spiteful, but never cherished a grudge. Like all creative artists he had ups and downs, moments when he lost confidence and became gloomy, sour — after his shock in Mexico such a moment extended many months — but (except for that experience) he would in an instant be bubbling over with new liveliness and cheer. He was loyal to all his friends — but devoured them totally, completely, utterly.

When in 1936 I flew to Moscow with Hell to consult him about "King Solomon's Mines", Eisenstein put us up in his flat. One of the two evenings, I had to leave for an appointment and his old nurse, who was still looking after him, was shocked and said to Eisenstein: "Fancy your guest going off like that and leaving the cabbage with the old goat!" The "old goat" did come into the "cabbage's" bedroom, but it was only to sit down on the edge of the bed and ask:

"Hell, why do you hate me?"

"Hate" was quite the wrong word to describe the shade of disapproval Hell mixed with her admiration for him; but, leaving this aside, she replied simply:

"Because you are so cruel."

He appeared perfectly satisfied. He had been afraid that she might have perceived some trait of which he was unaware and which he would have been ashamed of as a weakness. This, he immediately understood and did not mind.

I should not have said "cruel", but "ruthless". The artist, that is the quintessential artist, the outstanding artist-creator, must be ruthless. To achieve he must concentrate every sinew in himself on what he imagines, and on the acquisition of the skills and opportunities to realise it. Personal relations, friendships must be subordinated to it. Everyone he comes in contact with must be bowled over or fascinated, neutralised, or devoured and incorporated. Those who would share the work must, open-eyed, accept the treatment and ignore the thorns.

Bernard Shaw was often accused in his lifetime of writing plays about ideas, in which the characters are merely cardboard puppets cut out to present one or other point of view. This was untrue of course. Had it been true his plays would not be revived, for ideas have moved on and they would have little to say today. But one of the most profoundly perceived characters of his canon is Dubedat, the artist-rogue in *The Doctor's Dilemma*. Here we have the extreme case of the selfish artist, womaniser, sponger upon his friends, unrepentant debtor, exploiter and apparent heartbreaker of his devoted and loyal wife, but creator of divine paintings. He is desperately ill. The doctors can save only one person. They sit around and debate: is it to be Dubedat, or an alternative, a worthy and self-sacrificing nonentity of a G.P.? It is impossible to understand a man like Eisenstein without seeing in him a great deal of Dubedat. Not the cad, of course, or the immoralist — that was simply part of the artist-stereotype put in by Shaw to heighten the dilemma of the traditional choice: in a shipwreck in which only one can be saved, to whom do you pass the lifebelt?

But every really outstanding creative artist must be just as much a problem even if he does not display the conventional wickedness of Dubedat. The quality, however virtuous, he shares is Dubedat's seeming egoism that is not really egoism at all, the selfishness that is not for his own sake but because of his consecration to his task. Can others accept it? Shaw depicts a moment when, after Dubedat's death, the doctors stand around and sympathise with the new-made widow for all that they suppose she had to suffer at her husband's hands. She answers with a paean upon him and a declaration that living with and being useful to his labours had been bliss and the only thing that had given her life a meaning.

I do not intend to sing any paeans or to exaggerate, but I do not think that any of us who participated in even a little of Eisenstein's creative work grudged his devouring appetite or look on that association as a wasted period of our lives.

Sutter's Gold

Scenario
by
S. M. EISENSTEIN, G. V. ALEXANDROV
AND IVOR MONTAGU

Based upon the novel "L'Or"
by
BLAISE CENDRARS

NOTE

This is a first script. An Eisenstein scenario is usually somewhere between what is technically known in cinema practice as a "treatment", i.e. a mere description of the actions of the film not yet "broken up" into a succession of shots, and the final shooting-script with technical instructions for the taking of each shot. Although there are no technical instructions, and although each paragraph here might eventually have been rendered by a single shot or a group of shots, the first script in this case — "Sutter's Gold" — already represents, as do all Eisenstein's published scenarios (e.g. "Ivan the Terrible"), an advanced stage of visualisation: the succession of separate paragraphs conveys to the reader the succession of visual impressions which will be conveyed to him by the finished film.

The lay-out follows closely that of the original typescript.* Only minor corrections — to obvious slips — have been made. The text is otherwise unaltered from the original.

* See note on scripts, page 342

REEL 1

A song of California.
Some gay and joyous song that everybody knows.
The happy, laughing song continues while there passes a series of titles speaking of the days, the heroes and the marvellous adventures now bygone.
The titles approach their end. The song has vanished.
As the song diminishes in loudness there is heard presently only the gurgling splash of water. A tiny stream emerges from a fountain to gurgle down upon the surface of the bowl beneath, raising little bubbles. In the water is reflected an old Swiss church. Bells melodiously strike Six.
With the striking, the camera tracks back, disclosing the fountain square and church of a little Swiss town.
Before the houses sit old men with pipes, and old women busy with their needlework. An atmosphere of dream and sleep.
On the steps of a wine shop are folk drinking from large pewter mugs.
From some distant hill the voices in chorus of girls and vigorous young men are heard singing Swiss songs, perhaps yodelling.
The sun is setting.
"Eigh-h," grunt the old men.
"Ah-h," sigh the old women.
And the water still gurgles.
And the voices sound from the hills.

And the clock strikes the quarter.

On the stones of the road out of sight ring heavy footsteps.

The hands of the old women stop.

The mugs check in the air.

Pipes are drawn from mouths.

A figure approaches with his back to the sun, the folk screw up their eyes to see his face.

His face is not seen, but his silhouette with big hat, high boots and stick startles the old people.

Enquiring, they look at one another and then stare at the man.

The man strides along, looking at the houses, not the people.

A boy runs up to him and, answering his question, indicates a building:
"That's the police."

The old men and old women bristle at the word, in inquisitive agitation.

The man fumbles in his pockets, brings out a coin, hands it to the boy and enters the building.

Everyone gazes at the closed door. A group of girls blush and adjust their bodices. The youngsters look at the girls.

An old man purses his lips and beckons to the boy:
"Tss-Tss."

The boy shows him the thaler he has just received, several crowd round and look at it.

Suddenly the door of the police building flies open.

The man — Sutter — comes out and slams the door behind him, breaking its glass.

A dog begins to bark.

Everyone turns.

The man advances to the fountain, looks round, and stares at the people.

Pauses.

Spits in the fountain.

Scene:
Kühnenberg. Swiss village

cheap setting
~~used~~ using old
settings in ~~jo~~-
~~ning to them~~
details,
(fountain etc)
and two foreground house
Fountain: details.

8-10 old men
6 old women
4 girls
4 youngsters
5-6 children

Sutter. 1½

Sound. "Swiss" chorus. "Yodling"

Turns his back on the fountain and strides away with the same firm step with which he came.

The sounds die away, the figure disappears in the evening, there remains only the gurgle of the water in the fountain.

The inquisitive old man comes to the fountain and stares at the floating spittle:

"Mm-m-m-m."

The notes of the clock ring out striking the second quarter —

"Ting
    Tang
        Tang
            Tang...."

Dialogue in the police station conveying the fact that the stranger is Johannes August Sutter who has enquired for a passport and that this has been refused him.

The notes and image of a larger bell.

From the indication that this is a larger church, we understand that this is another and larger town.

The congregation is just leaving church.

A woman and three boys become distinguished.

The woman is merry and the boys are laughing.

The woman comes to a house and a little girl runs out to meet her, holding a letter in her hand:

"Mummy! Mummy!
Look!"

The woman takes the letter from the child's hand, enters room and reads at a table.

> *Wife!*
> *I've had to go.*
> *I've gone to seek my fortune.*
>   *Your husband*
>   *Johann August Sutter.*

She drops her head and elbows on the table. The children are seated around.

The woman is crying. The Angelus is ringing.
Dark.
Out in the dark other bells.
Peaceful bells.
The dance of little bells in a beautiful landscape. The growing light of morning, the beautiful air of morning, a mountain landscape.
Dawn.
A herd of cows is grazing. It is the cow bells that ring so peacefully and musically.
Among the cows in the grass sleeps Sutter, head on hand.
The rising sun, the sound of the cow bells and the breath of a nearby cow on his face awaken Sutter.
His movements are carefree.
He smiles at the sun, it irradiates his face.
He crawls to the edge of a rock and looks down.
Far beneath him he sees a little customs post. Perhaps a couple of soldiers eating soup. Sutter licks his lips and we can see that he is hungry.
Turning his head he sees the udder of a cow.
Without hesitation, he takes the teat in his hand, milks the cow into his hat, and drinks the warm milk with gusto.
On the road nearby walks a group of young artisans in picturesque Swiss costumes.
Sutter dries the milk off his lips, gets up, sees the lads and goes to meet them.
"Hullo, folks, where are you off to?"
"To Germany."
"To Germany," repeats Sutter, and spies a ripe berry in the grass. He picks up the berry, eats it and says:
"I, too, am bound for Germany."
He joins the group and merrily goes off with them, looking back to wave a light-hearted good-bye to Switzerland.

                                          FADE OUT

Mrs. Sutter in the street with her children.
Her smallest son shouts, she turns back and looks at him.
"Mummy, look, there's Papa."
She sees her little son before a poster.
Fear in her face, she hurries to the poster.
On the poster she sees the face of Sutter and a *Wanted* notice for his arrest.
The children cry happily "That's papa! That's papa!"
She shrinks in fear, turns away, dragging the children behind her.
Passers on the street, those on whose backs the morals of the town securely rest, look at her, some supercilious, some contemptuous.
She gathers her last self-control together and, bearing up under these eyes, hastens to her home.
Again the church bell, this time monotonously and insistently expressing the feelings in her heart.
The creaking of the door and the crying voice of the boy: "Mummy! But it is papa!"
A haystack. In the hay, the artisans are sleeping. Sutter is calmly and quietly engaged in emptying their pockets; and from one fast asleep he pulls off the coat and trousers, while the sleeper smiles beatifically.
After silently bowing his thanks to the artisans, he rapidly descends the ladder and makes off.
The snores of the artisans blend into —
— sound indefinite, confused and at first not clearly distinguishable.
Shouts, cracking noises, and hubbub of voices, music. These are the sounds of a bustling, idle crowd.
On the screen a wall set with many clocks. Pendulums moving in countless directions.
The tick-tock of the pendulums gives a rapid rhythm.
A placard with an inscription:

WHAT TIME IS IT NOW? A clock nearby it.
WHAT YEAR IS IT NOW? A flag at this level
   with the year on it: 1853.
WHAT CITY ARE YOU IN NOW? A label:
   NEW YORK.

We see a fair, a crowd reading the placards at one of the tents.

ALL THIS YOU KNOW YOURSELF...
BUT WHERE WILL YOU BE TOMORROW?
ONLY I CAN TELL.

From a pair of oriental shoes with tapering tips, the camera passes up to the blackened face of Sutter, pearls in his ears, clad in a costume of golden tinsel and painted feathers.
Music, whistling, the noises of the fair.
People gaze curiously at him.
The placard above his head:

BUT WHERE WILL YOU BE TOMORROW?

An old woman in spectacles, with a stick, rheumatism and a sceptical smile.
With toothless mouth, she enquires:
   "Well, fakir, tell me where I'll be tomorrow."
She laughs a gross laugh as he draws the tent flaps to behind her.
Chatter, singing, clamour, whistling of the fair.

Title: BUT YOU NEVER CAN TELL WHERE YOU'LL BE ON THE MORROW.

Seen from behind, a blacksmith shoeing a horse.
The blackened face of Sutter, this time blackened with smoke.
The puffing of the bellows, the clanging of the hammers, the sizzle of hot iron in water accompanying his work.

He is shoeing a horse.

The coquettish laugh of a woman.

Her coy face.

Sutter is helping her to try on high button-up boots.

His face dirty again, his hair once more tousled, Sutter is next pulling out the tooth of a horse.

Then tearing a tooth out of a man's mouth.

Giving with delicate steps a flute lesson to an immaculate little boy.

A butcher's shop. He is chopping meat.

He is selling in a corner portraits of Washington, and medallions from a tray.

All these passing episodes are in sound, the tunes of one single melody. The tick-tock, the shouts of the crowd, the noises of the town are all arranged in a specially composed Sutter march.

The sounds of the blacksmith's instruments, the girl's giggles, the neighing of the horse, the screams of the man losing his teeth, the flute, the choppings are all arranged in this rhythm although they retain their natural and recognisable sound.

At last the natural sounds fade and only the music persists.

Circus music.

A beautiful woman leaps out on a platform before a tent, and curtseys deep. With her is a large dog, English bobtail sheepdog type. She wears a frilled and glittering skirt. The dog is wearing a sailor's cap and smokes a pipe.

The dog climbs up on a chair to smoke his pipe. Curls of smoke.

The woman sings a song to the dog, addressing the song to it as though it were a man.

The matter of the song is a complaint of man's cowardice and lack of enterprise. And the refrain calls upon him to go out and seek new paths, fortune will smile on him.

To seek a new Eldorado.

The first verse may be sung as a circus song, with an erotic double meaning: carried away, the woman sings the second verse movingly with its surface romantic value.

Her voice is unforgettable, the tune simple and easy to remember.

The dog moves its paw to show its indifference to travel.

Sutter, holding a horse, stands rapt. His eyes burn as he gazes at her. He is enraptured by both song and woman, and for a moment at least, they catch one another's eyes.

As she finishes, the bystanders all applaud. He does not hear the applause.

One of his fellow circus employees calls to him.

At first he fails to hear.

Then, aroused, he lets go of the horse, turns and makes away in the crowd.

He catches the sound of a man at a booth standing and shouting a boxing challenge to the crowd. The challenge is to fight a giant Negro. The prize is shown, one hundred dollars and a young slave to the man who vanquishes the giant.

Sutter approaches the man and nods in sign that he will fight.

They enter the tent and the crowd surges in after them.

The woman reappears on the platform looking for Sutter.

She goes from tent to tent, and stops peering before the one where all is ready for the boxing.

"Seconds out! Time." The signal gong — Sutter begins to fight the Negro.

It is half dark in the tent.

It is overpoweringly hot in the tent, fiercely and pitilessly the fight is waged in the heat.

Waves of anxiety and joy fluctuate on the face of the woman according to the fluctuating fortunes of the fight.

Sutter fights like a demon.
All his energy, his desperation are in the struggle.
No rules or laws, everything goes.
Each strives to strike the other to the floor by every means.
Sutter strikes down the Negro to the floor.
The crowd shouting in bestial joy.
A savage-looking man hands the money to Sutter.
At that moment, the woman at the tent entrance shrieks.
All turn their heads. Police-officers. Such a fight is unlawful.
Sutter seizes the money and knocks over the one lantern.
All is dark. He lifts the edge of the tent, slips beneath and runs off among the ropes at the rear of the tents.
Whistling and clamour in the darkness.
A lantern, hanging on a wagon, nears the camera.
A crossroads. The man on the wagon — Sutter — stops it, jumps down, and looks into the darkness. He whistles as he looks. The dog that smokes the pipe runs towards him.
Behind the dog appears the woman with a little carpet bag; she is dressed for a long journey.
Sutter approaches her and speaks for the first time. He asks:
"Well?"
She nods.
He smiles, and takes the woman in his strong arms, lifting her onto the wagon. He lifts the dog after her.
The wagon sets forth on an unknown road, and from it comes the song that mocks those who are sloven and weak of spirit, and calls them to fare ever forward.
The farther goes the wagon, the more slender dwindles the song. The words are indistinguishable.
The wagon is out of sight and the song at an end.

REEL 2

Title: TWO YEARS LATER. FORT INDEPENDENCE.

The gates of the fort open upon the desert.

The garrison of the fort stands in formation in the courtyard.

The soldiers raise their guns in the air.

The commander of the fort gives a word of command. He speaks:

"Bon voyage to the pioneers."

A volley.

Sutter, and the circus girl.

Three missionaries, two military men and two women are setting forth together.

Nine persons pass through the gateway of the fort.

The gates of the fort close slowly, hiding from view the party that is riding away.

                        FADE OUT

The travellers sit in groups in a big boat among furs.

A slow panorama of desert lands passes by.

The circus girl — Mary — hums ever the same song.

Sutter speaks quietly of what he has heard of the far West, that in the distant land of the setting sun there is deep rich soil and fertile valleys.

He muses beside her, singing. He rejoices that they have strength and vigour enough to cross the desert and begin a new life.

"Wealth, happiness and fortune...."

— sings Mary.

Slowly swings by the wilderness.

The dreamy faces of our heroes.

Darkness.

"Good-bye."

"Good luck on the road."

— the travellers are saying to one another, as the expedition lands on the river banks.

Ship's boats are set on wheels and harnessed up. The big barge departs down the river. The expedition sets out into the empty desert.

Sutter is riding ahead. He whistles his favourite air.

"Good-bye. Good luck on the road."

— their two military companions are leaving them.

They are staying behind with the two women in a tiny fort.

They warn their continuing companions:

"Be careful ... the Indians are killing everyone ...."

"Good-bye"

— answers Sutter, and moves off.

Mary and the three missionaries are following him.

Snakes dart away from the track.

Beasts plunge into the bushes.

And now the track has come to an end.

Only the desert is ahead.

Sutter pulls up his horse in uncertainty.

Sutter considers.

Mary looks at him enquiringly.

They stand before three high wooden columns. These are Indian gods, totem poles. They are trees carved into the forms of men and winged beasts with fearsome expressions.

Sutter takes a coin out of his pocket.

He spins it. "Heads or tails."

He looks at his companions and tosses the coin into the air.

His eyes follow the coin and he sees it glitter against the deep blue of the sky.

"Hey!"

— suddenly shouts one of his companions, and Sutter ducks abruptly down on his horse, avoiding an arrow in its flight.

The arrow lodges in a totem pole.

Mary is the first to fire.

A group of Indians is galloping towards them.

Sutter and his companions shelter behind the poles and shoot.

Some Indians fall.

A scattered volley.

More Indians fall.

But the warriors have contrived to reach the totem poles, and there follows a fearful hand-to-hand struggle beneath the terrible faces of the totems.

A now relatively soundless, ferocious, merciless fight.

Broken only by the grunts of struggle and the groans of dying.

The desert is enormous and the struggling group is tiny in comparison with the endless immensity of the desert.

The Indians break and run. The few surviving Indians flee into the desert.

Two of the missionaries help a wounded colleague to mount, and, without staying for a word, they gallop back down the trail.

Mary shouts to them to stop. She wants to stop them.

They do not hear.

She bites her lip and tears come into her eyes.

And Sutter walks, searching on the ground for the coin on which he has staked his future.

He recognises the spot on which it fell.

Over it lies a dead Indian. He turns him, and kneels down to examine the coin.

Mary watches him in horror.

"We win!"

— shouts Sutter.

"Heads!"

He picks up the coin, rises and shows it to Mary.

Mary is content and smiles.

Sutter borrows the refrain of her song:

"Forward, forward, fortune waits you."

Abandoned by all companions, small and helpless in the

immensity of the desert, they leave the silhouettes of the Indian gods and set out towards the setting sun. The West is their goal.

Thunder ... clouds ... lightning ....

A deluge of rain ... a whirlwind of snow ... heat ... quaking earth ... a whirlwind of dust ... a blizzard of flies ... clouds of humming mosquitoes ... a forest of gigantic trees.

A sluggish stream. Out of the water onto the nearest bank are climbing two persons. It is difficult to recognise Sutter. His beard has grown, he is black with sunburn. Mary is thinner and dark, but beautiful with a new and wild sort of beauty.

Mary must change her dress. Her dress is wet. She has had to swim the river.

Sutter enters the forest to seek a way farther.

Mary enjoys the beautiful day, the cool earth of the banks, and she takes off her wet clothes.

She reaches in her small bag.

She can find nothing to change into while they dry.

Sutter penetrates farther and farther into the forest, trying to discover their best path.

Mary discovers in her bag a little twisted bundle of thin gauze.

She unfolds it on the ground, and takes pleasure in it, for it is her circus skirt, trimmed with flowers and glittering spangles.

She clothes herself in the gauze skirt and puts on Sutter's greatcoat: together they make a quaint costume. She looks at herself in the water and smiles.

And suddenly the smile leaves the image of her face.

She turns her head.

Between two enormous tree trunks there stands a young man, clad in ragged and furred leathers.

He is a trapper, a hunter in this wilderness.

He is hypnotised by the sight of the woman. His eyes, his face, his body are paralysed by the apparition.

Passion, determination and strength are in his gaze.

Mary turns away, seeking an avenue of escape in the opposite direction.

Two other trappers are piercing her with their eyes.

They have faces that are fierce, and greedy.

They are older and more cynical.

They gaze, as beasts gaze at a lump of raw meat.

And behind them the enormous trunks of the trees.

Unending colonnades of trees reaching their roof to the sky.

Barking and growling, a pair of enormous dogs jump forward towards Mary.

Terrified, she steps back and tries to hide between two of the big trees.

The dogs approach her. They bark no longer; they wag their tails and, reaching the woman, begin to sniff at her feet.

The dogs sniffing at her circus skirt.

Terrified beside the dogs, small and cowering in the ring of woman-hungry men, she looks around her.

The enormous forest.

Silence.

And in that silence only the woodpeckers at work, and the sound of their tappings is as the death-roll on the drums of a circus.

A shrill whistle. In horror she covers her face. The dogs retreat.

Near, the face of the young trapper:

"We have seen no woman for two years."

The young trapper gulps, and makes a movement to approach her, but in the same moment he catches his breath and sinks downwards. He has been stabbed.

The second trapper pushes him aside and draws the knife out from between his ribs.

He steps forward, but the third is near. Their shoulders collide, they look each other in the eye.

Suddenly they turn their faces back towards Mary.

A fourth trapper is dragging the resisting Mary into a nest of giant trees.

The two rivals rush towards him. Two shots from among the treetrunks.

One of the attackers falls, the other rushes in.

The one who dragged her into the tree nest, and the one who had rushed in, struggle, not with each other, but to embrace her, kissing her feet, her hands.

The injured man, wounded by the recent shot, drags himself forward, striving towards the struggle.

Mary succeeds in freeing her mouth, and a terrified, agonising shriek rings through the wood.

The echo rings again and again.

Sutter hears and turns, and runs towards it.

The men drag their burden further into the trees.

The woman's circus dog appears from the depths of the wood and hurls itself at the men. The other dogs attack it.

Sutter appears and rushes past the fighting dogs into the nest of trees, pistol in hand.

While we see the conflict of the dogs and hear growling and barking, we also hear shrieks and the sound of Sutter's conflict in the tree nest.

The woman's dog makes a circus leap onto a tree-stump, where it is out of reach of its antagonists, which leap up at it.

Feet in high boots drag painfully past the camera, the feet of a woman being carried trail after them.

The man's feet drag their burden past the stabbed and dying young trapper.

The young trapper sees with delight the feet of the woman trail past close to him. His face lights up as he sees, from one foot, fall a shoe.

A woman's rough travelling shoe.

The dying boy drags himself to the shoe with his last strength, his fingers reach for it and he presses it ecstatically against his cheek.

page 13 (continued) & 14, 15.
Forest

Sutter
Dog.
Italian Woman
4 trappers.
3 mastiffs (dogs)
1. horse

Lasky Ranch

NB. If enough water.
If not : 3 shots (swimming together with scene on page 11 (Boat), but "shore" and following on Ranch

2
(transparency)

Setting: 10 – 15 "big trees"
(about 15–20 feet high)

For double exposure some shots (without actors) in Yosemite [can be done during week end, or during cutting period.]

page 16-18   Desert

Several shots with
Sutter
Italian woman
Horse
Dog   in desert

2½.

3-4 "gigantic" artificial cactuses.
3. artificial bushes.

all the evening material in ranch.
6 - 7 small dogs ("acting" Koyottes)
8 modells of Koyottes with glittering eyes [in the dark]

His strength leaves the young man, and his head falls to the earth.

He dies with a smile on his face.

Sutter — it is he who bears Mary — arranges himself on the saddle of a horse, holding her in his arms.

He whistles the dog, it answers, barking, and joins them.

They continue on their way.

The horse goes slowly through the forest.

Mary is delirious in Sutter's arms.

She speaks of the Golden Land....

"Wealth, happiness and fortune wait us on our road" — sings Mary.

The wood is at an end. Bushes. Fields. Desert.

And in the desert it is spring.

The cactuses are in flower.

A myriad crickets chirrup.

Birds sing.

Deliriously Mary, her voice weakening, utters ever more and more fantastic words.

There is no horse any more. They have lost the horse somewhere....

Sutter bears her in his arms, growing more tired at every step.

There are no more cactuses, nor bushes....

Naked and infinite sands are around them.

Heat rises from the burning sands.

The dog pants, his long tongue hanging from his mouth.

Sutter is exhausted. He kneels and lowers Mary onto the sand. She lies, one foot shod, the other bare, lacking the strength to open her eyes.

Sutter sits near Mary, motionless.

The sun turns in the heavens.

The shadow of the unmoving Sutter turns around him, and then lengthens with the sinking of the sun.

Suddenly the dog starts, and jumps to its feet. It yelps and trembles.

Sutter comes to himself and raises his head.

A ring of black coyotes sits around them.

In the twilight the wild dogs are like darkened silhouettes, and their eyes glisten like those of cats.

Sutter tries to awaken Mary.

But Mary is dead.

The thin, tragic laughter of the coyotes startles him again.

He jumps to his feet and fires wildly in the direction of the laugh.

The coyotes run off in various directions.

Sutter mechanically reaches among his belongings for a spade, but fails to find one.

Finding nothing, he kneels on the ground and begins to scrape a grave with his hands, to the sound of the sarcastic laughter of the coyotes in the desert. The coyotes are in dispersed groups. They howl. They howl.

Mary lies in the grave. Only her face is visible.

Sutter looks long at the pale spot on the darkening sands.

The coyotes creep nearer.

No face now breaks the smoothness of the sand.

Sutter tries to get up, but checks as he catches sight of a torn fragment of the circus skirt. He picks up the fragment and straightens himself.

He takes his gun, holding it before him, and goes forward.

The dog jumps up, makes a movement to follow him, then stops, hearing a new salvo of laughter from the coyotes.

The dog turns its head back towards the grave. It is anxious and undecided.

Sutter departing in the distance. The coyotes close in towards the grave.

The dog, in desperation, howls and whimpers.

It moves its feet, uncertain where to turn.

Sutter is farther, ever farther away.

Frantic with despair, the dog runs to the grave, takes up

a fighting position, and, with its hair bristling wildly
   and baring its fangs, it faces the coyotes.
The ring of coyotes comes ever nearer to the grave.
The cat-like glimmer of their eyes now forms a circle.
Ready to die, the circus dog growls.
Sutter's figure grows ever distant and more distant, until
   swallowed by the shadows of the night.

REEL 3

Title: TWO MORE LONG YEARS HAVE PASSED OF TRAVEL AND ADVENTURE

A fragile schooner sails towards the camera across the
   open sea.
A view of the shore, an earthly paradise from far away.
The sails are being furled, the anchor cast into the water.
A boatload of persons detaches itself from the ship and
   approaches the shore.
As the prow of the boat touches the shore, there leaps
   from it the dog and, following the dog, Sutter.
He is well-dressed and equipped with baggage.
   "So this is San Francisco?"
Sutter's gaze wanders along the shore and he sees the
   lonely hills, some pigs, two or three dilapidated huts
   and a dying, fever-stricken Spanish friar.
Thousands of sea gulls and pelicans circle round the
   coast.
"So this is San Francisco?"
   — asks Sutter of two or three Mexican soldiers.
"This is San Francisco."
   — is the answer.
"But have you the permission of the Governor to land?"

— ask the soldiers of Sutter.

"No."

— says he.

"Well then, re-embark."

They take him by his collar and the seat of his pants, put him in the boat and push the boat into the water.

The soaked dog, shaking the water from its coat, jumps into the boat, while Sutter swears most terribly in Spanish, and the Mexican soldiers swear Mexican oaths back at him.

The imprecations do not cease, but change and change and multiply, while there appears on the screen the entrance to the Governor's house in Monterey, where Sutter is denouncing other soldiers who are refusing him admission.

On the verandah, in the midst of a bevy of ladies bearing sunshades and with squirrels on their laps — in those days it was the fashion for great ladies to keep squirrels in place of lap dogs — we behold Governor Alvarado in person.

The Governor is embroidering the portrait of Washington on an embroidery frame — in those days it was the fashion for great noblemen to go in for embroidery.

He hears the stir at the gate, listens, and explains to the ladies:

"It must be a foreigner."

Then, turning to the gateway, he calls to the soldiers:

"Let him in."

The soldiers obey.

Sutter arranges his clothes, gives his pipe to the dog and enters the gateway.

He introduces himself to the Governor as a captain in the French Army.

Glancing around him he sees everywhere portraits of Washington.

A bust. And, finally, the half-completed embroidery portrait on the frame.

Perceiving the Governor's interest in Washington, he at once begins to speak of him.

He pretends a great interest in Washington, claims to have friends who were friends of his, says that he studied him for years, and as he speaks there passes before the audience the series of tawdry pictures and medallions, and print handkerchiefs with Washington's portrait on them, that he sold as a huckster at the fair.

He pretends a perfect familiarity with the portrait of Washington and steps up to the frame, correcting the position of two pieces of wool to make the embroidery resemble more closely the portrait on the handkerchiefs, "improving the likeness".

The Governor and the ladies are delighted.

The Governor invites him to take a seat and be his guest.

The sentinels at the gateway look savagely down their noses.

The dog, too, is seated. On its haunches before the gateway, it smokes Sutter's pipe.

The soldiers glare with envy at the dog, and, as the smoke rises from its pipe, they savagely sniff the aroma of the weed forbidden to them while on duty.

"You should have land in our country, Captain."

— says the Governor to Sutter, patting him cordially on the back.

The lackey brings a box with seals and sealing wax.

The Governor completes writing a grant, seals it with his seal, and presents it to Sutter:

"Here's your land. Love it and tend it, Captain."

FADE OUT

The fingers of Sutter are crumbling between them a handful of earth.

Sutter looks about him.

Work, vigorous and energetic, is in progress around him.

Bushes are being burnt down, trees being cut and cleared.

page 19

Shore of San Francisco

Sutter
Dog
3 Mexican Soldiers
Spanish friar
2 pigs
Seagulls & pelicans.
Small boat.

½ somewhere on the shore, where there are lots of birds.
(NB.? Catalina Isthmus?)

page 20 & 21.

Monterey
Governor Alvarado
4-5 ladies
4 Mexican Soldiers
Sutter
Dog.

1½

gate-way

Loggia

Sound

gateway
palms
Loggia

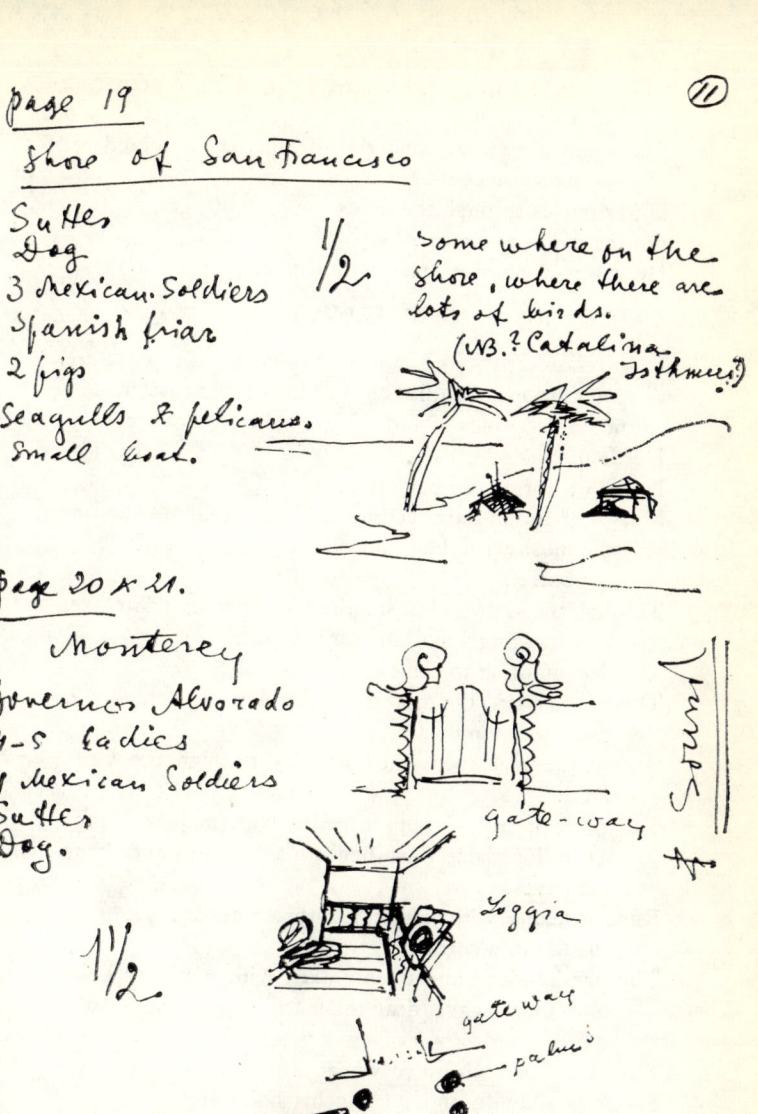

Indians, yoked to ploughs in teams of six, are preparing the earth.

Tents and grass huts; materials are being assembled for construction of the fort.

Sutter passes through the fields.

On the banks of a river.

He enters a gateway fixed with a nameplate.

NEW HELVETIA

In the courtyard sounds music of the drum and the flute, and groups of Indians are drilling to its rhythm.

In the fields groups of Indians are harvesting wheat.

Herds of cattle.

Herds of horses are pasturing.

Masses of Indians are feeding at a long trough, gathering the mush with their hands as it pours out of the rolling barrel.

Through the swamps one hundred and twenty white oxen are dragging a machine for the mill.

The first machine to come to California.

The whips crack, the drivers shout, the wheels creak with mighty clamour.

Slowly the machine wends its way through the virgin land.

Tall piles of fruit — apples, pears, watermelons — grow as Indians heap them beneath shady and over-hanging eaves.

Rude wagons with wheat for threshing are being unloaded in a corral.

The one hundred and twenty oxen with a mighty effort, and a last heave, drag the machine over the brow of a hill.

Mountains of unthreshed wheat grow higher and higher.

Sutter is shaving and parting his hair. He puts on the uniform of a captain and looks in the mirror to adjust his decorations.

The Indians who were taking part in the military exercises are now clothing themselves in soldier's uniforms.

They remove their scanty loincloths of bones and shells, and, for the first time in their lives, draw on trousers and shirts.

Their appearance is comical in this unfamiliar dress.

A signal sounds.

The Indians leap on their horses.

Sutter arranges their costumes and their deportment.

The attitude of everyone towards him is full of respect and veneration.

A German officer, their instructor, gives the command.

The group of Indians on horseback clad in gaudy uniforms, Sutter at their head, passes through the gateway of the fort.

A herd of wild horses is waiting to be driven into the enclosure that holds the unthreshed piles of wheat.

Sutter and his detachment pause. He gives the command for the threshing to begin.

The herd of wild horses is driven into the corral.

His soldiers rush forward and take part in the shouting.

Another signal and they are re-formed into marching order.

The wild horses, frenzied by shouting and the cracking of pursuing whips, rush in mad gallop, trampling and leaping on the unthreshed wheat, beating the grain upon the ground.

Pigeons, birds of all shapes and sizes, descend upon the grain in clouds.

A Sutter detachment encounters the expedition of General Fremont.

Fremont is astonished at the barbaric pomp of Sutter's greetings.

The two detachments approach the fort.

An orchestra of Kanakas plays on Hawaiian instruments the Marseillaise — in honour of Fremont's ancestry — and Sutter's favourite Swiss air.

The cannons of the fort fire a welcoming salute.
The horses in mad gallop are still threshing the wheat.
The train of white oxen arrives at the fort with the machine.
Amid boisterous "Huzzas" the flag of the United States takes the place of the Mexican flag on the mast of Sutter's fort.
A festival of rejoicing completes the occasion.
Milk in barrels, fruit in wagonloads.
Carcasses roasted on spits.
Wine flowing from wineskins, and drunk from huge bowls made of bull's horns and Chinese lacquer.
Everywhere, softly moving, neatly aproned Indian girls.
Sutter is at the height of his dignity and power.
He sits on the terrace of his house.
The dog, grizzled and heavy, sits near him.
Both of them are dreaming.
The day is drawing to its close, the sun sinking beneath the horizon.
Tired out with work and play, the retainers sleep upon the ground around.
Their satisfied snores sound upon the cooing air.
The cooing of well-fed pigeons.
The grasshoppers make their music in the grass.
A woman's laughter is heard from the bushes, where Fremont's soldiers are making friends with Sutter's girls.
The symphony of these sounds fills the air with a feeling of satisfaction and repletion.
On the table near Sutter stands a small box.
He takes from it the fragments of a tinsel skirt.
The dog lifts its head and wags its tail.
He stares at the glittering fragment and thinks of days gone by.
In the same little box there is a medallion.
In the medallion is a portrait of his wife and children.
In his two hands, the two relics of his past.

Coy and pleasing woman's laughter sounds low from the bushes.

Sutter stares at the sunset.

He replaces the fragment of gauze in the box, and retains in his hand the miniature of his family.

The Hawaiian guitars play a lyric and passionate melody.

Title: AFTER 14 YEARS OF SEPARATION, SUTTER SENDS HIS FIRST LETTER TO HIS WIFE.

                                              FADE OUT

REEL 4

Title: FRIDAY

On the ground is beating a merciless and ceaseless deluge of rain.

Title: THE 28th OF JANUARY.

The deluge continues.

Title: 1848.

The deluge.

Sutter writes, seated before an old writing desk.

The hopeless rain beats on the windows.

The gallop of horse's hooves is heard, beating through the rain.

Sutter lifts his head, rises to his feet, takes his gun and approaches the window.

The sound of the gallop approaches.

The door is flung open and, with a gust of rain, a man in dripping clothes rushes into the room oversetting two chairs.

"Marshall!"

    — shouts Sutter and runs to meet him.

Marshall is frenzied with excitement and out of breath. Exhausted by his journey, he finds difficulty in uttering his news.

But, through the broken fragments of speech, the fact gradually penetrates that what he has to tell is vitally secret, and he implores that the door be shut.

Sutter closes the door.

With trembling hands, Marshall takes a package out of his pocket, and tries to unfold it with his trembling fingers.

The door opens, in comes one of Sutter's clerks in search of something in a cupboard.

Marshall thrusts his package hastily back into his pocket and glares at the man.

The man, innocently and without hurrying, takes what he needs and goes away.

As soon as he is gone, Marshall shuts the door again. Comes close to Sutter, takes out the little package and begins to unfold it with ever trembling fingers.

Into the room comes a servant girl.

Marshall hastily hides the package.

He goes to the girl and thrusts her out of the room, slamming the door.

They fail to find the key, and Marshall takes a table and lays it across the door.

Again he takes out his package, and at last he unfolds it and shows it to Sutter.

His fingers, trembling, hold the paper, with, on it, some tiny grains of metal.

Title: GOLD?

Title: GOLD?

Title: G O L D ?

Hands completing a chemical test on the grains and Sutter's voice answering softly and definitely:
"Gold."

Sutter is standing at the table, with the gold and reagent in his hands and grief on his face. He repeats yet lower:
"Gold!"[1]

Title: GOLD.

Rushing up from small to fill screen and, in a simultaneously rising inhuman roar the word "GOLD!"

"Gold!"
— shrieks Marshall at the top of his voice, overturning the table, flinging the door open and rushing into the yard.

Sutter rushes to the window and opens it, ignoring the rain, and shouts after Marshall:
"Stop! Stop!"

But Marshall does not hear. Through rain and tempest he gallops on his furious way.

In the room with the overturned table, a cupboard also on its side, the rain coming unheeded through the window and the wind playing havoc with the papers in the room, the door flung open, stands Sutter, brooding in foreboding over the gold on the table.

A fresh gust of wind blows out the light. The dim outlines of the windswept room slowly *fade out*.

In a long *fade in*:

A grey and misty morning.

Sutter dismounts from horseback near his sawmill in Coloma where the first gold was discovered.

The Indians working at the mill are in the grip of superstitious horror.

They say the gold belongs to the devil, they know it of old, and they implore Sutter not to make use of it.

Sutter answers that in any case they must first complete the construction of his sawmill.

He urges them all to pledge themselves to keep the discovery secret.

They all pledge themselves to keep the secret.

And Sutter is on his way home.

He passes through the prosperous landscape of a happy countryside.

Wealth, fertility and contentment are everywhere.

The rain has ceased, the garment of nature is soft and sparkling. Myriads of raindrops shimmer in the sunshine.

Suddenly he encounters a group of working people with picks and pans for gold-washing.

Astonished, Sutter follows them with his eyes, then turns his horse and gallops to the fort.

Out of the drink store near the fort runs the storekeeper who hastens up to Sutter and shows him gold dust in the palm of his hand.

He asks Sutter whether it be gold or no.

Sutter inclines his head.

Shouting: "Gold! Gold!" the man runs into his store.

Sutter, nervous and ill at ease, rides through the gateway of the fort.

The storekeeper nails up the door of his store.

All he has is flung onto a wagon.

His help steals two of Sutter's horses from the corral.

The storekeeper drives off furiously towards the gold.

Two Indians working in a field are listening to the tale of a woman who, with much gesticulation, is telling them the news.

Flinging down their tools the Indians follow in the direction taken by the storekeeper.

The herdsman deserts his herd.

The husband abandons his wife and children. They weep and implore him, but he abandons them.

The schoolmaster leaves his school and his pupils.

Groups of Sutter's workpeople set out on the road.

Ever more and more people stop working and join them.

Fields and homes are a desert.

Sutter puts on his finger a ring with the inscription:

FIRST GOLD FOUND 1848.

On the ring are the arms of his native town.

Picks, shovels and crowbars begin to bite into the earth.

The sound of the sand moving in the wooden working pans, the dashing of water, begins to creep over the forests and the fields.

The sound of the picks, and the sound of the stones that are discarded from the working pans grows louder and louder.

Still the sound of the picks and the hoarse grate of the shovels scraping the stony ground is ever louder and louder, ever more and more insistent.

The sounds pervade the whole land.

And beneath this tearing sound the dominion of Sutter falls to waste and destruction from its own fertility and luxuriance.

The boughs of the fruit trees are cracking with their over-burden of ripe fruit.

Barrels are exploding with the over-fermentation of their wine and beer.

Horses, untended and not foddered, break out of their corrals and rush pasturing into the fields of wheat.

Cows fill the air with lowings of pain, their udders un-relieved, and, maddened, they break down the walls of their stables, trampling flowers and vegetables.

High-piled sacks of grain and flour burst with the tension of their long-standing weight and the grain runs down and scatters in the wind.

Dams overfull, locks broken down, the water of the streams rushing on its natural course.

Sutter, deserted by his people, wanders through this wasted desolation, hearkening to the symphony of the working of the mines.

"Gold". The word rings through the forest, and its echo goes ringing through the hills and canyons.

And then, from the depths of these canyons, arrives a symphony of new sounds.

These sounds are the sounds of thousands of feet tramping upon the stones.

The sounds of endless trails of creaking wagons.

The sounds of horses' hooves and the screeching of wagon wheels.

And the murmur of endless mobs.

The first wagon appears near the fort.

A rough and savage man tears out some flowers, and takes a pole for tent-making.

The sound of the approaching march grows louder and louder.

Sutter sits on a hill.

His old dog is pressed against him.

The sounds are quite near, he can hear human voices.

He hears that the people are come from far away, that there is no end to their human stream.

And through that sound is heard the beat of axes, felling the trees, the whistling of saws, and the falling of the trees.

Pigs are screaming in slaughter, and frightened ducks quack frantically as they hurry away from those pursuing them.

Sutter is maddened by these sounds. And now to them is added the renewed sound of the picks, and of stones piled high out of the river, stones encroaching and burying under them the fertile fields. Stones rapidly being built into mountains that crush under them all trace of the fertility that went before this terrible symphony of sounds.

Dark, and the crackling of a little fire at his feet that lights the face of Sutter sitting on his hill.

Colossal are the sounds of the mob that are giving his land to destruction.

Sutter is in an agony of despair.

And the saws continue to whine and the axes to fall, and

the trees to tumble and the picks to beat on the stones.

The oaths of the gold diggers in the heat of the gold fever.

These things madden Sutter, and he takes refuge in the darkness of the forest.

REEL 5

The gentle, melancholy bell of a Swiss church tower is tolling its song.

And, just as 15 years before, sits Mrs. Sutter at a table, her head bent lowered upon an open letter in her hand.

And, just as 15 years before, her children sit around her.

They are now 15 years older. Already grown folks, three youths and a girl.

And the letter speaks of "children".

And the letter urges "come to New Helvetia".

That is why Mrs. Sutter is distressed once more.

The pastor advises her to go.

He speaks with the utmost deference of her husband, who has remembered them after so many years.

Enters the children's schoolmaster. He returns from a visit to the bank and brings money — real money — to pay the debts of Sutter and the expenses of the long journey to the new country of Sutter.

The schoolmaster has heard tell of Sutter in his visit to the bank. He says that Sutter has discovered a new country. That over there, it seems, he is something of a William Tell.

All the little town is excited by the news and turns out to see Mrs. Sutter as she boards the phaeton with her family.

The townsfolk long wave their handkerchiefs and smile farewell to her as the phaeton leaves the town.

And among them are many of those who looked askance at her 15 long years before.

Mrs. Sutter reads the letter over and over again.

She lifts her head and pronounces the name of her husband:

"Johann...."

She is seated on the deck of a ship.

She gazes over the vast expanse of the ocean. She muses.

The ship is laden with people travelling to California.

Through their gossip flit the words: "Gold... California... Sutter... Sutter...."

"Johann...."

— whispers his wife.

"Sutter... Sutter... Sutter...."

— flits through the gossip of the travellers.

A woman sits near Anna (Mrs. Sutter). The woman speaks of Sutter admiringly and ecstatically.

She says that he is famous.

Everyone has heard of him.

Everyone speaks of him.

And now....

A young girl speaks of him, naively and lyrically. Of how marvellous, how beautiful is the hero so precious to her. She dreams of him.

An old man speaks of him. Of his riches. Of the infinite expanse of his lands. His herds. His gold.

A young man speaks of him. Of his strength. His courage. His energy.

Poets weave legends around him.

Gold is picked from his soil merely by stooping down. Pearls, diamonds are gathered by the shovelful. A land of fairy tale, a land fair and flourishing.

"California... Sutter... Sutter... Sutter...." pervades and dominates the tales on every lip.

Daylight, eventide and night follow one another upon the earth and, ever musing, sits the wife of this man.

And with the birth of her excitement there is born the first trembling sounds of a chord.

A chord ever strengthening and its tone ever rising upwards, trembling and sobbing.

The hands of Mrs. Sutter tremble.

And "Sutter ... Sutter ...." the world endlessly re-echoes.

The word emerges in speech of every tongue.

Sutter the King.

Sutter the Hero.

Sutter the Rich Man.

Sutter the Genius.

Sutter the Emperor.

— proclaim Indians, Chinese, Frenchmen, Russians, Czechs, Japanese and Spaniards each in their several tongues.

And out of this chorus of exclamations is formed a song, a song without melody, but a song solemn and rhythmic.

A motley crowd, a crowd of many nations, rushes to board the train.

They take the train by storm.

In the flood are Anna and her children. Her sons defend her from the pressure of the flood. But the flood sweeps them on.

"California... Gold... Sutter... Sutter...."

— the infinite voice of the mob.

"Johann....."

— the barely distinguishable voice of Anna, and a new surge of the crowd carries her further.

"Ss-u-tt-er ...."

— the hoarse rattle of a dying Negro. Foam on his lips. Swamp is around him, the tools of a gold digger are in his hands.

Cradling her baby in her arms sits a young mother, crooning a song.

"Sutter ... Sutter ...." is the burden of her song.

Locked in one another's arms sit a pair of lovers, murmuring a song.

"Sutter ... Sutter ...." is the burden of their song.

The rhythmical lilt of the wagon wheels. The throb of the engine envelops the wheel sounds but preserves the same rhythm.

Even the wheels pronounce the name.

"Sutter ... Sutter ...
Sutter ... Sutter ...."

Anna is seated at the open door of a baggage wagon.

The landscape passes before her eyes.

The wheels ever rattle the name, and increasing and increasing is the excitement of the woman and ever more marked is the trembling of her hands.

And again the chord.

The sobbing, long-drawn-out, crescendo chord, vibrating like her nerves, beating like her heart.

Anna closes her eyes and, in a broken voice, pronounces the same and ever the same name —

"Johann ...."

"Sutter ... Sutter ...."

— is caught up by a host of voices, singing, loudly and clearly, the song of Sutter and California.

Citizens of every nation, filling the train to overflowing and clinging to the buffers, sing that song.

Like a march sounds that song, and past, past fly the woods, the swamps, the villages.

Into the sky, to the uppermost clouds, mount the words of the song.

And a sailing boat emerges against the background of that sky.

Anna sits on the deck of the sailing boat.

The wooden deck of the ship creaking.

The waves dashing themselves against her sides.

The barrels rolling in her hold.
The wind whistling through the web of her rigging.
In every one of these sounds, there echoes, rings, re-echoes ever one and the same name.
The very elements chant the song of Sutter.
Lulled by the waves, Anna, dreaming, and motionless sits on the deck of the ship.
Under the song of the elements she sees the land of fairy tale.
Sees gold, and diamonds, and rare fruits and the fabled Eldorado.
Mounted on a snow-white steed, in the robes of a king, glittering and golden, Sutter — dimly visioned — rides — his land.
Nearer and nearer comes the horseback emperor.
And again the chord. The sobbing and vibrating chord mounting crescendo in its sobs, and trembling ever more rapidly and more rapidly, and more nervously and more nervously.
"Johann!"
— cries Anna, and comes to herself.
Her children are standing over her.
"Mummy...
Soon we shall be there."
— says her daughter.
Anna is gaunt.
Her eyes are sunken.
Her hair is grey.
Her strength is gone.
On a litter borne by two mules she continues on her way.
The children ride horseback.
Over the sand-baked plains.
Through forests, over hills proceeds their march.
At last they are before the gates of Hock Hermitage.
By some accident the gateway has not lost its pomp and majesty.

And a smile lightens the white face of Anna as she sees the gateway.

She closes her eyes.

And once more the soft sobbing chord begins its trembling crescendo. The chord rises higher and higher, mounts more and more pitifully and touchingly.

"Mummy, it's Papa....

Here he comes."

— says the daughter.

Anna catches her breath and the chord ceases.

Sutter is on a hill and the light makes him look majestic and beautiful.

In very fact he looks like a king.

Anna gazes at him with wide opened eyes.

"Johann..."

— contrives Anna with failing strength.

"Johann..."

She blushes and seeks to adjust a curl, to hide a wisp of grey hair.

"Johann..."

She shudders, then shrieks, bites her lips, closes her eyes.

A blow on the chord and the sobbing sound runs from its nadir to its apex and, reaching its highest timbre, shatters —

The chord bursts shrill.

And Anna falls back on the litter.

Death is on her face.

In the air sound the overtones of the shattered chord.

Sutter is on his knees before the body of his wife.

He is old, and the passing glory of his face has passed.

A miserable, broken, grey-haired old man.

"Father."

He hears a loud voice.

He lifts his head.

And in front of him stand his three sons.

page 21 (continued) – 24.   ⑫

Sutter fort ("New Helvetia)

7½ days

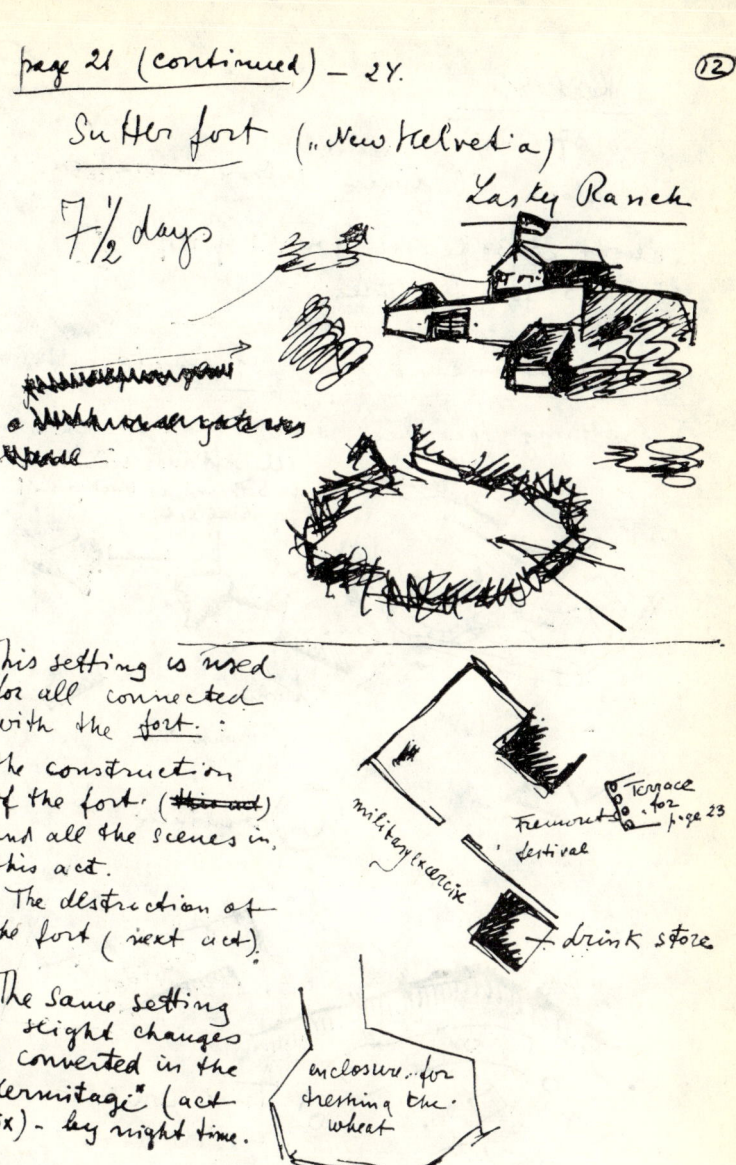

Lasky Ranch

This setting is used for all connected with the fort.:

the construction of the fort. (~~his act~~) and all the scenes in this act.

The destruction of the fort (next act).

The same setting by slight changes is converted in the "Hermitage" (act six) – by night time.

military exercise

Fremont festival

Terrace for page 23

drink store

enclosure for threshing the wheat

Reel Six

page 37
Saloon ordinary saloon decoration.

about 25-30 persons. [men & girls]
Frogs for frog-races.

San Francisco Street, square etc.

Setting for Reel Six & Reel Seven.

all outdoor scenes
in S.F. and as background
for trial setting.

turning house

Fountain

corridor

Trial court

Three enormous strapping sons, decisive and brimful of
 life.
"Father, we shall fight."
  — say the sons.
Sutter rises and braces himself and repeats the words:
 "We shall fight."

REEL 6

T ra-la-la ...
  ... tra-la-la."
    — sings a girl and her feet dance, tripping as care-
 free and as vulgar as the musical refrain.
A burst of male laughter, alike impertinent and gross.
The men are betting on frog races.
They wager little sacks of gold.
The starter stands in the middle of the room and calls the
 names of the gross unwinking frogs.
Gambling fever, the recklessness of the gold diggers
 pervades the room.
It is a saloon. The scene of drink, squabbles, dancing and
 gambling.
Drunkards are thrown out through the doors.
They fly out into the street and pitch in the dirt, among
 the goats and barrels.
Through the streets runs a man.
He runs up the steps of the saloon beneath the inscrip-
 tion:

SAN FRANCISCO
SALOON

Opening the door of the saloon he shouts a slang word
 boding peril and danger.

He holds up a paper and announces:

"Sutter has started a law suit."

Flabbergasted, everyone is struck dumb by the unexpectedness of the news.

And the terrible name of Sutter once more fills the air.

Terrific and fearsome as never before.

"Sutter."

Ten padlocks on a gateway.

Barns chock-full with goods and stock.

Enormous are his money coffers.

Ten padlocks on his gateway.

The still dumbfounded people in the saloon.

"Sutter."

An old face, firm and grim, approaches the camera with the increase in loudness of the word.

His hypnotising eyes strike awe and uneasiness in all beholders.

He stands in the window of his house.

His house is walled like a fortress, and at every defence slit stands a guard with four-barrelled gun.

A guard raises his gun and sights it.

A man runs along the darkened road.

One, two, shoots the guard, and the man falls with a shout, dropping the tools of a gold digger.

At the sound of the firing there leap up out of the bushes an Indian boy and a girl.

Three, four, fires the guard.

Incomprehensible and sorrowful words the Indian girl utters over the body of her lover.

The terrible silhouette of Sutter in the window of his house.

And the people in the saloon still stand dumbfounded.

And not only in the saloon.

On the streets.

On the square.

Through all these places rings and rings the news.

"Sutter is bringing a suit."

Claiming the land on which we live.
Claiming San Francisco.
"Sutter is bringing suit."
The sound of quills scratching on paper.
People writing, writing.
Mountains of paper, barricades of paper, flooding rooms and climbing onto tables, shutting out the lights of windows, cluttering up the floors.
Dressed in stiff and uncongenial coat —
— his eldest son directs scribes and secretaries.

Title: 17,221 PERSONS PROSECUTED BY SUTTER.

Sutter brings action against seventeen thousand two hundred and twenty-one persons. The newspapers are full of it.
And on the streets of San Francisco — fog.
Those strange streets on which houses are made out of ships.
Streets on which the evening lanterns are beginning to be lit. Lonely streets. But....
Appears a black figure in a strange black cloak and passes by, stepping on planks through the mud.
And two other figures, just like the first, emerge out of the fog.
And another group, also mysteriously clad.
A large boat appears out of the fog and stops at a wharf.
From the boat emerge ten or fifteen persons, as sinister as the others.
A second, a third boat draws up at the wharf, discharging its ominous cargo of persons.
"This will be no lawsuit — this will be a battle..."
— says one Negro to another, sitting on a barrel and watching the unloading of the sinister figures.
The black figures are encountered on the wharf, persons go with them into dark corners.

In the saloons, in the houses, on the streets everyone
   speaks of the lawsuit.
The gold diggers take their graduated turkey-feather
   quills and gold dust runs emptying out of them as
   ink runs onto other quills.
And scratch, scratch go the quills.
Dossier after dossier is written by the black-clad figures.
The sun rises above the town, the town is already in
   movement.
Scores of lawyers in black top hats elbow their way
   through the crowds.
Everyone's road today leads to the court of justice.
"This will be no lawsuit — this will be a battle."
   — says a sailor sitting on the roof of a house built on
   the deck of a ship.

Title: THE SUIT.

The President opens the proceedings.
Sutter and his sons and lawyers are on one side.
An army of lawyers on the other.
There are so many lawyers that there is no room for the
   defendants. The anxious defendants crowd the cor-
   ridors.
They crowd the streets outside.
The word is to the attorney for the prosecution.
Before him is an immense trunk full of documents.
One after the other the documents are presented with
   pointed gestures of the prosecuting attorney's hand,
   and, with the presentation of each document, is heard
   the sound of a faraway shell.
Shell after shell despatches the prosecuting attorney, and
   to every explosion answers the growl of the mass of
   his enemies.
"Yes."
   — demands the prosecuting attorney of his enemies,
   claiming the authenticity of each document.
"No."

— surges the growl of his hundreds of enemies.
"Proved."
— decides the President of the Court.
A new shell, and a new growling.
"Yes."
"No."
"Proved,"
— says the President of the Court.
Ever more frenzied the rage of the defendants.
Ever more overpowering the battery of the documents.
And suddenly there leaps up a tiny man who shouts vehemently and in a thin voice:
"No, no, no, no, no . . ."
— like a machine gun his strange hysteria sounds in the rising clamour of the crowd. And in the growling of the mob his sounds become indistinguishable and there remains only the machine gun rhythm of his speech.
A shell — the rattle of a machine gun.
A shell — the rattle of a machine gun.
Bombardment, explosions and so forth, all the actual noises of a violent battle.
The battle in full force.
The clamour of the mob.
The shaking of the fists of the four attorneys of Sutter and his sons.
Shouting, oaths, applause and whistling mingled all together in the sounds of the battle.
Then, dominating all the noise and battle, the oldest son of Sutter points through the window to his office, announcing that, heaped in there, are thousands upon thousands of grants and documents infallibly crushing the opposition.
The noise stops immediately, and everyone turns to look through the window at the office.
The noise and whispers in the corridors cease.
No one moves.

The voices on the square cease, everybody stops speaking and everybody looks.

The big building of the offices of Sutter's son.

Through the windows heaps and piles of paper.

But the battle has been resumed in the courthouse.

Sutter smiles for he feels victory approaching.

The whispers are resumed in the corridors.

And the nervous hubbub in the square.

Only one man stands like a statue, his gaze fixed on the office of Sutter's son.

Now there are three men staring at the office.

At the extreme moment of fury in the courthouse, two men fling a barrel of kerosene against the door of the office.

The barrel breaks and splashes kerosene all over the door.

A burning brand flies over the mob.

A sheet of flame immediately flies up and envelopes the whole house.

In one moment the entire crowd rushes towards the house.

All in the corridors press themselves against the windows.

In the midst of his speech the son of Sutter stops suddenly.

He rushes out of the room.

Sutter leaps up with a fearful curse against the scoundrels.

All precipitate themselves towards the window.

The son of Sutter rushes frantically through the mob into the house to perish with a shriek amidst the flames.

Alone, the tiny figure of the President preserves unruffled dignity. In a soft voice he pronounces the words:
"In view of new circumstances the suit is indefinitely adjourned."

Sutter turns and clenches his fists in mad anger at the President. But his two remaining sons grip him fast.

The mob is dancing round the fire.

Sutter breaks down in an armchair, and, accompanied by

shouts and whistling and the sound of the flames; the lawyers stiffly, coldly and ironically pack their papers by the light of the glow of the fire, nodding to each other with the firelight on their faces.

REEL 7

Title: A MAN CAN BE FIVE YEARS OLD.

A five-year-old boy smiles from the screen.

Title: AND A TOWN CAN BE FIVE YEARS OLD.

View of the five-year-old San Francisco from a hill.

Title: 5

The number is painted, cut out of paper, fixed on doors and on gates.
The number is hoisted on the masts of ships, and drawn aloft on flags.
The number is made in decoration on garlands and banners.

Title: FIVE YEARS OF SAN FRANCISCO.

The town is making ready for a festival.
The town is gaily decorated, and on the spot where stand the remains of the burnt offices a rostrum has been erected.
The firemen clean their engines.
The artillery clean their guns.
The cavalry clean their horses.
Some persons are engaged in decorating their homes when somebody casually mentions the name of Sutter.
Sutter — Sutter — the founder, the pioneer, the patriarch — he must be the central figure of our feast.

Groups assemble, delegates start out.

Sutter is old, morose, deep in his reading of the Apocalypse.

The group of delegates approaches the gateway. The two sons parley with them, reluctant to admit them.

Aroused, Sutter starts up from his reading, takes out his pistols and faces the door.

The door swings open.

Disclosed, facing him, two ranks of five-year-old children, white-clad, with sashes labelled SAN FRANCISCO.

"Sutter, Sutter, he's our hero.

    Father, Father of our State."

    — immediately begin the children, in a mechanical childish pipe.

Behind them smiling delegates —

    "Tomorrow is the Jubilee of the town.

    You are to be the hero of the Jubilee.

    Honour is in store for you, Captain Sutter."

Sutter does not want to go.

The people are insistent.

The sons seek to persuade him.

Sutter is silent.

Disregarding, they surround him and lead him cheering to the phaeton.

Horses taken out, they drag along the phaeton.

His sons are with him.

He is morose and mistrustful.

He looks at the people with fear and mistrust.

Nervously he moves round his finger the ring of the first gold.

                              FADE OUT

At the outskirts of the town a crowd is waiting.

Across the main street of the town is a triumphal arch.

Out of the town comes a detachment of soldiers.

Out of a tent steps Sutter in a new general's uniform.

His two sons behind him.

To the sound of music and shouting the people greet him and run towards him.

Fearfully and suspiciously the old man disbelieves the welcome of the crowd.

The people raise him on their hands.

They raise him above their heads and take him to the town.

Under the decorated triumphal arch.

Through the ranks of soldiers.

The people sing the song of Sutter.

The joyous, swelling song of California.

From the balconies and roofs above float flowers and streamers.

On the square all is ready for the parade.

The soldiers are in formation.

The rostrum is crowded with dignitaries.

They sit the General on a white and fiery steed.

Behold, Sutter rides a snow-white steed in a glittering uniform.

But — otherwise than in the imagination of Anna.

Acclamation as he nears the rostrum.

The Mayor of the town presents Sutter with a document appointing him General.

The soldiers and the officers present arms.

People shout and throw their hats in the air. Women throw their bonnets.

The artillery discharge a salvo.

The ships an answering salvo.

The bells peal in the churches.

The orchestras play furiously.

The banners wave in the windows.

Flowers cover the ground near the feet of his horse.

His two sons like adjutants by his side.

Sutter raises his hand.

All is quiet awaiting his voice.

"Thank you."

And the shouts break anew in the sky.

Showers of fireworks break in the evening sky.
The town is filled with light and laughter, music and rejoicing.
Only the face of Sutter is ever fearful and mistrusting.
Beset by waves of enthusiasm and music rides the old man through the streets of San Francisco.
And the song of California, the joyous song is on every man's lips.

FADE OUT

The festival is over.
The town has returned to everyday.
Banners and garlands are taken down.
It is early in the morning and the streets are yet empty of people.
Sutter is in the street, adjusting his stirrup with the heavy movements of an old man.
In a lonely square, the only sound is the gurgle of the fountain.
A man is running across the square.
The man runs to Sutter and hands him a paper, shouting: "General, you have won your case."
Sutter tensely and silently reads the paper, and as he reads the line of his shoulders straightens, his figure grows youthful and more forceful, and the expression of youth appears once more on his face.
When he has finished the paper, he raises a joyful face and —

Title: JUSTICE

and
"Justice!"
— shouts Sutter in a voice of thunder, as he leaps into the saddle with the agility of youth.
His horse rears in the air.
His horse rears in the air with the unexpected impact of the youthful leap of Sutter.

The horse dances on the ground while Sutter speaks to the man.

He tells him that he must not lose a minute, he is on his way to Washington to ratify the decision.

He laughs with a laugh of thunder.

He laughs who had never laughed before.

His laughter rolls through the streets and re-echoes at their uttermost ends.

People awaken and rush to their windows.

Like a madman laughs Sutter.

Catching sight of the fountain, in an echo of his young hooliganism he spits into the fountain.

"Justice!"

— shouts Sutter and sets off in mad gallop down the street.

People run to the fountain and look astonished after him.

Sutter is bubbling over with joyful laughter. He laughs and sings and whistles in the measure of his horse's pace.

Happy is the tinkle of the bells of the bridle of the horse.

Happy are the sounds of the effort of the belly of the horse.

Beautiful is the road before him.

The people are holding meetings in the square.

"He has won his case. He has won his case."

"We are ruined, ruined."

And not only on the square.

At the corners of the streets.

At the blind ends of alleys.

In the tone of their phrases more and more menacing become the people.

More and more nervous are their shouts.

People are drinking whiskey in the saloons. The bartenders are serving spirits free.

People are growing drunk, and, with the spirits, springs up a growing bravado.

Already a drunken man is shouting and waving his fists.

The drunken crowd shouts with him, its words are not distinguishable.
But distinguishable is the menace in its tone.
The shouter jumps down from the rostrum and makes towards the street out of the town.
The crowd surges behind him.
"Forward — forward —"
— Sutter sings vigorously to the joyous rhythm of his gallop.
"— fortune waits you."
And the little bells of Sutter's horse tinkle to the tune of his song.
The sound of the hooves, the jingle of the harness of the horse, the sound of the wheezing in the horse's belly blend in a single composition like a gay triumphant march.
It is Mary's song, the song of adventure, but now the music sounds in joyous and energetic tone.
Higher and higher winds the road, and on his way stands a Spanish mission of the hills.
On the terrace of the mission sits a group of unmoving Indians, and like a still statue stands a tall figure of a friar.
Motionless, they all gaze at one spot over the forests and the mountain trees.
The gay Sutter jumps down from his horse.
"It is you, Captain."
— says the friar.
"General, General —"
— shouts Sutter and stops, turning his head and looking in the same direction as everyone else.
The reflection of an enormous fire hangs upon the clouds.
The reflection grows brighter and brighter, and the glow becomes more and more intense.
"It is your house that is burning, General —"
— says the friar.
"A-h-h... Scoundrels!"

— shouts Sutter and, turning the head of his horse, he gallops back along the road on which he came.
Once more tinkle the trappings of the horse.
And once more the sound of the hooves, and the sound of the pantings of the belly of the horse.
But now full of fear and anxiety are the rhythm and the tune.
And in the tune mingles the sound of the burning.
The crackling of burning wood.
The pitiful tinkle of breaking glass.
The roaring of falling roofs.
Shots.
Shouts.
And the roaring laughter of the mob.
And again the jingle of the harness.
And the rattle of the hooves on the stones.
And the panting in the belly of the horse.
The tinkle of the bells and the short gasping pants of the horse.
Sutter arrives at the bridge he has crossed once before.
The bridge is burning, Sutter gallops through the water.
The horse is losing its strength.
The fire illuminates the terrible gallop.
With the crackling and roaring of the falling buildings, the horse shudders and falls.
Sutter jumps to his feet.
And suddenly all is quiet.
Sutter stands alone in the field. His eyes are closed.
He opens his eyes. A fearful picture of the ravages of the fire is before him.
The smoking ruins of his house.
The silhouette of a half-broken stove.
The silhouette of a naked half-burned tree, and, hanging from a branch, the figure of the man who first told him of his victory.
Eagles and vultures are tearing at the dead bodies of cows.

And the wind flutters the scorched leaves of his Apocalypse.

A black desert around him.

"Thank you —"

— says Sutter, and age and tiredness come into their own.

His old and broken figure ambles away in the direction of the sunrise.

The strange and broken figure of the old man wanders through the streets of the town.

He passes restaurants, gardens, hotels, shops bearing signs with the inscriptions:

SUTTER HOTEL
RESTAURANT SUTTER
SUTTER STREET

He does not see these notices.

Without any contact with them, he passes by.

And he approaches the building of the courts of justice.

As he sits on the steps of its enormous staircase —

— he rearranges his General's orders on the now old and dirty uniform and asks himself:

"Am I a General?"

— and he answers himself:

"Yes, I'm a General."

Down the steps comes running a tiny newspaper boy.

He runs towards Sutter and holds out a sheet:

"General — you have won your suit."

He shows him the sheet.

But Sutter does not look at the sheet.

He straightens up his figure from the ground, but he cannot straighten his old, old back.

And suddenly the chord begins to sob. That same dying chord that tore the life of Anna.

Sutter hearkens to it.

The scrunch of sand, the noise of picks.

The macabre laughter of the coyotes.

And again the sound of the human avalanche rising through the air.

And the death chord running tremblingly to its crescendo.

Sutter is aroused, an expression of triumph appears upon his face.

"August..."

— he hears the whispering voice of Mary.

"Johann..."

— says the dying voice of Anna.

The sounds grow stronger and stronger as the strength leaves Sutter.

His diabolic laughter joins the other sounds.

The shriek of his son dying in the fire.

The song of the elements about Sutter.

The rolling of the wagon wheels pronouncing his name.

The roaring of the mob.

Orchestras.

Salvos of cannon.

All increases in one majestic symphony whose content is the life of John Augustus Sutter.

And as the symphony sounds ever louder and louder the weaker grows his body.

"Hurrah-h!" sounds on the highest fortissimo of the symphony, even transcending it.

Every sound is shrill, every note is piercing.

Ringing above all is the note of the breaking chord.

And suddenly every tune stops.

"Thank you."

— says Sutter, falling, as he dies, upon the steps.

The camera rushes up the steps.

The entrance to the courts of justice.

A big empty room. Empty chairs.

His little black figure on the wide immensity of the flight of steps.

The sun advances on its eternal way, and an enormous shadow of the court of justice lies like a black curtain across the steps.

And a voice unknown, from a place unknown, speaks the
    words:
    "People die.
    Facts are covered in the dust of history.
    Legends are forgotten."
The shadow creeps and creeps, ever more and more
    covering the stairs, and in its black darkness disappears the dead Sutter.
"Legends are forgotten.
    But songs —
    Songs remain!"
And as the words THE END appear upon the screen,
    there is heard the sound of the joyous lively song
    that everybody knows, the song of California.

An American Tragedy

Scenario
by
S. M. EISENSTEIN, G. V. ALEXANDROV
AND IVOR MONTAGU

Based upon the novel
by
THEODORE DREISER

NOTE

This also is a first script.

In this case the first script represents a more advanced stage of preparation in one respect, less in another. The action and characterisation is worked out in much greater detail, as befits the more complex theme of *An American Tragedy*. But the paragraphing, though it represents carefully and in detail the succession of the *action*, does not yet so clearly or precisely prescribe the exact eventual image-succession.

The paragraphing here again substantially follows that of the original typescript.* The next, save for minor corrections to slips in the typescript — is likewise unaltered from the original.

* See note on scripts, page 342

REEL 1

1.
Darkness.

The low inspired voice of a woman is heard rising and
 falling in the singsong of a chanted sermon. Gradually there mingles with the voice the sounds of the
 city and the noises of the street. The siren of an ambulance — the anxious ringing of a streetcar. The
 characteristic cries of newsboys. The tooting of auto-
 mobiles. Gruff music through radio horns. With the
 ever-increasing sound of the various noises, views of
 the city flash upon the screen. Views that express a
 well-defined contrast. The infinite contrast between
 the chant of the sermon and the life of the city.

And the woman's voice continues, exalted, speaking of
 the harm of drink, of the horror of sin and of the
 love of Jesus Christ. A small thin chorus follows the
 voice of the woman as she starts singing the 27th
 hymn:

"How sweet is the love of Jesus."

As yet we see neither the woman whose voice is
 heard, nor those who sing with her.

2.
Of the many indifferent passers-by, there are one or two
 who listen to the sound of the song . . . . Persons slow
 their walk and look in the direction of the hymn.

3.

A group of curiosity seekers gathered at the corner of a narrow street, they are busy watching.

4.

The crowd watches pityingly. Various of its members speak of them in varying ways. Some mock them — "You'd think they could find a better racket than this." Others pity them ... Yet others patronise them ....

5.

Finally — the street missionaries. An old man with thick grey hair; a woman large, heavily built; and their children, two little girls and a boy of about seven — CLYDE GRIFFITHS. It is they who are singing the psalms.

6.

One woman wishes to know why they drag their children along with them. And a second woman clinches the comment by adding: "Better for them to be sent to school." The children, uninterested, listless, devoid of enthusiasm, their eyes astray, sing their hymns of praise while their parents try to gather alms from the little group of curiosity seekers. No alms are given.

7.

The bystanders disperse, and the missionaries, folding up their music, pick up their small organ and move away into the cavernous darkness of the towering narrow street.

8.

Seven-year-old Clyde — sensitive and ashamed of his surroundings — looks no one directly in the eyes.

9.

The family of missionaries moves slowly down the street.
"I think they were kinder today," says the mother.

10.

They approach a dingy low-built old-fashioned building, over the door of which hangs a sign *Bethel Independent Mission*. The rest of the family disappears within the small doors of this building and only Clyde remains on the threshold. He hangs back because street urchins are making fun of him and his family — because he irks to answer them and pay them out for their mockery. But no words come to him, and with a typical movement he shrinks into himself.

11.

In sorrow, and hurt by the insults, he turns from the laughing children and runs across a dark and dirty courtyard towards an old, steep iron fire staircase at the back of the mission; like some small hunted animal he runs up the staircase to a platform.

By the platform, crouched on the steps, is his sister, seated there motionless.

12.

Esta, his elder sister, who played the harmonium on the street corner, is crouched on the steps; she peers through a stone gap between the houses onto the street, alive, bathed in light. Clyde sits down beside her as though hypnotised; as though enchanted, the children stare at this tiny piece of noisy life, listen rapt to the sound of an old waltz, the strains of which float up from an unseen restaurant. They look, listen and dream.

FADE OUT

13.

And again in the darkness the same feminine voice rising and falling in the cadences of a singsong sermon. Now Clyde's mother is speaking of the Life of Man — the child that becomes a youth — and the years that pass and the youth that becomes a man; and again the darkness dissolves and we see the favourite nook of the children, but now in their places are sitting a youth and a young girl. Clyde is now about sixteen or seventeen years old, and the girl a year or so older, but the impression remains enchanted as before. There are more lights on the street, its noises are louder, its movement more bustling. From the restaurant we now hear the quick lively tune of a foxtrot, but the expression on the youth's face has remained the same and there is the same weary sadness in the eyes of the girl....

14.

In the restaurant is being played the well-known dance the chorus of which is formed from the hackneyed repetition of a cry of Hallelujah, and from below, in the mission building, rise, interrupting the woman's sermon, the same cries but with another intonation and another feeling — Hallelujah. And as the same yet different cries of Hallelujah clash, the tremendous contrast forms a discordant dissonance that rouses Esta and the boy Clyde, who start at its sound. They descend the iron stairs.

15.

Opening the yard door into the mission, they pause just within it.... The mother has finished her sermon and, with sincere exaltation and faith, bids her listeners sing the last psalm:

> "If ye have faith — as a grain of mustard seed,
> Ye shall say unto this mountain; Remove

>   hence to yonder place; and it shall move;
>   And nothing shall be impossible unto you."

Finished, she asks her followers to sing the chorus.

16.

Clyde is miserable. He wishes to leave. His sister presses his hand and, though equally unhappy, she nevertheless goes docilely towards the harmonium. The congregation gets ready to sing.... They clear their throats — (*cough!*) .... They blow their noses and shuffle their feet.

Clyde, hatred in his eyes, turns his head from the spectacle, and goes into his own room, slamming the door behind him. His mother looks up in concerned surprise.

17.

Inharmoniously and out of tune the congregation begins to sing.

18.

Clyde sits down on the bed, hiding his face in his hands.

19.

The mother sings with deep faith and religious feeling. Sleepily, droningly sings the father .... The congregation sings hoarsely and out of tune.

20.

Clyde jumps off his bed, grabs his hat, brushes the dust off it with his sleeve, and leaves the room with decision.... With firm steps he walks past the crowd of singers, and his anxious mother, continuing to sing, follows him with surprised eyes. Esta at the harmonium is likewise startled by his behaviour. Clyde goes out into the street and moves, firmly resolved, in the direction of Life — in the direction of light and movement; and the further away he gets from the mission the less clearly does he hear the discordant tune, and the stronger grows the sound of the street and the brighter grow its lights.

21.

He passes the show windows of a sports-goods store.... The windows, and glass showcases set out into the street, crowded by dummy figures of the well-dressed in white bathing suits, tennis dresses, white golf suits — brandishing all manner of sports weapons. Clyde drifts amid the maze of these white society dummies.

22.

He passes a drug store, where, amidst dazzling shine of metal and white porcelain, the soda fountain is being manipulated by a youth of his own age clad in white cap, tunic and apron. Clyde stops, as a group of young girls, laughing and joking, take all the seats at the counter. The youth jokes with them as he mixes his syrups and creams like a circus magician, flipping his glasses and spoons like a juggler. Clyde sees that one of the places at the counter is empty. The young girls smile enticingly, but the fewness of the copper coins he has extracted from his pocket make him turn and go in the opposite direction.

Now he passes close to a gasoline station, where boys of his own age, in white dungarees, are cleaning the windshields of magnificent cars, filling the radiators with water and pouring gasoline into the tanks.

23.

His path lies past the bright entrance of a cinema. Boys of his own age in ushers' uniforms of white, trimmed with gold, like those of lion tamers, stand there seeming to him more magnificent and splendid than generals in uniform. Past all these boys, so beautifully groomed, so proud and self-assured, slinks Clyde in his little darned old suit, his haircut as of a day long past, his manner as of a crushed, maimed soul.

24.

Suddenly the sad weariness leaves his bearing, and alert attention enters his expression.... At first a little cautious, then musingly uncertain, then resolute, he looks at a sign glued to the glass pane of the door of a store. The sign reads *Boy Wanted*. Clyde is undecided but at last he takes hold of the doorknob to turn it. The door is locked, and now Clyde sees a postscript on the sign *Apply before 6 p.m.* He looks around him and sees on the clock of the city hall — 10.

25.

Out of the mission, straggling, the last remnants of the congregation are making their way onto the street. Clyde enters the building, he passes through the hall, there is no one at the harmonium, the harmonium seat is empty, the mother is talking to a miserable group of persons about to leave.

26.
The deserted harmonium.

27.
The father preparing dinner.

28.
The deserted harmonium.

29.
Clyde enters his room. Approaching the chest of drawers

he takes out his money box and jingles it next his ear. It is of papier mâché, a worn child's money box in the form of a pig; it contains only a few pennies. Now he takes out of his pocket the money that was insufficient to buy him a soda and thrusts it, coin by coin, into the slot. As he restores the money box to the chest, he catches sight of himself in a mirror, approaches it and scrutinises his reflection.

30.

From under the bed he pulls out an old album with a collection of illustrated newspaper clippings, on which are represented heroes of the world of sport — of fashion — dancers — entertainments in which girls and boys of his own age participate. He looks back into the mirror and compares himself with the pictures.

31.

The mother, a coffee pot in one hand and a mug in the other, approaches his door offering him his dinner.

32.

Clyde starts at her voice, hides the pictures, and, having learnt the object of her knock, refuses his dinner. When the steps of his mother have died away, and the squeak of the closing kitchen door has reached him, Clyde proceeds with his strange occupation. He combs his unruly hair, pours on it some oil out of a bottle, and then parts it like that of one of the boys in the pictures. He ties his tie into a bow, and, tearing a little piece of material from the curtain, tucks it into his breast pocket. When he now surveys himself again in the mirror, he smiles in satisfaction at the marvellous change in his appearance.

At this moment comes an anxious knock at the door.

Clyde neither starts nor shrinks in the manner customary

to him. With firm step he goes to the door and he
asks what is the matter without hesitation. From
behind the door in a voice uneasy and trembling,
unusual to her, his mother asks him to let her in.
Clyde half-opens the door, and his mother looks into
the room over his arm, asking him whether he has
seen Esta. Clyde is surprised at her question and
her manner.

"We can't find her," says his mother.

At that moment enters the father, and, as though confirming the words of his wife, says that he has hunted
through all the places outside, where she usually
goes and he can't think where she can have got to.

33.
The deserted harmonium.

34.
Clyde dashes into the little room of his sister.... Her
things are in disorder. The signs of a hasty packing.

35.
The parents are speaking of asking help from the police.

36.
From out of the bed in the room next door peep the
frightened younger children.

37.
On the pillow of his sister's bed is pinned a small note.
Clyde finds it. Before he has time to unfold it, his
mother stretches out her hand for it. Having read it,
she pales and says:

"She's run away with someone. I thought she was
happy here, but evidently I was wrong."

Only now does the mother notice the change in her
son. Only now does she notice his changed way of

dressing his hair, his tie, and his grown-up appearance. And Clyde suddenly, in an unfamiliar voice, speaks. An outburst full of bitterness. He speaks of the futility of his existence. He says he wishes to work, but he doesn't know how to do anything because he hasn't been taught anything. He says his parents have done nothing for him, not even written to his Uncle Samuel who has a big collar factory and might have taught him to work. They haven't even done that. He raises his voice and says that he won't go on living like this, that he wants to work and he will work.

38.

While he is engaged in this outburst the younger children creep out of bed and approach their mother. She drops wearily into an armchair. Clyde stops suddenly and runs out of the room. The mother is quiet under the blow of these unexpected events. She notices the children, puts her heavy arms around them, and tells them what they should say if anyone should ask where Esta is. She has left to visit relatives in Tonawanda. This will not be quite true but we may say it because we ourselves do not know the whole truth. Go pray to the Lord and go to sleep.

39.

And in the yard, on the platform of the fire escape, trembling with emotion at the scene he has just gone through, Clyde — now alone — stands gazing out over the town, the mysterious town that has swallowed up his sister, where one by one the lights twinkle and go out.

REEL 2

1.
Dawn creeps up over the city.

2.
And already Clyde stands, in the pale light of the dawn, in front of the store with the notice *Boy Wanted*.

The store is not yet open.

Clyde waits and waits, until life begins slowly to waken on the street.

At last the door of the store is opened from within, and a youth appears, wearing spectacles and clad in a white smock.

Clyde asks him: "Is this where the boy's wanted?"

The youth shakes his head and grins. Clyde, disappointed, points to the notice. The youth laughs, takes it down from the glass doorpane and explains that he's the boy that was wanted; he got taken on yesterday. The fortunate youth withdraws into the store closing the door behind him and Clyde, discouraged, sits listlessly down upon the steps.

An angry-looking individual opens the door and comes out:

"What do you want?"

— he asks of Clyde. Clyde explains again that he wants work. Crossly, the man replies that he has nothing for him. Taking a second glance at the boy, he notices his good looks and offers him a hint:

"You look a smart lad. Why not try the hotel round the block?"

He gives Clyde the name — Squires — of the staff manager, but warns him not to say who sent him, and as Clyde, his spirits soaring, moves away, the storekeeper calls out:

"But don't give them my name."

3.

Clyde stops at the corner to write down the name Squires.
> As he does so we see that he makes orthographical mistakes indicating the imperfection of his education.

4.

Across a yard into which the hotel garbage is being thrown and where coal is being unladen for the heating of the building — through the door where dirty linen is being checked into a van and by sculleries where dishes are being washed, Clyde passes into the office of Mr. Squires.

5.

"We need good-looking boys," says Mr. Squires to a red-headed youth with freckles all over his face standing before his desk.

"Sorry," says the boy.

"Next." From Mr. Squires.

Clyde, entering the private office, plunges into the midst of telephone calls, the signing of cheques and forms. Mr. Squires' every attention is wrapped up in calls and errand boys. He looks up at Clyde standing there and sees in a glance all he desires to know about him. He tells him rapidly the conditions of work, calls a boy and sends Clyde with him to be fitted for his uniform.

6.

As Clyde takes off his shoes with their patched soles, he is ashamed of them and of his darned socks — ashamed of his soiled and mended underwear as they take his measurements. The youth who is his guide looks superciliously at him, and keeps his eyes fixed upon him, which tends only to increase Clyde's embarrassment.

The name of the boy is Ratterer.

"You gotta be back ready to start at a quarter to eight this evening," says the boy.

FADE OUT

7.

FADE IN

Clyde's hand is seen grasping the papier mâché money box and breaking it against the window sill — the fragments tumble, and the hand picks up the coins from among the fragments.

8.

Active hands, busy hands cleaning all manner of people in all manner of ways. Hands stropping, shaving the razor blade down a soap-buried cheek, trimming the hair with great snips of the scissors — hands busy polishing boots with a boot brush, and the great hand of the city clock pointing to 7.35.

9.

The basements where the hotel boys get dressed, little elbowroom and plenty of noise. Boys are busily slicking their hair down — scenting themselves with a dash of eau-de-Cologne — giving an extra shine to their shoes — tilting their caps at an angle, just so — and smoking cigarette after cigarette. In a corner sits Clyde, uneasy and bashful. He is washed, his hair is cut, he is spick and span in his new uniform. He is terribly anxious, as a schoolboy before an examination — as a soldier going into battle. Ratterer enters towards him, looks him over authoritatively with the air of a superior being — fixes Clyde's tie, pulls at his uniform — fixes his cap at the right slant over his eyebrow and then starts to give him instructions. Having adjusted Clyde's clothes, unconsciously noticing him as clean and neat, Ratterer becomes friendly. He sits there at his ease, his knees crossed, flicking the ash off his cigarette with a finger of the hand that holds it. Clyde sits on the very edge of the bench, his knees apart, striving to control his anxiety. Ratterer begins:

"In the morning the blinds have to be pulled up — at night they have to be let down — at sundown switch on the small light and always put fresh water in the closet."

10.

As Ratterer speaks we see on the screen the mechanical routine of an hotel boy's duties.

A day-boy pulling up the blinds.

A night-boy letting down the blinds.

Ratterer continues: that when the room is ready one can stay by the door a few moments before leaving, and if this procedure results in a tip it must be gratefully acknowledged —

and if it doesn't one must show no trace of disappointment and bow oneself out.

And as he continues we continue to see the illustrations of the routine.

And Ratterer continues: that no matter what happens, the guest is always right, and he adds that, in a good day, if all goes well, Clyde may possibly make as much as six or seven dollars in tips.

11.

Six or seven dollars! Clyde is speechless with joy.

12.

The signal bell, and Clyde stands in single file with the other boys ready for duty.... A second bell and the boys go through a small door, through which as it opens is heard penetrating a buzz of voices and the

distant music of the hotel orchestra. The army of
boys approaches large gilt doors and, as these are
flung back, Clyde is plunged into the maelstrom
and dazzle of a gorgeous gilt and mirror hall decorated for a ball.

13.

Immediately by the doors whence he has emerged is a
cloakroom. Piles of rich furs heap upon the counter.
A woman beside him flings back her mantle and
emerges from it, white and naked by contrast. The
silks, the exquisite dresses, the precious stones and
elegance bewilder and increase the anxiety of Clyde.

14.

On the highly polished floor of the vestibule of this hall
stands the file of boys ready for orders.

15.

To Clyde, these are not boys on duty but almost the
Guards at the changing of the guard at Buckingham
Palace. He feels that this is a parade, at which he
will be promoted general at least.

16.

The parade is finished, groups of the boys disperse in
their several directions, Clyde is in a group that sits
down on a long bench waiting for calls.

17.

Barely have they sat down when a bell rings — from out
of a small window an order is given, and the first
boy in the line runs off to fulfil it.

18.

Bell after bell, order after order, boy after boy — the
long line of boys keeps moving up as those at the

head move up, returning to sit at the tail when their tasks are completed. As, little by little, Clyde sees himself approaching the head of the bench his anxiety grows stronger and stronger. His movements are more nervous and there is a bewildered expression in his eyes.

19.

And on the background of the accompaniment of bells — of orders being cried out — of the music from the restaurant and the laughter of the guests — occasional fragments of Ratterer's continued instructions continue to penetrate to us: "You gotta use the employees' elevator" — "Even numbers are on the left of the corridor, odd numbers on the right."

20.

And Clyde approaches nearer and ever nearer to the end of the bench — and the bells ring ever more frequently and the tempo of everyone's movements hastens and speeds. It is his turn now. He trembles in his anxiety like a race horse at the "Off". A bell. An order rings out: "Number 500" — Clyde dashes up the short flight of steps to the gates of the elevators on the Bel-étage.

21.

The employees' elevator is full.

22.

At the last moment he squeezes into a neighbouring elevator. The doors shut to, deadening the sound of the orchestra, the laughter and noises of the great hall.

23.

The elevator is packed with men in evening dress. Clyde is wedged into the midst of satin lapels and stiff white cuffs. The elevator goes up and up, leaving behind it the sound of the ever-receding music. The glitter of the evening dress suits and the polish of the men only increase the anxiety of Clyde. The elevator stops. Clyde squeezes aside to let someone in and then darts out himself.

24.

The doors of the elevator swing to behind him, and Clyde is left, solitary, in the carpeted silence of a long empty corridor. At first he runs quickly, but then more slowly for it seems sacrilege to run on the soft sinking pile of this carpet.

25.

He stops before the big double doors of No. 500, brushes his hands over his hair, gives a twist to his tie, to his cuffs, and knocks.

"Come in," is heard from behind the door.

26.

Clyde opens the door. It is dark in the room; only one light shines from behind a screen. A man's hand with money in it reaches out from behind the screen and a masculine voice is heard telling him to go buy a pair of garters.

"Pink ones," adds suddenly a woman's voice from behind the screen.

"Yes, sir," stammers Clyde in his confusion and runs down the corridor towards the elevator.

27.

A Negro boy is in it, guiding the elevator, and together they start going down. "New?" enquires the Negro. "You'll soon get used to it," and, learning his errand gives him directions for finding the hotel shops.

28.

The doors of the elevator slide open, Clyde rushes out. The doors close behind him.

29.

Clyde is in the shop. The woman behind the counter is finishing wrapping the garters and hands Clyde, together with the package, a bill and a ten-cent tip. Noticing his pleased surprise she tells him that every time he buys anything there he will receive 10 per cent commission.

30.

Clyde rushes out of the shop. He is lost in the series of great halls. Through Morocco — through Venice — through rooms in Empire and in Gothic style, through samples of all the world he hurries frantically. At last he is back in the main entrance hall, filled with guests in their gorgeous dresses. He threads his way through the great crowds, and once again at the last moment manages to squeeze into the elevator.

31.

The elevator is crowded with ladies. Amidst the expensive dresses and perfumes and the nudity of the bared backs stands the trembling Clyde, his excitement having passed all bounds.

32.

A bell. Clyde dives through the bevy of ladies and stops before No. 500. The door opens, and in front of the decorated screen stands a man in radiantly glittering dressing gown. Clyde bends and obsequiously hands him the package, the bill and the change. The man absent-mindedly takes the package, puts the change into his pocket, and screws up and throws away the bill — then he looks at the garters and then at Clyde. Exactly as instructed, Clyde stands in the same place, shifting from foot to foot. The man throws open his dressing gown with a gesture, takes a fifty-cent piece out of his vest pocket and gives it to Clyde. Clyde cannot believe it. He is numb with astonishment. To look at the garters the man turns on the light, and with the click of the switch the room suffuses with brilliance, as the glow of happiness suffuses Clyde's face.

"Fifty cents."

An unknown voice is heard screaming it and a smile almost of exaltation brightens the whole face of Clyde.

"Fifty cents."

Still louder screams the strange voice, and together with the cry the orchestra is heard playing a wild, happy march. As though at High Mass the music peals forth, and the hotel resembles a mighty cathedral. Like an organ swells forth the huge proud volume of music and a tremendous chorus of human voices rends the air asunder behind the whole small being of the youthful Clyde, clasping in his fists his fifty-cent piece.

33.

And as the screen fades and grows darker, so the mighty notes of the music grow fainter and their sound slowly fades —

34.

And there rises the image of the poor mission hall and the sound of its congregations singing psalms.

35.

Clyde runs through the mission hall into his room, closing the door behind him.

36.

He goes to pick up his money box but it is there no longer. Only the fragments of it are upon the sill. Then he unclenches his fist and in the palm of his hand are to be seen silver coins to the amount of several dollars.

And with the same gesture as that with which the man had thrown back his dressing gown and given Clyde his first tip, Clyde now throws back his coat and thrusts the money into his vest pocket. Then, slapping his pocket with his hand he looks at himself in the mirror and smiles his first smile. And together with this first smile are heard from behind the door the strains of a joyous song such as "Everybody's happy."

REEL 3

1.

It is a morning, and boys are filing through the office of Mr. Squires. Mr. Squires sits at his desk and each as he passes lays a dollar on the table, to be greeted sometimes by a nod. Mr. Squires appears casual, but we can see from his glance that he is watching carefully to make sure of his tribute. The little dollar pile grows and Clyde adds his quota.

"Quite at home now, eh?"

— greets Squires as he pockets the money.

"Yes, sir," replies Clyde and goes.

2.

Clyde goes into the dressing room, smokes a cigarette, and in a carefree knowing way, dons his hotel uniform. With a practised hand he smooths his hair, flips the ashes off his cigarette, ties his tie and laughs at the cracks of his colleagues, among whom is Ratterer.

A bell is heard, and the boys get into line.

3.

As on the first day, they all go into the hall, but the hall now no longer seems as grand to Clyde. A morning, businesslike atmosphere pervades it — emptiness — severity.

The tempo of the successive bell-ringings is no longer frenzied, but slower, deliberate. And as bell follows bell, there passes before us, in glimpse after glimpse, the fragments of life as they pass before a bellhop, the moral face that society presents to him. The boys seated on the bench are quietly yawning and bored.

4.

A bell.

Clyde jumps up and runs to the office.

A happy and bright couple of newlyweds ask for a room. The clerk tells them the number, and gives Clyde the keys. Clyde takes their luggage and leads them to the elevator.

5.

In the room, obedient to Ratterer's instructions, Clyde goes through all the necessary operations. He opens the blinds in the windows, checks the electric bulbs, sees if there is ink in the inkpot, water in the pitcher, and goes into the bathroom.

Left alone, the couple kiss.

Obeying Ratterer's instructions, Clyde changes the water in the carafe.

At the sound of the running water, the newlyweds start and look guiltily at Clyde, standing in the doorway.

He smiles back in answer to their smile.

6.
A bell.
A second boy on duty jumps up.
He carefully knocks on the door of another room. "Come in," a voice is heard to call out. The boy enters. He is carrying a large bundle of newspapers.
Once in the room he sees through the half-open door into the bathroom. In the bath, her back to him, sits a woman combing out her wet hair.
"It's our wedding day today," says the woman.
Her husband grunts unintelligibly in answer, and starts picking out the papers he wants from the boy.
The woman, seeing a youth, gives a scream. The man laughs at her fright and hides himself behind the paper with the callous expression of one who thinks such modesty from her unnecessary at her age.

7.
A third bell.
A third boy on duty jumps up.
With a tray on which are bottles of soda water he enters the room. Within it, all is in dreadful disorder. A gramophone — empty bottles — cards — and from behind the back of an armchair can be seen the feet of a sleeping man. A woman is lying in bed and abusing a second man who is pouring a drink for himself out of a hip-flask. The woman, having said what she wanted to, turns her back on him.
"Behave yourself," the man says, as he sees the boy enter.
The woman in irritation, to spite him, throws her blankets off her, sits up and chucks the boy under the chin.
Sensing a quarrel, the man gestures for the boy to get out.

8.
A fourth bell.
A fourth boy on duty, handsome, sunburnt, closes the door behind him. In the foreground of the room he has entered are baskets of flowers. He hears a woman's

voice, as if calling out his name. He straightens up, and smiles a knowing smile.

Sitting in an armchair, the woman motions with her hand. On it are numerous bracelets, rings, and her fingers hold a long cigarette holder.

The fourth boy on duty approaches her.

9.

Three bells ring one after the other.

Three boys jump up and run off.

In a room stands a woman, who is sobbing in terrible distress. Mr. Squires is annoyed, he is scolding her as she packs her things into a trunk. The woman says: "What a fool I've been — and he walking straight out like that and leaving me," and at that moment the three boys enter.

The woman finishes writing out a telegram, and a boy takes it, then waits for the money. The sobbing woman searches in her purse and cannot find any money. Mr. Squires takes the money out of his own pocket and the boy runs out into the corridor.

10.

The fourth boy circumspectly leaves the room of the woman with the cigarette holder, and, folding a bundle of dollars, hides them in his pocket.

11.

"We can wait two or three days, but you will have to change your room," Squires motions to the other two boys to take away the sobbing woman's luggage.

In another part of the room two stout Negro women are pulling the bedding and table cloths off the beds and tables.

12.

Clyde and Ratterer are going down the stairs carrying trunks.

"You haven't forgotten," says Ratterer, "that we're going out tonight?"

"Oh, no," answers Clyde.

13.

From the room vacated by the deserted woman we can hear the laughter of the Negro maids, changing the linen.

One of the plump women pinches a bellhop who has just come into the room.

14.

In the room where they undress, the boys, finished with their duties, are changing their clothes, and laughing at one of their number who is imitating the sobbing woman.

Ratterer is biting his lips in anticipation of the night-out; showing an imitation of the "Danse du Ventre" to Clyde, comically exaggerating the snake-like movement, as a sample of what he is to see that evening. "And gee, next week, Clyde, that will be a time. I know a fellow who's a gardener and the people there will be away. We can take their car easy, one of the fellows here can drive. And we'll get some girls and we will have a time! Don't forget."

Having divested themselves of uniform vests and caps, the boys are dressing in smart evening dress, hats, fastening up the fancy bows of their ties, fixing their silk pocket handkerchiefs, and fastening the laces of their shoes in extravagant bows. They powder, scent themselves with eau-de-Cologne, oil their hair, put cigars into the pockets of their vests and, in such a costume, Clyde looks like an illustration for a fashion magazine.

15.

At the back of the huge hotel, with merry jokes and an important stride, a group of the boys goes by, dressed up like men. The group disappears in the darkness.

16.

The window of Clyde's room. Dawn behind the window. And in the room a lamp is burning and in a sitting position on the bed, his mother has fallen asleep waiting for him.

17.

Clyde, coming in from the street, cautiously opens the door to the mission building, over which hangs a sign: *How Long Since you Wrote to your Mother?*

18.

On tiptoe Clyde walks through the big empty hall, past the empty harmonium. He quietly enters his room, goes to the mirror and studies his dishevelled look consequent on the riotously spent evening. Suddenly he notices the lighted lamp, turns to the bed and sees his mother. Her open eyes seem to have been watching him. But they had been unseeing, she had other thoughts. Startled, he is confused by awareness of his appearance, and quickly starts to take out the bright links from his cuffs.

"Clyde," he hears his mother's voice.

The mother is sitting on the bed, she looks long at him with strange eyes. Clyde is worried. He hides the bright cuff links, but the mother remarkes nothing about him, she says:

"Clyde, couldn't you help me find some money?"

And her rough, big, coarse hand passes over her face.

"You see — Esta — has been left by the man who ... by her husband .... She is in a terrible plight — I will sell your father's ring, then you know — we have — a silver jug and plate — but it won't be enough."

Clyde's surprise and worry pass. He begins to feel the superiority of his position. He puts his cuff links back, and with an intonation which is still humble but has a different ring in it, promises to find money for his mother. His mother asks him to add five dollars a week for the rent of his room, so that with this money she can pay back the money she has borrowed. Clyde agrees half-heartedly and makes a sour face.

"You see, mother, I don't earn very much and then I wanted money rather specially next week," he says.

FADE OUT

19.

A luxurious open Packard drives out of a garage. Ratterer, dressed in smart evening dress, closes the garage doors. At the wheel sits a boy of about sixteen or seventeen years, dressed as elegantly as Ratterer. Looking about them, they turn into an alley where two of their companions (one of them Clyde) and four young girls, powdered and dressed up, are waiting for them. They take their places in the car, and Ratterer says to the boy at the wheel:

"Well, there — no one saw us — I told you it would be safe as houses."

And, with a grinding of gears, the Packard starts off.

20.

A young girl is sitting on Clyde's knees. She presses close to him, and he derives from her contact a trembling sense of pleasure. But Clyde is inexperienced, he is shy. The car goes rushing by pretty roads, the girls squeal at every turn, pressing closer to the boys. Time passes. They have gone far.

The sun is setting, and the boys look at their watches. "We must be getting back now," says Ratterer, "or we shall be late for work."

And with a risky movement the Packard is headed round. Looking at his colleagues, Clyde slowly grows more certain of himself and, seeing how they press the girls closer to them and boldly kiss them, Clyde embraces his companion who, helping him, kisses him herself. The car stops at a railway crossing, letting a long freight train pass by. Ratterer is nervous and tells the driver:

"Step on it — there'll be a fearful bawling-out."

When the last freight wagon opens up the road for them, the car at a mad speed dashes through the evening darkness, along the wet roads.

21.

The first snow is falling. The wet flakes cover the windshield and close the eyes of those in the car. At a street crossing they cannot pass because of the steady traffic across. It is five minutes to six on the watch. The boys no longer embrace the girls, they are anxious, nervous, beat their knees with their hands, twist their watches in their hands, stamp their feet on the boards, and wait for the moment to get across the crossing. At the very first opportunity, at high speed, the car flashes past and dashes into an alley. At the turning, from out of a corner, a little girl comes out, and the car knocks her down. Terrified, the driver, his face livid with fright, accelerates his speed, and the car, humming like an aeroplane, dashes past.

"Stop that car" — "He's killed a child" — "Stop, stop!" "Stop them!" Cries and whistles are heard from the alleys, and, humming ever louder, the Packard goes ever quicker with its terrified occupants.

"Switch off the lights!"

cries Ratterer, and the driver turns the switch to off. Without lights, through the dark alleys, the car dashes on. The sirens of police motorcycles are heard behind them. Hearing these sirens, the driver pushes the speed up to the very highest the car can go.

22.

The sirens are heard ever nearer and a group of motor-cyclists come dashing into the camera.

23.

Skidding at a turning, the Packard is thrown against the pavement, jerks sideways, cuts into a mound of stones and wooden boards, and, crackling with a loud noise, it turns on its side.

24.

Clyde jumps to his feet, having been thrown out through an open door, and, trembling with fear and foreboding, looks around him. The roar of the police sirens approaches nearer, becomes more and more terrifying. Wiping the blood off his face, Clyde runs into a narrow alley between tall buildings, climbs over a fence, over a mound of bricks, runs through a lot of dust and rubbish and reaches the outskirts of the town, where the prairie begins. Looking back, he sees, through the curtain of falling snow, the lights of the city, hears the roar of the police sirens, the whistles, the cries. He sees behind him the ruin of his job, the scandal that cuts him from his home. Clyde trembles and, turning, goes away into the fields, hiding in the thickly, fast falling snow.

REEL 4

1.

The darkness lightens to disclose the anxious family of Clyde intent upon a letter.

The letter is the first news they have received from him for a year. In it he has related something of his difficulties and fears following the Packard accident;

his scraping of an existence from town to town. Now he is working in Chicago, a small job and he is sorry he cannot yet send money.

The family is deeply moved. The father stares in front of him. Clyde's mother pauses, and puts down the letter. She cannot finish it.

The little girl ends the reading of the letter.

At the end of the letter is set *Chicago*, the date and the year.

2.

The letter fades out and we see the city of Chicago and, resplendent on one of the buildings, is an electric sign. The sign outlines a collar, a collar gorgeous, in apotheosis — straight lines of light, like a fiery star, like a halo, shoot out around it, bursting and extinguishing like the opening and shutting of a fist. And ever and anon, beneath it, shows the illuminated signature: *Samuel Griffiths*.

3.

The camera pans down, and we see a man with a travelling bag beside him on the pavement and an umbrella. His head strikes the background of the lighted collar and over his shoulders bursts out the illuminated sign: *Samuel Griffiths*. He is standing outside a sort of residential club, a hostelry much more sober of exterior than the hotel of previous reels.

A porter runs up to him, takes his grip away from him, and follows him through the doors of the club.

4.

Having checked-in for a room, he hands a visiting card to the clerk. The name on it is: *Samuel Griffiths*.

5.

Once in his room he rings down, asking that newspapers be brought him, and, while waiting for them, he looks out of the window, pondering upon the advertisement of his wares.

A boy comes in with the papers. He offers him a tip, but the boy, shifting as if embarrassedly on his feet, refuses to accept the money, saying:

"Excuse me, sir, but are you Mr. Samuel Griffiths?"

"Yes," answers the surprised guest.

"Well, excuse me, sir, my name is Clyde Griffiths. My father is your brother."

"Oh, indeed!" exclaims Samuel Griffiths, glancing at him shrewdly. Clyde bears this inspection. He has been through a good deal. He is thinner and more subdued, but still sensitive-looking and handsome.

6.

In the corridor an employee of the club, in the same uniform as Clyde, is vacuuming the carpets. On the stairs, a second servant in uniform is polishing the brass balusters. A third servant is washing a large windowpane, through which can be seen the city, and the advertisement of the collars.

7.

Clyde is standing deferentially before Samuel Griffiths, who, patronising and seated, is bringing a homily to an end:

"If you want to get out of the rut and be somebody, and care to come down to our part of the world, I think I should be ready to give you a chance to show what you have in you and what you are capable of."

Clyde, but still deferential, thanks him with warmth and then, hearing a bell in the corridor, hurries out of the room.

8.

The interior of the Griffiths' household. The family — his wife, son Gilbert, and daughter Bella, are breakfasting.

"Well, what is he doing now," Gilbert, displeased, desires to know.

"He serves in a club in the capacity of a messenger boy," Mr. Griffiths answers.

"But father says he is very, very much like you, and much handsomer than any of our other cousins."

"Bella!" — her mother stops her.

"I still can't understand," says Gilbert, who really has a strong resemblance to Clyde, only looking a little more sullen and less docile, "why father takes on people when we have difficulty in keeping those who already work for us. Besides I can imagine what will be said when people know this messenger boy is a relative of ours."

"It is too late now to do anything," says the mother. "He's arriving, and you had better try to control your rudeness."

9.

Neatly, if inconspicuously dressed, with a small grip in his hand, Clyde approaches the gates of the Griffiths factory. The watchman takes him for Gilbert, opens the gates for him, and greets him:

"Good day, Mr. Gilbert."

"Excuse me, my name is Clyde. But I should like to see Mr. Gilbert," Clyde answers with an embarrassed smile.

He passes through the gates.

"Well, what do you want?" the secretary asks, without lifting her head.

"My name is Clyde Griffiths. I have a letter with me from my Uncle."

And the secretary, lifting her head, does not know how to act, so surprised is she at the extraordinary likeness of Clyde and Gilbert, whom she quickly rings on the telephone.

Having heard the answer, she says: "You may enter," and

leads him to a door, with the sign: *Mr. Gilbert Griffiths*.

And having entered, Clyde sees himself as he likes to imagine himself. It is Gilbert — his cousin.

Both lose poise at the resemblance.

10.

Telephone bells ring — machines are working — the collars run along endless bands — men and women are busy with different kinds of work — smoke comes out of the factory chimneys — the typewriters click in the Griffiths factory.

11.

The discomfort of Gilbert shows itself in an icy coldness, the discomfort of Clyde shows itself in a nervousness and hesitation in speech. The gulf between them has grown wider with the advance of the conversation.

In Gilbert's office, the conversation continues.

Gilbert: "Father tells me you've had no practical experience. You don't know accounting?"

Clyde: "I am sorry to say I do not."

Gilbert: "You don't take down shorthand, or something like that?"

Clyde: "No, sir, I do not."

Gilbert: "In that case it will perhaps be best for you to start working in the shrinking room; that is the department in which the first stage of the business takes place. By this means you will be able to learn our trade from the very beginning."

Gilbert presses a button, and in answer to it, a well-dressed young woman with a scowl on her face enters.

Gilbert: "And so, good-bye, Clyde. Mrs. Bradley will tell you all you want to know, and tomorrow you must be at work by 7 a.m."

And without shaking hands, Gilbert bows officially to Clyde.

12.

Clyde comes out of the factory gates and walks in leisurely fashion along the streets.

13.

And all at once he finds himself before an imposing mansion, with bronze deer in the garden and marble lions over the entrance gate. It attracts his admiration.

"Can you tell me please — whose house is this?" he asks of a passer-by.

"You don't know? Why that's the home of Samuel Griffiths, one of our leading citizens."

"Thank you," answers Clyde and, though rendered puny by the contrast, yields himself to the luxury of reflecting on his connection, however humble, with this gorgeous family. The mansion slowly fades in the darkness.

14.

And in the darkness the factory looms roar, and the steam machinery hisses, and out of the clouds of steam appears working a perspiring, wet, miserable-looking Clyde.

He seems unable to get the hang of his work. The material boiling in the kettle keeps falling off his tongs, and spraying his chest with boiling water; he is despairing, lost, and helplessly looks around him.

The foreman comes to his help. He emphasizes the name "Mr. Griffiths," sits by him and starts to explain and show him how to handle his work. Around Clyde are working experienced men, their movements are calm and sure. And, after seeing them, we realise how little suited Clyde is to this work, how unhandy he is in character, how difficult he finds it to be in this low-built, stuffy room, among red-hot kettles, clouds of steam and the roar of the machines.

And when the factory whistle blows, Clyde sighs deeply with relief.

15.

Weary and exhausted he comes into his room and sits down on the bed. The furnishings of his room express everything that is dingy and horrible in a boarding-house existence. No more comfortable, in reality, than those of his room in the mission, they differ only in being more oppressive.

A knock at the door, his landlady enters, asks him if there is anything he wants. She accents his name "Griffiths" in snobbery.

"There's a letter for you, Mr. Griffiths," she adds, and hands it to him.

The letter is an invitation.

Dear nephew,

Ever since your arrival, my husband has been away or busy. Now he is less occupied and we should be very glad to see you if you could come to dine tomorrow, Sunday. We will be quite alone, no guests. And there will be no need to dress.

Your aunt,
Elizabeth Griffiths.

16.

Once more Clyde stands before the gate with the marble lions and the gardens with the bronze deer. But now he feels as though possessed of the magic key. He brushes his hair back, flicks a speck of dust off his carefully pressed dark suit, fixes his tie and rings.

A maid opens the door and leads him to the drawing room.

The room — filled with different kinds of furniture, bronzes, candelabras, little statuettes, flowers, covered in carpets, with beautiful draperies — amazes Clyde.

He looks about him, and hears the swish of a silk skirt.

The swish approaches. Coming down the wide staircase

can be seen a pair of feet, and the swishing of the silk dress increases. Mrs. Griffiths is coming down the stairs, a thin, faded, sweet-tempered woman.

"So you are my nephew," she says, coming up to Clyde.

"Yes," answers Clyde.

"I am very happy to meet you — welcome," Mrs. Griffiths greets him in formal manner.

"How do you like our city? We are very proud of our street."

— begins Mrs. Griffiths to the embarrassed youth. She is interrupted by the arrival of Griffiths himself, who takes Clyde in with a penetrating look, and says:

"Well, it's good you came. It means you got fixed up. Everything was done for you without me?"

"Yes, sir," answers Clyde.

"Well, that's perfect. I'm glad. Sit down, sit down."

The rattle of feet fast descending the staircase, and Gilbert, in evening dress with a coat on, plunges into the hall. He speaks to his parents, ignoring Clyde except for a nod.

"Well, I'm going out now, mother," he says in an even voice.

"Are you sure you have to go? You know Sondra Finchley is coming back with Bella and she wants to see you."

"No, I have to go."

He gives a quick side look at Clyde as if to tell his mother: You know why I'm dining out tonight, pecks her forehead and hastily goes out. The signal neither escapes Clyde nor increases his self-confidence.

Dinner is announced, and Clyde walks with his aunt and uncle through several large rooms, all satin and mahogany, each stiffer than the last.

Dinner is not a success. Conversation flags, and Clyde is painfully uncertain in the various social graces such as bestowal of the napkin and correct selection of the fork. As unobtrusively as possible he endeavours to wait for the example of his relatives, but he is conscious that they are conscious he is waiting.

Dessert has been reached when there is the sound of a car drawing up at the door, of the doors being opened and a burst of laughter and barking comes into the room.

Gaily into the dining room come three girls, and pause in the doorway. They still wear their wraps, one of them is Bella, and one, in the centre, holds two wolfhounds on a leash. The newcomers had checked at the sight of the stranger, but Mr. and Mrs. Griffiths rise and welcome them. Mrs. Griffiths explains to the centre figure — Sondra Finchley — that Gilbert is not in, he had to go out, at which news Sondra makes a movement of annoyance.

Never has so gorgeous a being previously appeared before Clyde. Her white dress, the orchids on her shoulder, the straining wolfhounds make her appear as a being from another world. He of course had risen too, and hovered, partly expectant that he would be introduced.

But most certainly not.

Perhaps not consciously, but certainly inwardly relieved at escaping for a moment from the need to entertain him, uncle and aunt have forgotten his existence. He is supremely conscious of his ostracism, of the gulf that yet separates him from such incomparable denizens of Paradise, as he gazes at this girl, like a firework bursting in the darkness, like a saint glowing upon an altar. And her figure is covered in mist, growing thicker every moment, and whirling upwards in its movement. She is hidden in white clouds, and these clouds expand.

17.

And now they are the cloudy bundles of hot steam coming out of the factory kettles, and in this steam

Clyde is working, perspiration running down him, and frightened by the noise of the machines.

Samuel Griffiths, surrounded by his managers and secretaries, is coming down the factory stairs into the cellar. He makes a wry face, as he sees how one of the workmen, bent over the can, is stirring small pieces of material in the boiling water. The workman has little strength left, his face is burnt mercilessly as well as his hands, he groans from his efforts and his pain. When the workman turns away from the can, and turns to Samuel Griffiths, he recognises in the workman — Clyde.

Wet with perspiration, in a torn shirt, his chest bare, with hands swollen and red from the steam — the nephew stands before the uncle. The uncle turns his head and sees Gilbert, who looks so like Clyde, but crimped and elegant.

18.

Embarrassed and not knowing how to act, the uncle goes upstairs. Entering the director's office, he turns to Gilbert and says to him:

"We must transfer Clyde to another department. After all he is a relative of ours and we cannot keep him there. Heaven knows what people will be saying about us."

Gilbert is about to disagree. The uncle adds:

"Besides, he looks so much like you."

Gilbert no longer dissents, and taking his hat and coat, Samuel leaves the office.

19.

In the outer office the telephone rings. The secretary listens with the receiver, and says:

"I understand. From the cellar department, workman 70 is to be transferred to you? I understand. Yes, Mr. Gilbert."

20.

The foreman approaches Clyde and tells him to go to the director's office. Clyde takes off his wooden shoes, his leather jacket: over his torn shirt he puts on his coat, and then goes up the stairs.

21.

He enters Gilbert's office. Gilbert, more kindly than before, tells Clyde that he has given permission to have him transferred to another department, as he feels he has gained enough experience in the cellar. "Instead of fifteen dollars weekly — you will now receive twenty-five dollars. My father, your uncle, wishes it to be so."

Clyde mops the perspiration off his forehead, and his face brightens.

Gilbert, as distant as ever:

"We have decided to give you a trial as manager of the stamping department. The work is easy and does not require any technical knowledge. But you must show qualities of character. There are twenty-five girls working in that department and you are responsible for its moral tone. Our rules absolutely forbid any relationship outside the factory with any female employee and we expect you to set an especially high example by your conduct owing to the fact that you are related to us. Now you have got your chance, do not allow yourself to be disturbed by working in the presence of so many girls."

At the very first words pronounced by Gilbert, his office disappears from the screen, and in its place we see girls stamping collars. Slowly they all drop their work, and their heads become turned in one direction. And as Gilbert's words are heard, on the screen we see more and more of them, and the stronger grows their coquettishness, and the more concentrated their gaze —

And as the gaze of twenty-five pairs of eyes flirtatiously centres on one spot, we hear Gilbert's voice — "You must not get acquainted with these girls, and must never meet them after working hours. Have you understood all I have told you? Do you promise to do as you have been told?" And at that moment all the girls turn.

"Yes, sir," answers Clyde's voice, and on the screen we see his figure, elegantly dressed and severe.

In a pose of expectation Clyde stands face to face with twenty-five young girls.

"How do you do?" the chorus of young girls greets him.

"How do you do," answers Clyde.

REEL 5

1.

Springtime. On the ledges of the factory windows coo pigeons, through the panes a river is sparkling in the sun, and within the factory is the noise of looms and the hissing of steam machinery.

2.

Five and twenty girls of differing characters, of differing types, are working behind long tables stamping mountains of snow-white collars. One of the young girls throws open a window — startled, the pigeons fly away flapping their wings, and the mechanical noise of the looms has become softer as its sound loses itself through the open window in the spring-clad gardens and fields.

3.

As a breath of sweet fresh spring air enters the room the girls breathe in deeply its freshness and sigh with relief... They are all young, all in their own way are charming and pretty... And the eyes of all of them are constantly focussed in one direction. Thither, where stands the head of the department. The twenty-year-old Clyde Griffiths.

4.

He is dressed in a well-cut suit with a smart modern tie. He is handsome, and that is why the girls' eyes are so often directed towards him. But Clyde tries not to look at the young girls. He remembers Gilbert's warning and with all his strength tries to be indifferent and unapproachable. But the sweet spring breeze is coming through the open window and fills the room. The pigeons return to the window ledge, joyously the looms work on, and because of the spring warmth the girls open up the collars of their blouses and turn up their sleeves, but Clyde tries to remain cold and severe.

5.

Noticing the light-heartedness of his workers he goes to the window and shuts it in order to emphasize his severity. His movements are clumsy and cramped for he feels upon himself the gaze of five and twenty pairs of youthful eyes.

6.

One of the girls, Roberta, while watching Clyde, makes a mistake, stamps the number on the wrong side of the collar. She nervously approaches Clyde with the spoilt article in her hand and tells him of her error. Clyde tries to be serious and reserved. He dares not look into the young girl's face — he gives her instructions with face averted — but when the girl's naked arms come forward in passing him the collar he cannot help but lift his head and meet the shy admiring look of Roberta.

7.

The factory whistle blows. The joyous crowd of girls comes out of the factory gates, runs up and down the stairs. Some of the girls are being met by their sweethearts, but Clyde, looking out of the window, notices that Roberta moves down the street unaccompanied, alone.

8.

Over the factory chimney in the evening mist a full moon rises. Alone, Clyde strolls along the boulevard.

9.

Alone, Roberta sits on the river bank.

10.

At the entrance to a cheap dance hall Clyde stops, hesitating and thinking to enter, but at that moment the foreman of the shrinking room greets him: "Good evening, Mr. Griffiths." The foreman goes on his way but his respectful "Mr. Griffiths" still lingers in Clyde's mind, and it brings before him the image of the wealthy house of his uncle with its bronze deer in the garden, and its marble lions on the gates.... And accordingly he does not enter the cheap dance hall, but, turning around, moves off.

11.

Roberta is in her room.... She turns off the light and looks out of the window at the smiling spring moon.

12.

And Clyde is sitting at his window sill and likewise looks at the same moon as it gently hovers over the chimneys of the factory.

13.

And again the machines beat. Once again five and twenty
young girls are busy stamping collars . . . . Again the
girlish eyes embarrass Clyde. It is hot in the building. From the heat and the sweat and the thickness of
the air, everyone is filled with languor and weariness,
languor is in the heat of the machines, languor fills
the eyes that grow more amorous and Clyde with
greater difficulty holds himself in hand; and when
suddenly his gaze meets that of Roberta he does not
lower his eyes but smiles, in a sudden unexpected
smile. And to his smile answers a smile of Roberta.

14.

And the machines beat on. And in their work the girls'
hands flit to and fro, and on the bench float mountains of snow-white collars, and more and more often
Clyde's eyes meet Roberta's. They meet in those moments when the other girls are not looking. They steal
seconds from the quick tempo of factory work and,
accompanied by the dull roar of the machines, the
monotonous beat of the stamps, the hissings of the
steam, their gaze speaks a dumb language miming
the sympathy reciprocated.

15.

The heat of the sun grows stronger. It is hot in the building . . . . The girls languidly speak of young Clyde
and build fantastic tales around him and his wealthy
relatives, tales of his imagined luxurious life, the
while Roberta listens, looking with pride and affection at his handsome figure, and flashing a happy
smile at him at a convenient moment.

16.

And on the white ceiling, and on the whitewashed walls
of the factory the sunlight plays in bright pools re-

flected from the river. These pools of light leap and dance to the sound of the machine in quick rhythm and fantastic composition, and then slowly the noise of the machines dies and in the water we see the calm surface of a lake on which is reflected Clyde as he comes rowing in a skiff.

17.

And on this body of water the same exquisite rays of light dance their way. Also on Clyde's face, and on the sides of his little boat, just as they did on the walls and ceiling of the factory.

18.

Boats pass by with couples in them, with singing, with the strumming of a banjo, or guitar, and through this atmosphere of love Clyde drifts along alone and lonely. His boat drifts slowly along through the tangle of water lilies, quite near the shore. And on the shore, at the very brink of the water, stands a young girl; her hat is off and she is admiring flowers.

19.

Clyde stops rowing and watches her. And when the boat comes abreast of her she lifts her head and Clyde sees her smiling face.

"Miss Alden! Is that really you?"

"Why, yes. It's me," smilingly answers Roberta, but she is startled and seems a little afraid.

"Are you spending the day here?" asks Clyde. And noticing that she is watching the water he adds:

"Would you like some of these flowers?"

"Oh, yes," answers the girl and looks surprised.

The dark hair of Clyde is wind-blown, he wears a sports vest short-sleeved and open at the neck, and one of the oars is lifted high above the water. All this makes the girl inwardly tremble, and in order to cover her confusion she gives him a charming smile.

20.

She looks out onto the lake and sees a boat pass by in which are sitting a youth like Clyde and a girl like herself.... And all over this lake similar boats drift by, and in each one of them are just such identical couples.

"Oh, please take a seat in the boat," she hears Clyde invite her.

"Why yes, only I have a friend with me here and besides it might be better for me not to, it may not be quite safe."

"Oh, but of course, it's safer to sit on dry land," laughingly Clyde answers her.

21.

Boat after boat... Couple after couple... Song after song float down the water past them. And, suddenly anxious, Roberta cries out:

"Grace, Grace. Where are you?"

From the woods in the background a voice is heard answering:

"Hallo. What's the matter?"

"Come here, I want to tell you something."

"No, you'd better come here. There are marvellous anemones over here."

"You know what we'll do? We'll row down to where she is. What do you think of that?" asks Clyde.

"Why yes, certainly," answers Roberta, and suddenly bashful, in concern, once more asks him:

"You're sure it's safe?"

"Quite safe."

22.

Roberta jumps into the boat and Clyde helps her so that she shall not fall.

"Do you know, I had just been thinking of you.... I had been thinking how nice it would be if we were rowing together on this lake."

"Is that true, Mr. Griffiths?" Roberta wants to know.

And Clyde, shyly reaching forward, strokes her hair.

"Don't!" Roberta says, frightened, and becomes more reserved and colder towards him.

23.

And, together with a crowd of other boats, their boat drifts along among rushes under the shade of thick-leaved boughs into nooks by the shore.

24.

And along the water's edge are heard youthful songs — the chords of guitars .... And the sun begins to set. Evidently Roberta feels cold for she has come to sit next to Clyde .... Evidently he has not noticed how their boat has become tangled in the rushes and that they are now left alone .... And, as in the hotel, on the long bench of waiting bellboys, Clyde was filled with trepidation, so now once more he is filled with trepidation, from the fullness of his youth, from the presence of the young girl by his side, from the secluded nook ... And he kisses her. She tears herself away from him, frightened, saying:
"Mr. Griffiths."

But Clyde, made happy by his daring, excited by his conquest, smiles as he smiled that day when he earned his first money, and heard that grand music, that majestic — swelling — hymn in the hotel. And the echo of that music rises in the tune of a dance hall distant on the other side of the lake.

25.

And paying no attention to her exclamation, to her fright ... at the sound of that conquering march he turns his boat to the shore where Roberta's friend is waiting.

26.

Forgetting all, forgetting where he is and what he is...
   he wanders through the woods and across the fields,
   through streets and alleys, walking to the tempo of
   the ever swelling march....

27.

And when he has shut the door of his room, he speaks
   quietly but exaltedly: "To live! To live! How good
   that is."

REEL 6

1.

No longer does the river glisten behind the factory
   windows.
The long factory windows are closed — to shut out the
   cold, whistling wind....

2.

Silently the girls go about, stamping their endless train of
   collars. Silently, with concentration, Clyde is working in his little office. No longer do Roberta's eyes
   and his meet in affectionate understanding — they
   are like strangers — at least as such they conduct
   themselves.

3.

The factory whistle.....
From out the gates, the hands make their way....
In the jostling crowd, Clyde and Roberta come face to
   face with each other, but they do not wish to acknowl-
   edge each other's presence. They look past each
   other. And they separate, each going his and her
   separate way....

Clyde to the right....
Roberta to the left....

4.

The gates of the factory close....
And its lights are turned out....

5.

The tower bells play in the evening air and the street lamps light up one after the other....

And when one of these lamps goes on — it throws its light on the shivering figure of Clyde. He lowers his hat over his eyes, and walks into the mist.

He is waiting — back and forth by the railing he walks, wrapping himself tighter in his coat to save himself from the severe gusts of cold wind.

6.

Into the light of the lamp Roberta enters. She carefully looks around her.

7.

Clyde calls her by a tender intimate little name.

8.

He gives a peck of greeting on her cheek. Not because he is indifferent but because he is still shy and respectful. He kisses her once more and whispers to her.

When, across the pavement, the figure of some passer-by goes past, they stop their love-making and press against the dark corner, remaining motionless until the figure has disappeared.

"It's getting very cold," Clyde says. "I don't know what we're going to do. Isn't there some place where we could sit down?"

"Couldn't we go to a movie or a cafe?" asks Roberta. Clyde shakes his head and answers: "They might see us."

9.

Another passer-by. Once again they stand still in their dark corner.

10.

When the steps of the stranger die away, a new gust of wind makes Roberta and Clyde shiver from the cold and he says: "What do you think? Couldn't we go to your room for a little while?"

"No, no, no, that wouldn't be right." Shaking her head and frightened, Roberta answers him.

Clyde takes out his watch and lights a match — 11.30.

"No, no, we might be seen," continues Roberta.

But Clyde is excited and resolved. He links his arm through hers and together they go down the street towards her home.

11.

Roberta begs him not to come near her house but Clyde is insistent and stubbornly leads her towards it.

12.

"I can't see why we shouldn't go in out of the cold."

"No, you oughtn't to come in, Clyde. It may be all right in your set, but I know what's right and what's wrong, and I don't want it."

Clyde's face sombres and Roberta looks at him, scared at her own firmness. The tense minute-long pause is broken by the hysterical bark of a little dog.

Clyde: "If you don't want to let me come in and sit down a few minutes...."

Roberta: "Oh, it isn't that, but I can't. I'd like to but I can't. You know it's not right," and she puts her hand on his shoulder.

Clyde shrugs his shoulders, turns away and says: "Well, all right, let it be so, if that's how you want it," and he makes a movement with his shoulders throwing off her hand.

"Don't go away. I love you so Clyde. I'd do anything for you I could," and she embraces him.

"Yes, yes," roughly answers Clyde, and tearing himself from her embrace he goes off into the darkness. And at that moment someone kicks the little dog and it gives out a long painful wail.

13.
Roberta, bewildered at his departure, cries out loudly to him in despair: "Clyde, Clyde!"

14.
But he does not turn back.

15.
Filled with despair the girl, not knowing what to do, remains standing stock-still in the same place.

Clyde has not stopped. Quietly the door of the house opens and a woman looks out inquisitively while her hand pushes the wailing dog away.

16.
Further and further away, fainter and fainter, Clyde's footsteps are heard disappearing.

17.
"Don't leave me," Roberta cries out to him in a voice full of tears. Then she runs after him. But after running a few steps she stops and, frightened, looks around her. The footsteps are no longer to be heard, nor the dog's wail.

Roberta feels weak, she sits down, sobbing, upon the ground. One by one the street lamps fade and her sobbing grows weaker.

18.
Rain lashes the factory windows — The looms beat

harshly and unpleasantly — Heavily hisses the steam machinery — And even and anxious in the hands of the girls is the sound of the stamp as it falls.

19.

Pale, Roberta is working nervously and uncertainly.
Motionless, Clyde sits over his papers.
It is no longer cosy in the stamping department. It is bare and empty.... Not many hands remain.... Little merchandise.... Empty tables.... Empty shelves .... And that is the reason why the sound of the machines is so unpleasantly grating.

20.

Rain falls behind the windows.

21.

Roberta tries by every means to catch Clyde's attention, but she herself does not look at him.
There is an increasing nervousness in her movements and an increasing number of mistakes in her work. She is nearer and nearer to complete despair, and suddenly she sees —
Clyde is smiling to the other girls.
Clyde is flirting with her neighbour.
Her head is spinning. The roar of the machines fills her ears. The beat of the motors is as fast as the beat of her heart. She is unable to hold out.
She runs off to the girls' rest room, where, on a little piece of paper torn from off the table, she writes a note: *Come.*
And they go to her home.

22.

As they come in together, she switches on the light and it floods the dingy parlour that is her apartment.
"Oh, this is nice," says Clyde. "I never thought it

would be so cosy." She takes off her coat. "We'll have a fire in a minute," she says and kneels to adjust the coals before setting light to it. He kneels on the mat to help her.

They are close together. So close their elbows touch. She half turns. He lets his head drop on her shoulder and raises his hand to stroke her hair. Putting her arm round his neck, she presses her lips to his head and then speaks: "Dear . . . ."

23.

And when in their embrace the two young bodies come into contact and the hands grope for one another in a sudden new desire, that majestic music that Clyde hears in the happiest moments of his life bursts forth once again. And when they stop their kisses for a moment, behold, the ceiling of her little room has opened to the heavens and so have the walls.

Marches of victory.

Hymns of happiness are rending the air asunder. And they no longer know where they are because fantastically beautiful but absolutely incomprehensible things crowd in upon them, and they laugh a young and infectious happy laugh. And while the fantastical compositions with the underlining of music change from one to another, her voice, in an anxious whisper, is heard to say: "But never, never! If anything should happen . . . You won't leave me?" And Clyde likewise in a whisper, answers her: "Never — I'll never leave you."

24.

And again they are standing facing each other at the door of her little room; now they are saying goodbye, and once again Clyde repeats: "I will never, never leave you."

Kissing her before he leaves, he goes out into the street.

25.

But still Roberta's face holds traces of anxiety as, through the window, she watches his disappearing figure.

26.

And for the first time Clyde walks off like "a real man". His head is proudly held up and his hands thrust deep into the pockets of his coat.

27.

He passes by a big luxurious automobile.

"Hallo! Are you walking?" he hears a voice. "If you like I can give you a lift." Sondra Finchley is saying these words, looking out of the window of the automobile.

Clyde turns away.

Sondra, astonished, says, "Oh, excuse me. I thought it was Gilbert."

"I beg your pardon, it is I," he answers, taking off his hat.

"There's no need for excuses, I'm very glad to see you. Please get in and let me take you wherever you are going."

He would like to leave and takes a few steps backwards, but Sondra, desiring to cover the mistake she has made, insists: "But do come, Mr. Griffiths."

Embarrassed he goes to the car and sits beside her.

28.

At that moment the chauffeur returns with a package and she asks Clyde where she can take him.

29.

The car makes its way quickly along the road. "I didn't realise that you were mistaking me for my cousin," Clyde says in his embarrassment.

"Don't speak about that any more. Tell me rather why do you never go any place?"

"I'm working in the factory and have very little time," answers Clyde.

Sondra's conversation, flirtatious and flippant, ends in her promising Clyde to get him an invitation to a dance that is to be attended by the very best society of the town.

The beauty, charm, dress and manner of the rich girl overwhelm Clyde with admiration and he cannot take his eyes off her all the ride long. And Sondra, looking at him, notices his charm and good looks. They smile at each other, but at that moment the car comes to a stop at the corner of his street.

30.

The chauffeur opens the door of the car and Clyde steps out.

"Till soon," answers Sondra in reply to his thanks.

31.

And the car disappears behind the bend.

32.

Clyde remains standing still on the empty street and listens to the ever fainter noise of the car.

"Mr. Griffiths," he hears once again the name as she pronounces it. "Griffiths", repeats Clyde to himself, standing there frozen between embarrassment and a new pride.

REEL 7

1.

Hands are fastening the laces of patent leather shoes — then the same hands lift higher, dusting an almost invisible speck off the crease of the trousers — then higher still, as they button a black dinner vest. At last they give a final twist to the black bow tie, and in all the glory of his new tuxedo, drawn to full height, we see the figure of proud Clyde, polished, smartened and finished by Roberta. Now she is giving a final comb to his hair. As she lays down the comb she says: "If I can't keep you all to myself, if I must share you with the Griffiths, I'll make you as beautiful as I can."

She helps him on with his coat and white silk muffler, hands him his brand-new silk hat, and escorts him to the door. As she hugs him in a kiss: "You'll think of me tonight, won't you dear?" she says. He is gone.

2.

The first snow of the year is falling, and Clyde, to protect his new suit, opens his umbrella.

He pauses beneath a lamp, takes a card from his vest pocket and rereads the text:

The Now and Then Club
Will hold its First
Winter Dinner Dance
At the Home of
Douglas Trumbull
135, Wykeagy Avenue
On Thursday, November 4.
You are Cordially Invited
Will you Kindly Reply to Miss Jill Trumbull.

It is to this address he is going, not to the Griffiths. Turning it over, Clyde rereads a note written on its blank side:

Dear Mr. Griffiths:
Thought you might like to come. It will be quite informal. And I'm sure you'll like it. If so, will you let Jill Trumbull know?

Sondra Finchley.

Having read the note, Clyde tucks it away carefully in the pocket of his vest and resumes his way.

Past the amazed inhabitants of the poor quarter, Clyde walks beneath his umbrella, filled with pride and self-satisfaction.

3.

Handsome-looking cars stand before the entrance to Jill Trumbull's home. A group of chauffeurs, chatting among themselves, make room for Clyde to pass through.

He rings at the front door. Behind it can be heard happy laughter and conversation. The door is opened. The servant takes his hat, coat and umbrella from him and, once inside, Clyde finds himself face to face with Jill Trumbull.

"I know you. You're Mr. Griffiths. I'm Jill Trumbull."

— and on this they shake hands.

"Miss Finchley hasn't arrived yet, but I'll do my best as hostess until she comes."

4.

She leads Clyde through several rooms, introducing him to various girls on her way. "This is Mr. Clyde Griffiths, a cousin of Gilbert Griffiths, you know." The girls, who are speaking to attendant swains or otherwise engrossed, nod and smile politely with a — "How do you do" — "So pleased to meet you," and turn back to their companions, completely uninterested.

5.

Finally, guided by Jill, Clyde arrives at a big fireplace at the end of the room where stands, resplendent in white waistcoats and tails, a group of unoccupied males. Here, with another muttered introduction or two, a little laugh and an "excuse me" she leaves him to return to her welcome of other newcomers.

Clyde stands on the rug in front of the fireplace. Beside him on the rug stand the males, tall, wide-chested and stiff, their hands behind their backs and their feet separated. They survey him dully, while he endeavours to control his nervousness.

6.

Into another room, adjoining at some distance by wide-opened doors, Sondra enters in a dazzling white dress. Her entry causes a stir, Sondra is always a centre of movement. "Is Griffiths here yet?" she asks eagerly.

Through the intersecting doors Clyde can be seen on his rug. He shifts about nervously, the stiff society young men are reminiscent of the maze of society dummies in the glass window cases between which, earlier, he drifted.

Sondra calls Jill and her friends to her. "He's presentable, isn't he?" she says. "He's better-looking than Gilbert. We must take him around a bit. Gilbert will be furious. Oh, what a lark!" A rustle of silks and satins, gay approval and the group starts laughing forward.

7.

Clyde looks up. Across the room he sees Sondra advancing, more beautiful and resplendent than ever. He feels a thrill at her approach.

Sondra greets him and surrounds him with a bevy of girls, who have crossed the room in her train. He is at once the centre of the whole group. All are eager to cultivate Clyde, the idea of spiting someone else through him appeals to them.

"We shall have the first and the eighth dances," says Sondra with authority. "And I want you to dance with Jill, Betty, Clara ...." naming several of those around.

8.

The strains of the first foxtrot are heard coming from the ballroom and Sondra leads him to the floor for the first dance.

The orchestra plays rapidly; embracing Sondra, adoringly but gingerly, as if he held something too precious to be real, Clyde allows himself to be swept into the dance among the crowding couples.

Rapt by the rhythm, he is beginning to stammer his appreciation to Sondra, when she gently disengages herself and he is swept up, first by one of the girls whom she led to greet him — then by another —

— from one to the other he is swept, dancing with each a bare moment. Snatches of their conversation reach us. His partners pretend a roguishness. One: "You're better-looking than Gilbert." Another: "I saw you going into the confectioner's on Central yesterday. Were you getting something for your girl?" (This one alarms him.) And another: "Sondra thinks you're handsome." (Clyde thrills.) "She told us she means to see a lot of you."

9.

And once again Sondra is with him. The jazz continues.

10.

The jazz diminishes and dies.

In the factory rest room. A gust of giggles. Roberta is taking down her coat from a peg. The other girls, also preparing to leave, are laughing and gossiping. "No wonder Mr. Griffiths looks tired. I'll bet they stay up late at those parties. Dancing night after night." Roberta starts, and, concealing her interest, asks a question: "Don't you never read the papers? Why those young society people all went to two dances last night, on from one to the other. And they had Mr. Clyde's name down," is the answer. Roberta, the gossips turned aside, glances at a note crumpled in her hand: *Dear, I have to dine with my uncle again tonight. You understand, don't you.* Her fist grips round it. She bites her lip, her face is white.

And the music of the dance begins to rise again.

11.

Clyde is still with Sondra. The growing band music rises abruptly to sound ever faster and more gay, now fortissimo.

To the fortissimo of the band, he whirls into a poem of the days that follow. A poem of dancing, laughter, joy. A poem of loving glances, smiles, hinted caresses. A poem of Sondra's gorgeous wardrobe. Today she is clad in black silk, tomorrow in fluffy white, or again in glittering silver. And always Clyde is dancing with her. Or they sit on a couch, or they stand in a glassed winter garden, or they dance together in a lighted ballroom or in an intimate club. And as their poem of love progresses, its rhythm becomes ever happier, with the happier tempo of the music and the increasing brightness of the light.

12.

In his top hat, in his muffler, in company with a wealthy youth and girls, Clyde is passing, in a luxurious car, through the streets of the town. With a wave of laughter the car stops under a street lamp at a corner, and, excited, dishevelled, Clyde jumps out. Another burst of laughter and the car disappears.

13.

Clyde turns the corner and sees a light in Roberta's room.

14.

Sighing wearily, Roberta drops onto the bed.

15.
Clyde, standing on the porch, starts to push the outer door, it opens.

16.
Quietly Clyde enters Roberta's room. She turns a tear-stained face to him. "Clyde, where have you been? We haven't been alone together for weeks. What has happened?" Clyde feels uncomfortable, so makes a show of irritation. "I told you, I've had to go to see my uncle. You know what it means to me. You know I can't possibly refuse." Suddenly, unexpectedly, she jumps up, grabs a bundle of newspapers and turns towards him. "You're lying to me, Clyde." With difficulty keeping back her sobs, she shows Clyde the chronicle of his social life. One, two, three balls, more — and in each *among those present* appears his name.

Scared lest they wake the family of the proprietors, they quarrel in whispers. Whispers of passion, but now not of passionate love.

"You were with Miss Finchley," says the girl, and this drives Clyde to lose his head. He runs up to Roberta, takes hold of her shoulders and brings her face nearer to his, looking straight into her eyes.

And, seeing his face, his dear face, so close to her own, Roberta involuntarily forgets his neglect, and the old joy and tenderness for him appear in her expression.

And as the familiar charm reawakens, Clyde, instead of striking her or scolding her as he had intended, kisses Roberta. And when she throws back her head it seems to him as though he is being held in the arms of Sondra. His fingers clenched in her hair, with new strength and new passion he kisses Roberta.

17.
From the street we see the light go out behind Roberta's

window. Nearby, from some source unknown, the laughter of a little child is heard in childish glee.

FADE OUT

18.

FADE IN

Once more the noise of the looms in the factory, the hissing of the steam machines, and the sound of the stamps marking the collars.

It is dark outside and the electric light is searing. It outlines sharply unusual shadows on the faces of those working.

Roberta at her worktable is pale, sad and anxious. She watches Clyde, striving to catch his eye. But Clyde will not look at her.

Roberta takes a torn slip of paper and writes upon it a note: *Clyde, I absolutely, absolutely must see you today. Please come to see me after work, or meet me somewhere. It is essential. Roberta.* Taking a basket of collars she passes by his desk and, unseen by the others, throws him her note.

As Clyde finishes reading the note he sees Roberta's face, nervous and full of anxiety. With a slight nod of the head he agrees to meet her. He glances at a memorandum pad on his table, inscribed: *10th January, Dinner at the Griffiths,* and once again nods to Roberta.

19.

Slowly the noise of the machines dies and the jigging melody of an old-fashioned dance fills the air.

20.

Clyde and Sondra are dancing one of those old-fashioned, rapid jig-time dances in which everyone has to take part together, and which consist of circles and pairs.

A Christmas tree and Christmassy decorations are in evidence. To the sound of handclaps beating with the music, Clyde — now in tails — and Sondra advance, jigging, towards the centre of the room, and circle hands on hips and back to back in one of the figures of the dance.

By the walls a group of old ladies, made-up, powdered, overdressed, scrutinise Clyde and criticise his manners and success in society. They say that the Griffiths have started receiving him only because it became impossible for them not to do so when he was received by everyone else. Their smiles at the Griffiths' discomfiture are vinegar.

To the merry, frantic children's tune, Clyde and Sondra whirl round in the frenzied closing figures of the dance.

21.

The music stops with a burst of laughter. Clyde and Sondra run out into the hall and throw on their wraps and coats.

22.

Outside the snow is pouring down and is slushy underfoot. Cars move away from the entrance.

23.

Sondra and Clyde are in a car together. Sondra is driving. The car pulls up outside her house. She looks at him through half-closed lids and proposes: "Why don't you come in, Clyde. I'll fix you up a cup of hot chocolate before you go home. Do you like chocolate?" "Oh, yes," says Clyde.

24.

The kitchen amazes Clyde by its luxury, its cleanliness, the glitter of its copper dishes and the large Norman-style fireplace with bright logs burning in it. And Clyde says, spontaneously and sincerely: "What a marvellous kitchen!"

"Do you think so? Aren't all kitchens the same?" Sondra asks as she busies herself with the chocolate. She also looks around the walls of the kitchen and brings her gaze to a stop before the closed dresser. Having thought for a moment she goes to the dresser and opens wide its little doors.

An arsenal of crystal and silver services. Tumblers and goblets that amaze Clyde by their number and glitter. And Sondra picks out the handsomest tumbler for chocolate, pouring the chocolate out of a jug into the tumbler, she sits down beside Clyde, near the fireplace, and says: "Isn't it cosy here?"

"It's very lovely with you here, Sondra," says Clyde.

"I'm pleased you're satisfied," Sondra answers smiling tenderly, and each notices the good looks of the other and both keep silent, not knowing what to say or what to do.

"You've been very anxious to tell me something," Sondra asks in a very low voice.

"I'd like to tell you a lot, but you forbid me to."

"I know what you'd like to tell me." Both get off the bench and he takes her hand in both of his. Clyde looks at her as a faithful believer would look at a holy relic and under this gaze she lowers her eyes and Clyde, who has never done so before, puts his arm about her and kisses her.

At the moment of this kiss the silver seems to glitter dazzlingly on the open dresser — the burning logs crash throwing up sparks like fireworks, and for a few seconds Sondra allows herself to be embraced. Then she gently pushes him away without any anger and smilingly says:

"Now you must leave, do you hear?" "Are you angry?" asks Clyde.

Smiling, she shakes her head: "It is very late."

And Clyde makes a gesture with the hand, as does a sportsman answering the ovations of a many-thousand crowd.

25.

The handsome crystal tumbler stands on the table filled with the untouched chocolate.

26.

With a firm tread, humming the melody of that "hymn of happiness", that same melody which passes as a theme motif through all his happy days, Clyde walks down the street, already deep in snow, smiling to passers-by. The snow is whirling down and pouring, a frenzied whirling blizzard.

27.

He carefully enters the porch of Roberta's home and knocks at the door. The door is immediately opened and Roberta, still dressed in her day-dress, lets him into her room.

28.

Her face is so very sad and frightened that it makes Clyde scrutinise her closely. "Do you remember, Clyde, you said that if ever a misfortune happened to me... you would help me?"

"A misfortune?" asks Clyde, and he sees how Roberta sits down on the bed lifting her hands to the waist of her dress.

And again from some unknown source is heard the mocking joyous laughter of a child.

REEL 8

1.

A druggist's sign. The show window of a drug store. In it, among the array of medicine and bottles, the cardboard cutouts of nurses' figures and happy feeding children; this is an advertisement for milk, that for purgatives or candy. Hanging over the glass of the drug store doors, a bright illustrated sign of a naked little boy and his sympathetic father. Looking through the window is a nurse and her little charges, the children laughing, their attention caught by a gaily-coloured advertisement.

And at the entrance to the drug store stands Clyde, uncertain and embarrassed. He looks through the glass, trying to inspect the clerk behind the counter, and he sees —

2.

— a woman stands behind the counter, a saleslady.

3.

Clyde grits his teeth, looks around him, and crosses the road, stopping at another drug store. Looking inside, he sees a man. Trembling with anxiety, he enters, and at the same time through the radio loudspeaker is heard a song sung by children in a treble. Through the window we are able to see Clyde approach the counter, take off his hat, and, embarrassed, ask something of the druggist.

And as Clyde's embarrassment increases, so does the volume of the children's voices increase in the song over the radio. The druggist having listened to Clyde, shakes his head, and Clyde comes out onto the street. And at that moment, as Clyde opens the door of the drug store, the radio children finish singing, and are heard laughing over something in sheer exuberance.

4.

With quick steps, Clyde crosses past some little knots of children playing on the street. He stops at yet another drug store, and looks in through the window.

5.

A grey-haired, bewhiskered man is sitting there reading the newspaper. Next to the drug store is a phonograph shop. In its show window are cutouts of children and dogs listening to a record. And, within the shop, a record is being played of a child's recitation, touching and yet at the same time slightly comical.

Turning away from the window, Clyde enters the drug store and —

While the child's voice from the radio shop continues declaiming how it loves its father and its mother, the sunshine and the forest, Clyde once again takes off his hat, bends over the counter, and he repeats his question to the elderly man. And we see the grey-haired man grow angry, wave his hands about and raise his voice at Clyde; what he says we cannot hear through the glass of the window, but we do see Clyde grow confused, excuse himself and come out onto the street again.

6.

With quick steps Clyde makes his way through the noisy, busy streets. The lights are now lit. Gleams of light appear from the buildings, as lamps are turned on, illuminating the various signs, advertisements and illustrations in the shops. In the background is an enormous advertisement for milk, the huge, laughing head of a child. Clyde stops before it, thinking where

to go. He looks around him — on the roof of a tall
building a children's jelly is being advertised.

7.

As though feeling pursued by all these advertisements and
signs, Clyde retreats into a dark alley. He still walks
slowly, not knowing where he should turn. He has
to stop at the corner of the street to let a heavy truck
pass by, and as the truck passes, he notices that he is
facing an obscure little drug store. Something, perhaps a man-of-the-world air in the bearing of the
druggist, inspires him with confidence. An expression
of resolution comes into his face, and he enters....

8.

An ambulance with its red cross and long whining siren
dashes through the little street. The whine of the
siren dies away.

Clyde comes out of the drug store; as soon as he has
passed from the view of the druggist he thrusts a
small packet that he is holding deep into his coat
pocket. He looks happier and his walk is firmer. He
goes back through the streets he has passed, his hand
firmly gripping the package inside his pocket.

It is late. The lights fade, and in the growing darkness the
laughing posters of the children are no longer visible.

9.

Clyde goes into Roberta's room. She is so frightened and
worried over what has befallen her that she no longer
pays any attention to her looks. She is untidy, dressed
in a provincial-looking dressing gown and her movements are bewildered and absent-minded.

Clyde opens up the package, and takes out a bottle from
it. Roberta snatches it from his hands, lifts it to the
light, and reads the instructions on it. "We must hope
that it will all plan itself out," Clyde says. They

arrange that the following day, on his way to the factory, he will pass Roberta's house, and if everything works out well, she will raise the blinds, if not, the blinds will only be drawn halfway. He kisses her, but his tender words are only mumbled.

"Oh, Clyde, Clyde!" Roberta cries, as she is left alone.

10.

A Clyde who now appears much relieved enters his own room, to find waiting for him on his table several small packages from a smart shop. He reads an accompanying note from Sondra, her good wishes and greetings. These parcels she has sent him in token of their friendship, and in them he finds the smartest ties, and dainty handkerchiefs to be worn in the pocket.

11.

Roberta is lying on the couch in her room. Her cheeks have fallen in — the pupils of her eyes have grown immensely large — her face is as white as linen — there are deep blue circles under her eyes and the lips are parched. Suffering terrible pain, Roberta lies there on the couch.

12.

The blinds of Roberta's room are drawn only halfway.

13.

And Clyde stands looking at them on the other side of the street in horror and consternation.

14.

The blinds are drawn only halfway.

15.

Clyde goes down the street and stops at a men's goods store. He stands for a few seconds before the door, obviously nerving himself for a terrific effort, and suddenly goes in.

16.

He pleasantly greets the salesman, clearly an old acquaintance. Absent-mindedly picking out a tie, he lets drop, as though a matter of little importance — "By the way — I wanted to ask you about something. Perhaps you could tell me. One of the workmen at the factory, a young fellow recently married, is very much worried over the condition of his wife."

The salesman's face has grown annoyed; Clyde goes on, his nervousness, which he still endeavours to conceal, increasing:

"I don't know why they always come to me about such things — they seem to think I am very experienced —"

But Clyde's laugh rings false. The salesman continues to smile with that smile that clearly covers annoyance, and he gives an even greater attention to Clyde, who adds: "I'm new in this city, I don't know anyone, and so I can't help him. But you've been here a long time, so I thought you might be able to put me in a position to advise him."

The salesman looks around him, then comes nearer to Clyde and says: "Of course, I will be glad to help you, Mr. Griffiths. Continue, what is the matter?"

And they start to whisper in very low voices, too low for the words to be distinguishable. Clyde is seen taking out a notebook, and writing down an address. Then he sighs with relief.

"I'll tell the man not to mention anyone's name," Clyde says as he thanks the salesman and exits from the shop.

Left alone, the salesman opens his eyes wide and whistles. He is in possession of a fine piece of gossip and he knows it.

17.

Stealthily, to avoid remark, Clyde once more enters the house of Roberta. A lamp is turned on in her room. From outside the window, we hear Roberta's voice speaking: "No, Clyde, I won't go alone. I'm too afraid. I shouldn't be able to explain anything to him. I shouldn't know what to do, nor how to begin or anything. You must go with me and we'll tell him everything together — or I won't go at all. No matter what happens."

"Hush! Hush!" Clyde is heard to say, and then the words grow indistinguishable.

And indistinctly, maybe from one of the top floors, are heard the feeble cries of a sick child. The child moans pitifully. And against the light of the room lamp of Roberta, Clyde's silhouette is seen as he pulls down the blinds, and it grows dark all round.

18.

Roberta is half lying on the bed. Clyde sits opposite her on the couch. Pale, thin, Roberta stares at the light of the lamp, and says slowly: "I'll let you go." But, having said this, she is unable longer to restrain herself and large tears trickle down her wan face.

In the painful pause that follows we hear that someone is walking down the corridor, shuffling in bedroom slippers. Doors creak and we hear that an attempt is being made to soothe the child. Roberta turns off the light. A pause.

In the darkness, they continue their conversation. She must not be a drag on him, Roberta says, she is ready to face it and afterwards she will try to make her way alone in the world. Not quite alone, says Clyde, he will earn more money and be able to help her. No, says Roberta, she knows it will be alone and she is ready. But what if the doctor be unwilling? . . .

Again they hear the wailing of the sick child, a monotonous, low wail and sit silent, staring unseeing.

19.

And they still stare unseeing, but now they travel in a streetcar, and their stare is at the blank unreflecting windows, behind which lies the town in darkness.

"Did you find out where the streetcar stops — we won't have to walk far?" asks Roberta.

"It's quite near. A quarter of a mile, not more," answers Clyde.

An atmosphere of misery surrounds them as they sit in the streetcar. That cold and cut-off feeling of being the only passengers in a streetcar passing through dark and isolated streets. The hoarse clanging of the streetcar bell.

"Is he old or young — do you know?" asks Roberta. Clyde shakes his head.

"It would be easier for me if he were old."

They are silent again. Again the coldness and the enervating clanging of the bell.

"Oh," moans Roberta, "if only the doctor is willing."

The streetcar passes into the darkness.

20.

Roberta is seated in the depths of a huge armchair in the doctor's room. Through the half-opened door of his consulting room the doctor and his family can be seen finishing a copious dinner. Roberta is nervous. Now the doctor is washing his hands in an adjoining room. Roberta closes her eyes.

The old doctor is in the room. He is absent-minded. "What is your complaint, how can I help you?" he asks. Roberta opens her eyes. She makes as if to answer, then, abashed, drops her head.

"Calm yourself, child," says the old doctor and, passing the table, he comes and sits down beside her.

"Your name? Mrs...?"
"She answers: "Howard."
"Wife of Mister...?"

21.

Clyde, nervously walking up and down the pavement, before the doctor's railing. He stops, bites his lips, rubs his hands and nervously looks up at the house.

22.

The doctor stands in the centre of the room, and says to the confused Roberta:
"To start with, my conscience will not permit me to comply with your request. Secondly, such an operation is dangerous from a medical point of view, without even taking into consideration that I should be breaking our State laws as well as ethical laws...."

With an effort Roberta stands erect, she presses her hands together in anguish.

"You do not understand! You do not understand!" Roberta says, trying to keep her tears back. "I told you an untruth, I have no husband; it must be done, it must be done!"

23.

Clyde feels as though he had been lashed by a whip; he slips behind some shrubs with panicky, quick movements, as he sees an automobile pass by.

24.

The doctor's door slowly opens, and Roberta, broken by his refusal, comes out. Mechanically she goes out into the street and goes past the shrubs behind which Clyde is concealed. He watches her, and from the way she is walking, and the expression of her face, he realises what has happened. But he dare not leave his hiding place, because of the cars passing down the street, and the pedestrians on the pavements.

25.

Roberta, as though hypnotised, goes further and further down the street, unseeingly, having forgotten about Clyde.

26.

When the street empties, Clyde runs after her and joins her at a deserted spot.

At his question, Roberta only shakes her head, and wipes the tears from her eyes. Completely bewildered and helpless, they both stand there.

"You can leave me after, but now — you have to help me — you have to —"

And she starts to cry again. Clyde does not answer, and merely drops his head. Roberta is wringing her hands, she shakes her head and continues pitifully:

"Oh, don't you see, I can't be alone with a child on my hands, and no husband!"

27.

And around them, a new spring. Over the factory chimneys appears a soft, full May moon.

28.

They reach Roberta's house.

"You said yourself you don't know anything else we can do and every extra day is dangerous for me. There's nothing left for it, you must marry me — right away."

Cowardly, and in his anxiety really sorry for her, Clyde nods his head in confirmation of her words. In agony of realisation he closes his eyes.

His eyes closed, standing alone in another place, on another street, Clyde nods his head.

REEL 9

1.

In a ravine, near the road, a miserable, half-fallen-in, poor farmer's house.

An old woman is washing the laundry by the porch of this house; behind the open window Roberta finishes a hat she has been making. She tries it on, and talks to the old woman:

"What would you say, mother, if I suddenly got married?"

Continuing with her washing, the woman laughs at Roberta's question, and shakes her head.

"Oh, now I understand why you needed a new dress. Who is he?"

"I can't name him — yet, mother. But I think it will be soon."

"Oh!" says the mother, surprised and pleased.

2.

And at this moment an old, broken-down cart to which a thin, bony horse is harnessed, comes up to the house.

"Good day, Father," says Roberta.

"Hello, Bobby," answers a tall thin man, his tired worn face smiling up at his daughter.

The mother leaves her washing and goes across the dirty yard towards her husband. And Roberta, resting a piece of paper on the window sill, starts a letter.

3.

But when she begins to think, the happiness fades from her face, there is sorrow in her eyes and for a long while she looks through the window, her hand holding up her head.

Misery, dirt and poverty are to be seen through the window.

The letter:
> *Darling Clyde — It was hard for me to leave alone — as you know. But I am trying to calm myself, and now that we have decided everything, and you will come for me —*

— is written on the sheet of paper.

Along the dirty glass of the window, buzzing, crawl flies trying to escape into freedom.

But everything here is lovely — green trees, everything is blooming.

And again Roberta looks with sorrowful eyes through the window of the poverty stricken house. Among the darkness and the dirt of the yard one thin flowering plant is blooming. Several weak little trees are visible behind the fence.

I can hear the buzzing of bees in the garden under my window.

Roberta whispers to herself what she has written.

4.

"Bobby, you are wanted at the telephone," she hears her mother's voice from the street. She runs out of the house, crosses the road, runs into the entrance of a post office. Excited, gasping for breath, she asks over the telephone:

"Clyde, is it you? Oh, it's terrible, terrible, Clyde. I can't stand it any longer."

— and, after hearing his answer, made in a voice of excuses, she continues the conversation:

"Oh, don't be angry. Clyde, don't be angry. I don't know how to control myself. But whatever happens, you must, you must do what we planned, Clyde. I'll write you a long letter, because it helps me when I write to you. Clyde!... Clyde!..."

She hears no answer through the phone, calls him several

times, calls out his name, then, disappointed at the unfinished conversation, hangs up the receiver and closes her eyes, because the tears are rolling down her cheeks.

5.

Slowly Clyde hangs up the receiver, and exits from the telephone booth onto the verandah of the restaurant of a summer resort. He is in white tennis kit, a flower in his buttonhole, well-combed and handsome.

"Hurry, hurry, Clyde," Sondra cries out from a sports model standing in the road by the restaurant.

Clyde's dark expression is replaced by one of pleasure, and on the run he jumps into the centre of the car, into a group of young girls, merry and bright.

6.

Roberta returns, entering the door of the decaying farm.

7.

As the car drives, it drives into a new dream with Sondra, this time a dream of the joys of sport and the bright outdoors. Swimming, dancing, diving, racing, shooting, golf, tennis all are blended into a pictorial symphony that matches with a symphony of music, laughter and the natural sounds. And each is instinct with Sondra, and the personality of Sondra, and contributes to her growing charm for Clyde. Each scene, also, occasions some opportunity for intimacy. Now, on a tennis court, 15-love, 30-love, 40-love rings out, the syllable of "love" accentuated. Now he is pleading with her, on the crests of the waves, as they swim side by side, to run away with him, now immediately and, though she refuses, the coquetry of her refusal chases the gloom from his eyes.

Ever the composition of the symphony rises, increasing their intimacy, and at last, as final movement, they are once more in a car, and we see flash past a white roadster, in the front seats Clyde and Sondra.

8.

In the back seats is a group of laughing young people. The car stops at a crossroads, and Sondra asks Clyde to find out the road from someone.

9.

Clyde goes down into the ravine, to a miserable, dilapidated house; on the post in front of it he sees the proprietor's name written in printed capitals TITUS ALDEN on a small board.

Clyde is scared, hesitates and is about to flee, but Roberta's father comes up to him and asks him how he can be of help.

"How can we get to Twelfth Lake?" Clyde asks hurriedly, impatient to retreat.

And the sickly old man starts a long, slow, detailed explanation. And Clyde, barely hearing him, sees the pitiful ruins of the old house, and then, averting his head from it, he sees at the crossroads the dazzling car, and the laughing Sondra.

10.

Without waiting to hear the end from Alden, he runs back to the car, white and with compressed lips. He is anxious, and his hand trembles as he points the way, and Sondra surprised at his alarm quickly starts up the car.

11.

The car, with a roaring of its powerful engine, flies past the house. The father stamps heavily in. Roberta looks up from her letter and asks casually:
"Father, who was it?"

"I don't know, Bobby. Some rich no-accounts who lost their road."

The sound of the engine fades as the car recedes ever farther away.

FADE OUT

12.

Clyde throws open the door of his rooms. He is still white, still worried, still distressed. He goes up to the table and sees on it a letter, in Roberta's handwriting.

Annoyed and without pleasure he opens the envelope, and turns immediately to the last lines:

We must get married. I insist on it. I have the right to. You have allowed all this time to pass in silence and unless I hear from you before noon Friday all your friends shall know how you have treated me. But I will not wait and suffer one hour more.

Dazed, he stares at the letter, then lets his head drop forward onto it, his eyes closed.

Then he raises his head again. His hands pull the letter towards him.

And as it moves it discloses a newspaper that lay beneath it. Immediately in front of him is the paragraph:

ACCIDENTAL DOUBLE TRAGEDY AT LAKE PASS UPTURNED CANOE AND FLOATING HATS REVEAL PROBABLE LOSS OF TWO LIVES.

He reads it at first mechanically, without comprehending.

The girl's body has been found but remains unidentified. The second victim has not yet been recovered. Fifteen years ago in this spot a similar accident occurred, but the body of the man was never found.

13.

Clyde finishes reading the article, throws the paper off the table, turns out the lamp, and sits wearily down on the couch. And suddenly he hears a whisper:

"And what if Roberta and you —"

And in the dark corner, he imagines he sees an overset boat. Jumping up, Clyde turns on the light.

He sits down on the couch again, nervous and shivering, he picks up the paper he had thrown away and rereads the article. And while he is rereading it with wide-open eyes, the whisper from afar gradually creeps up till it forms the word: "KILL".

In a strange, gradual way the phrase spoken by the whisper forms and forms until at last it pronounces and repeats the whole word: "KILL! KILL!"

And from this moment the action begins to work along the line of the thoughts of a distracted man, leaping from one fact to another, suddenly stopping — departing from sane logic, distorting the real union between things and sounds; all on the background of the insistent and infinite repetition of scraps of the description in the newspaper.

In this scene, in which the idea of murder is born to Clyde, he acts separately from the background, which keeps changing after him, either dashing in a mad tempo when the background is slow, then falling when there is no reason to fall, then unsteady on a rock, then transformed into stone-like motionlessness in the midst of a busy street.

With the aid of the technical use of transparencies this effect of an inharmony between the actions of Clyde and his surroundings can be attained. Around him is first his room, then a street in busy movement, or the lake, or the mean dwelling of Roberta, or the summer residence of Sondra at Twelfth Lake, or the machines in the factory, or running trains, or the stormy sea, in each setting of which he moves, his movements being discordant with the scene.

And the same with the sounds. These are likewise distorted, and a whisper becomes the whistle of a storm, and the storm cries out "Kill", or the whistle of the storm becomes the movement of the street, the wheels of a streetcar, the cries of a crowd, the horns of motorcars, and all beat out the word: "Kill! Kill!" And the street noises become the roar of the factory machines, and the machines also roar out "Kill! Kill!"

Or the roar of the machines descends to a low whisper and it whispers again: "Kill! Kill! And at this moment a pleasant, unemotional voice slowly reads the newspaper article: *Fifteen years ago a similar accident occurred, but the body of the man was never found.*

14.

And at the climax of this symphony of madness Clyde jumps out of his nightmare, perspiring, dishevelled, excited. He runs to a telephone booth and calls up Roberta. Through the phone he speaks to her in a hoarse voice.

"This is Clyde."

He tries to put tenderness into his voice but in his effort there is too much affection. His voice, through the phone, sounds loving and soft; it seems unbelievable that a man in his state of frenzy could be so kind.

"I'll come to you, Roberta darling. You must wait for me two days. The 3rd of July I'll meet you at 15th Station at eleven o'clock, and we'll go rowing on the lake, and we'll get married, we'll get married."

And with trembling hand Clyde hangs up the receiver, and he leans against the wall, so as not to fall, while Roberta's sorrowful face lights up in trust and happiness.

REEL 10

1.

On a small railway station, away from the crowds of people, Roberta is sitting on her trunk.

2.

Clyde is seen coming along a side street leading to the station. He is walking slowly, carefully, making himself inconspicuous behind the trucks of baggage, pausing behind large baskets — he sees Roberta and, concealed, watches her.

3.

Roberta is pale and thin. She looks pathetic, and is dressed in a new, homemade costume. Her hat is also new.

Clyde's face expresses both shame and dislike. Nevertheless, he takes a few steps forward, so that she may catch sight of him.

Roberta sees him. A happy look comes into her face and she goes to the ticket office to buy her ticket. And as she leaves the office —

Clyde approaches it, and buys his own ticket.

She watches him, notices his light-grey suit, his new straw hat, the highly polished shoes, his grip and his portable camera. And a feeling of pride floods her at the sight of him. She smiles, and turns her head away from him, pretending to be a stranger, as though she did not know him.

Clyde starts, because it seems to him that an old man in a worn suit, with a bird cage wrapped up in paper, is looking at him with suspicion, not taking his eyes off him.

Clyde's knees are weak, and his hands are trembling. While waiting for the train he paces up and down the platform, starting nervously at every engine whistle.

4.

With a great roar the train pulls in.

Roberta gets off her trunk, lifts it. In her present condition it is heavy for her. Besides, the day is very hot.

Clyde sees this, but, turning away, he enters the first carriage.

Roberta gets into the last carriage.

5.

Clyde places his grip on the rack, hiding its initials *C.G.*

6.

Roberta, smiling happily, sits down by the window, in the sunlight.

7.

The piston on the engine wheels starts to shadowbox in the shadow of the engine on the platform as the train starts to move. It leaves the station.

8.

The wheels of the train beat out their usual rhythm, and to Roberta they sing joyfully. She likens it to the rhythm of the wedding march. She smiles up at the sun, the fields, the rivulets that fly past.

9.

Clyde is sitting in a dark corner of the compartment. He is quite near the engine, and its roar, its hiss and the chime of its bells fill him with dread — their sounds appear dark and sinister to him — and in their rhythm he can only hear the awful word "Kill — Kill —"

10.

The rhythm of the wedding march, the joyous beat, struggles with the rhythm of death. "Kill — Kill —"

beats the engine to Clyde. Full of hope is the rhythm to Roberta. The conflict rises, the tension grows faster, faster — until, suddenly —

11.

A long and piercing whistle of the engine.

The rhythm ceases and the train stops at a station. Clyde gets out of the first carriage.

Roberta gets out of the last one.

By different paths they leave the station, and meet in a deserted alley, where there are no passers-by.

12.

Clyde smiles, and the artificial, difficult smile makes his face look like a mask.

Roberta is radiant, and trustingly she approaches him.
"We could get married here. There's a mission down the street. What do you think?" asks Roberta.

And Clyde listens to her, and in listening he hears the voice of the preacher at the mission. The cadences intoned are as the singsong of the mission of his youth, and as he listens it changes to the singing of a hymn, and the thin voices of bystanders take it up as in his youth, and this fills him at once with a great shame and disgust and the desire to move further away.

"No, let's wait till Sharon, after we've been to the lakes," he answers.

And Roberta is so happy she does not think of opposing him, nor does his conduct seem peculiar to her, and she follows him.

13.

A large bus is travelling along a wooded road, it slows down at the turns and enters second gear as it goes up the hills.

14.

Roberta and Clyde are sitting side by side in the bus.

Roberta is bright with joy and, even in her simple costume, looks like a bride on her way to the altar.

Clyde's face is also smiling, but his knees tremble and he is unable to calm himself.

The bus conductor approaches with the tickets. Clyde purchases two, exactly counting his money.

15.

The bus plunges into a deep forest. Its wheels cross the quick-running streams, its noise frightens the young rabbits and chipmunks as they run across the road, its horn echoes loud in the forest.

16.

The bus conductor asks him: "First time here?"

But Clyde, in his nervousness, is unable to answer.

"Yes, we're here for the first time," Roberta answers for him.

"Going to the lake at Big Bittern?" asks the conductor.

And suddenly Clyde breaks into the conductor's question, apparently for no reason at all. "Tell me, are there many people there today?"

And, having asked this strange question, Clyde, embarrassed, does not hear the conductor's answer to it.

17.

The surface of Big Bittern.

Pools of the inky black surface of the silent water. The dark reflection of the pines.

Boats trembling on the motionless surface of the water. Their gunwales against a rude landing stage at the foot of steps rising to the small hotel. The beautiful panorama of the lake.

18.

Standing by the landing stage are Clyde and Roberta. They have just descended from the bus.

"How pretty — how beautiful it is!" exclaims Roberta.

Suddenly the hotel proprietor appears from behind the bus. Sprung into view as if by magic, he busily praises the weather, greets his guests.

Clyde notices that there are few people about and none to be seen upon the lake. Too late, he notices that the proprietor, praising his kitchen, has taken his grip from him and that Roberta is following the proprietor into the hotel. He makes a movement as if to get the grip back, but thinks better of it, and with a strange, hypnotised step, follows them.

19.

Open, the white pages of the hotel register stare threateningly at him.

Clyde grows paler; setting himself, he signs a fictitious name — *Carl Golden* — keeping his initials (*C.G.*) and adding *and wife*. Roberta, noting this, feels a pang of joy that she hides before those in the hotel.

"It's very hot. I'll leave my hat and jacket here — we'll be coming back early," says Roberta and she leaves both on a hanger in the hall.

20.

Losing his head and ignoring these incidents, Clyde takes his grip from the surprised proprietor and goes towards the boat stand. As he places the grip in a boat, he explains to the man: "We have our lunch in it."

Too preoccupied to note a remark by the boatman, he helps Roberta in and, taking hold of the oars, pulls off from the shore.

21.

Thick pine forests line the shore, and behind them are to be seen the tops of the hills.

The water of the lake is calm and dark.

"What peace, what tranquillity" — says Roberta.

Rowing, then stopping, Clyde listens to this silence, looks about him. There is no one around.

22.

As the boat glides into the darkness of the lake, so Clyde glides into the darkness of his thoughts. Two voices struggle with him — one: "Kill — kill!" the echo of his dark resolve, the frantic cry of all his hopes of Sondra and society; the other: "Don't — don't kill!" the expression of his weakness and his fears, of his sadness for Roberta and his shame before her. In the scenes that follow, these voices ripple in the waves that lap from the oars against the boat; they whisper in the beating of his heart; they comment, underscoring, upon the memories and alarums that pass through his mind; each ever struggling with the other for mastery, first one dominating, then weakening before the onset of its rival.

They murmur as he pauses on his oars to ask: "Did you speak to anyone in the hotel?"

"No. Why do you ask?"

"Nothing. I thought maybe you might have met someone."

23.

The voices shudder as Roberta smiles and shakes her head in answer, playfully letting her hand fall into the water.

"It isn't cold," she says.

Clyde stops rowing and also feels the water. But his hand springs back as though it had received an electric shock.

24.

As he photographs her, they preoccupy him. While they picnic, or pick water lilies, they possess him. As he jumps ashore a moment to put down his grip, they rise and torment him.

25.

"Kill — kill," and Roberta, happy, freshened by her faith in him, is radiant with the joy of living. "Don't kill — don't kill," and as the boat drifts almost soundlessly by the dark pines and Clyde's face is racked by the struggle within him, there rises the long-drawn-out booming cry of a water bird.

26.

"Kill — kill" triumphs and there passes through his mind the memory of his mother. "Baby — baby" comes his childhood and as "Don't kill — don't kill" rises he hears "Baby boy — baby boy" in the so different voice of Sondra, and at the image of Sondra and the thought of all that surrounds her "Kill — kill" grows harder and insistent, and with the thought of Roberta importunate it grows still harsher and shriller, and then the face of Roberta now, aglow with faith in him and her great relief, and the sight of the hair he has so loved to caress and "Don't — don't kill" grows and tenderly supplants the other and now is calm and firm and final. Ending the conflict. Sondra is lost forever. Never, never now will he have the courage to kill Roberta.

27.

And we see Clyde as he sits in blank despair and the misery of renunciation. He raises his face from his hands.

An oar drags in the water. In his left hand he holds the camera.

And Clyde's face is so wild with misery and so stricken by the struggle that has passed behind it that Roberta crawls anxiously towards him and takes his hand in hers.

28.

Clyde opens his eyes suddenly and sees near him her anxious, tender face. With an involuntary movement of revulsion he pulls back his hand and jumps up quickly. As he does so the camera, quite accidentally, strikes her in the face.

Roberta's lip is cut; she cries out and falls back in the stern of the boat.

"I'm sorry, Roberta, I didn't mean to," and he makes a natural movement towards her. Roberta is afraid. She tries to get up, loses her balance, and the boat oversets.

29.

Once more rings out the long-drawn booming cry of the bird.

The overset boat floats slowly on the surface of the water.

Roberta's head appears above the surface.

Clyde comes up. His face showing terrible fright, he makes a movement to help Roberta.

Roberta, terrified by his face, gives a piercing cry and, splashing frantically, disappears under the water. Clyde is about to dive down after her, but he stops, and hesitates.

30.

And a third time the long-drawn booming cry of the far-away bird.

On the mirror-like calmness of the water floats a straw hat.

The wilderness of forest, the motionless hills. Dark water barely lapping against the shore.

31.

A noise of water is heard and Clyde is seen swimming to the shore. Reaching it, he first lies down upon the earth, then slowly sits up, forgetting to lift one foot out of the water.

Gradually he begins to shiver, the shivering increases, he pales and makes a familiar gesture, that gesture that he makes when frightened or suffering. He shrinks into himself and hides his head in his shoulders. He notices the foot in the water and lifts it out. He begins to think, and with that, stops trembling. And the voice of his thought:

"Well, Roberta is gone — as you desired — and you didn't kill her — an accident — liberty — life —"

And then very low, tenderly, as if whispering into his ear, the voice says:

"Sondra."

And Clyde closes his eyes. And in the darkness:

"Sondra."

Her laughter and her tender voice.

"Sondra."

32.

Clyde is feverishly clothing himself in the dry suit from his grip. Into the grip he packs the soaked suit, and then, getting up from his knees, he stretches to his full height, standing in the rays of the setting sun.

33.

The sun hides behind the hills, behind the forest. The reflection vanishes from the lake, and all becomes darker and darker.

34.

Through the increasing dread of the darkling forest, Clyde is making his way, his grip in his hand. He starts, alarmed by every noise, he is frightened by the cries of the night birds, he fears the moonlight penetrating between the thick branches of the trees, he fears his own shadow and the shadows of the fantastic forest.

He desires to see the time on his watch in the moonlight, but, when the lid is opened, water falls from it and he finds out that it has stopped.

He plunges ever deeper into the thickening darkness of the forest, when, as he stumbles from behind a massive tree trunk, he comes suddenly upon three distorted gigantic obscure figures of men.

Yet more suddenly a lantern flashes out upon him. In its beam his face shows the extremity of terror, fixed with the horror of the damned. A boy's voice calls cheerily: "Hello," but, without giving himself time to realise the lack of menace in it, he plunges frantically into the brushwood.

The light is extinguished, but not before its movement has given us a fleeting glimpse of peaceful creels and fishing rods. While the trampling of Clyde's feet, the cracking of twigs, hurriedly grows ever distant and more distant, as he vanishes in the blackness of the night.

SLOW FADE OUT

REEL 11

1.

The prows of motorboats. The prows of motorboats filling the screen as they dash past throwing up clouds of spray.

Bright sunlight — glittering water — happy songs — the sound of banjoes and harmonicas — laughter, shouting and the sound of the engines of motorboats.

A small fleet of motorboats, with bunting gaily flying, cuts through the water.

The boats leave behind them a foaming track.

In the boats are young people, in bathing costumes, singing, laughing, playing.

2.

On the deck of one of the boats Sondra is lying. Clyde, in white, sits by her side.

Sondra's attitude is the incarnation of serene, carefree happiness. Clyde is gloomy; weighed down by terrible oppression, he is trying to appear normal, but his thoughts are elsewhere.

Sondra sits up. For a moment she forces herself to be serious. She says gently:

"You haven't been yourself, Clyde. All yesterday and today." Then she bends forward and whispers: "I know why you're worried. You're embarrassed about money. Please don't tell me about it. Just take this. I've got it ready specially for you."

And she presses into his hand a small folded roll of dollar bills.

Clyde categorically shakes his head in refusal, but Sondra stops him by kissing him, and, profiting by the moment, slips the money into his pocket. With an effort, Clyde is trying to take the opportunity to shake off his depression. They are engrossed in each other.

3.

A young man playfully rocks the motorboat from side to side, and water pours in over the gunwale. Neither Sondra nor Clyde notices the water.

A shrill girl's voice screams out in mock fright:

"You crazy fellow, do you want to drown us?"

This sudden scream startles Clyde off his balance. He pales and tries to keep his eyes away from everyone.

A young man calls from another boat:

"By the way, has anyone read yesterday's papers?"

Clyde becomes tense, he raises himself on one elbow.

The two boats run parallel. The young man reads out loud from the paper. His reading fluctuates, as the relative level of the boat fluctuates. "Two persons rowing on the south side of Big Bittern were drowned yesterday. The body of the girl has been recovered, but up to a late hour last night the body of the man had not been found."

Someone asks:

"Anyone we know?"

Clyde's head is spinning, the sounds around him grow chaotic and only the throb of the engine accompanies the throbbing of his heart. He lets himself fall back on a cushion by Sondra's side.

"What has happened to my boy? Why is he so pale?" Sondra asks of him, as she strokes his hair.

4.

The two boats are joined by others that try to outrace them. Happy shouts of excitement, and all aboard concentrate on the effort of the race.

The first boat cuts into the sandy shore, and everyone on board topples one into the other. Noisily, with exaggerated complaint, they get into the shallow water and clamber ashore. Boat after boat lands on the island.

5.

It is evening — and on the sandy shore a camp has been built. Tents have sprung up — great fires have been lit — and the whole young crowd is merry and sentimental. The camp makes one think of Indians and the flares of the fires are reflected in the night water.

Clyde and Sondra are sitting together on the shore. They are kissing each other and have forgotten all else in their own happiness. They are part of a group round an immense fire. The night is warm and this, combined with the warmth of the fire, has enabled the party to keep on their bathing suits. At one end of the group a chorus of gay voices is singing an harmonious song, and the song re-echoes faraway along the lake and in the surrounding forest.

And as on the occasion of their first intimacy, during the talk in Sondra's kitchen —

The burning logs splutter, and numerous sparks fly up into the air towards the stars.

The gloaming, the flittering firelight, the nearness of Sondra, combine to lull Clyde into a sense of peace. The echoes of a new song float across the lake and off into the woods.

Sondra and Clyde kiss again.

Keeping her head near to him, Sondra whispers .... At last she has come to a decision:

"I've made up my mind, dear. Come what may, we shall run away, we'll run away together."

6.

They stand up. Of a sudden, all his fears are reawakened. Realisation of what the morrow may bring floods back in full force. He stands cold, perplexed. Sondra leaning on his shoulder, her arm in his, they walk over to the outside of her tent.

"Darling," says Sondra, and they embrace. Standing at the door of her tent, a long embrace, clasped in each other's arms and mouth on mouth. Clyde feels it is the last time he will ever kiss her.

Sondra detaches herself and stoops into the tent. Clyde stands still for a fraction of a moment, then turns and stumbles frantically away, out of the firelight, into the further circle of the wood. His strength leaves him, and he lowers himself on the ground, resting rigid where he sits.

7.

Dawn.

His back against a tree, in the selfsame position, sits Clyde, sleeping. He stirs stiffly, his eyes open.

A few paces away, his back also against a tree, leans a tall bony man with enormous whiskers and a large felt hat. His chin is resting on his chest.

As Clyde stirs, the large man speaks. His voice is slow and calm:

"Your name is Clyde Griffiths, I suppose."

And as he speaks he holds an enormous revolver gently dangling.

Clyde, rousing, looks desperately about him, at the paths, at the lake, at the revolver and, after a moment's reflection, says:

"Yes, that's my name."

The man raises the revolver and shoots in the air. Clyde is still. The man is listening. Faraway comes the sound of an answering shot.

8.

Two young men, bathing in the water at this early hour, pause. One says: "Hey, listen to the guys shooting game out of season."

9.

"Fine, Mr. Griffiths. Excuse the revolver. My name is Kraut — deputy sheriff of Cataraqui," says the tall man.

He puts the revolver back in its holster and adds: "I have an order to arrest you."

Clyde, inwardly sick, does his best to assume a surprised and disinterested expression:

"I don't understand," he says.

10.

A boat touches the shore not far below where they are standing. A man jumps out of it. A thick-set man who knows what he is about. Others follow him.

11.

Clyde goes on:

"But of course, if you have an order to arrest me. I will follow you, but I — I don't understand."

The thick-set, energetic man has approached, he seizes on
    Clyde's remark:

    "You don't, eh? And you don't know anything about
a drowning on Big Bittern, do you, or Miss Roberta
Alden of Biltz?"

"No, no," Clyde answers nervously, terrified at the question.

"My name is Orville Mason. I represent the law," says
    the thick-set man, aggressively.

In a barely audible voice, Clyde replies:

    "You're suspecting me of murder. I wasn't there...."

"And you never met three people, Thursday night, coming
    from Big Bittern, going towards the harbour three
miles away?" says Mason.

"No, sir, I wasn't there."

The attorney takes one of Roberta's letters from his
    pocket, flourishes it in the air and waves it before
Clyde.

    "And you don't know anything about it, eh? And this
letter eh? Found in your trunk, among your belongings, in your room — you don't deny it's a letter
from Miss Alden, eh?"

With a tremendous effort and outward calm, Clyde replies:

    "Yes, I knew Miss Alden, I don't deny that. But I
had nothing to do with the drowning at Big Bittern, I
wasn't there."

At this, Mason, irritated beyond measure, exclaims:

    "Oh, very well then, you've decided not to talk, have
you." And to Kraut: "Take him away."

Kraut takes out a pair of handcuffs.

"No, you don't need those. I'll follow you," says Clyde
    hastily.

12.

Kraut takes a step down the path towards the camp.

    Clyde makes as if to follow him, but at the second

step he pauses, rooted. Mason looks at Clyde, then at the camp and sizes up the situation:

"Oho, so that's how the wind blows, is it? Too thin-skinned to be shown up before his lady and gentlemen friends. Well, there's nothing for it but to see if any of them know more about it than he does. Take him to the camp."

Kraut puts his hand on Clyde's shoulder. Clyde struggles and says, "No, no, you don't need to take me down there."

"Bring him along, boys," says Mason. Kraut grips Clyde. Mason approaches and thrusts his face towards Clyde: "Well then, suppose you answer some of my questions — come clean and quick, and at once, or down there you go!"

Clyde wilts and, his lips trembling, nervously admits: "It was an accident, that's all. I didn't kill her. I didn't turn the boat over."

Mason puts his hands on his hips and exclaims: "Ah, now we're getting somewhere," and attacks him with a new question.

13.

A sheriff's officer amid a group of young people in the camp. The young people are in various stages of early morning undress, some in sweaters after bathing, a girl in pyjamas with hair uncombed, and so forth. Steam rises from cooking utensils.

The officer is explaining that they have come for Mr. Griffiths.

14.

Sondra peeps out of her tent and overhears. She comes nearer.

15.

The officer explains that the case is as clear as daylight, there's absolutely no doubt about it. They have letters from the dead girl, and letters from another girl too, which gave them the hint to follow him to the camp.

16.

Sondra's eyes are open, she is frozen in horror.

17.

Just beside the camp, not far from where they stand, Mason, and Kraut with his hand on Clyde's arm, are getting into a boat.

18.

Sondra screams: "It's not true — it couldn't be — Oh, Clyde —" and, turning white, she faints.

19.

The cry reaches Clyde, where he sits in the boat between two officers, opposite Mason. At the sound of it, he shuts his eyes and lowers his head.

20.

There is a bustle of movement in the camp. A young man beside the unconscious Sondra says: "Well, that puts the lid on our party."

21.

The boat with Mason and Clyde is small in the distance, speeding across the lake. Within it Mason is still attacking Clyde with questions. Clyde is still stubborn.

22.

The camp is being dismantled. Tent pegs are uprooted, tents are coming down.

23.

A private apartment in the hands of the police. In a distant corner of the kitchen, which has been transformed into a temporary morgue, the presence of the body of Roberta under an obscure linen sheet can be rather guessed than distinguished. Two doctors in black stand nearby it, having completed their postmortem. Titus Alden, the father of Roberta, stands, in set and savage grief, against the wall. Others are in the room.

One doctor says to another: "The wounds on her face were not of sufficient depth to be fatal."

Then the first doctor turns to Titus: "Was your daughter married, Mr. Alden?" "No, doctor, she wasn't — why do you ask? . . ." And from the expression of the doctor everyone realises that she was about to become a mother.

24.

At this moment heavy footsteps sound in the corridor, the door opens and in comes Clyde, followed by the sheriff's officers and Mason, who goes over to the table. A gasp. All those who were within the room: Roberta's father, the assistants, the doctors, the secretaries turn and glare at Clyde. A murmur. Titus Alden rushes forward and raises his arm to strike Clyde, he is restrained. "Murderer!" he cries out.

Mason is examining the evidence like a wolf upon a scent. At the sound, he half-turns, still intent upon his examination and calls to the officers: "Take him out of here." The door shuts behind Clyde and his escort.

25.

Titus Alden steps into the centre of the room towards Mason and speaks in a low voice, desperately. At first Mason has his back turned to him, but as soon as he has heard a sentence he turns and listens with marked attention.

The old man: "I want you, Mr. Mason, to punish the scoundrel. I want to see him suffer as my poor child was made to suffer. He killed her. I have no money to help prove it. But I will work. I'll sell my farm."

Mason has risen and now stands majestically before the father; speaking to him but in reality addressing the crowd behind him, he pronounces: "Go home, Mr. Alden. I promise you, as the representative of the law in this country, that no time or money or energy on my part will be spared to bring this crime home to the murderer and to see that he reaps his just reward. And you won't need to sell your farm, either."

A member of the crowd calls enthusiastically: "You are right, Mr. Attorney. You're the kind of judge we all need."

And several persons approach Mason and shake his hand, saying: "You must have greater authority, Mr. Mason. We shall do all in our power to see you get it." Slapping him on the back and encouraged by Mason's smiles, the people leave the room.

26.

Mason is left with his assistants and detectives.

They go to a cupboard and bring out milk and sandwiches, talking among themselves as they do so. An assistant says to Mason: "This case will be the making of you Mr. Mason. You'll walk away with the fall election for judge."

"You mustn't speak like that, Fred," says Mason. "We mustn't mix up politics with things like this, but of course fate can be very convenient."

He wipes his mouth and puts down the milk glass.

"To work," he says and goes out of the room.

27.

Only one of the detectives now remains in the room. He is a thin man with a lugubrious countenance. He approaches Roberta, pulls a corner of the sheet off her face and admires her beauty. He passes his hand over her hair, looks long at it, and something like a tear seems to glisten in his eye. With one finger he plays with a curl, then, he severs it with a knife and tucks it away reverently into his pocketbook. As he leaves the room, he turns out the light.

REEL 12

1.
Gilbert lifts his head from the newspaper, curls his lips in a sneer and says:
"I said so — I said so."

2.
In the factory, the girls who worked with Clyde are reading another newspaper, and in this paper is a portrait of Clyde, and, in headlines, the news of his arrest.

3.
On the tennis court, friends of Clyde's are reading a third newspaper, and in this one too there is a portrait of him, and the details of his arrest.

4.
Gilbert, having read another article on the same subject, hands the paper to his mother. She glances at Clyde's portrait in it and hands it to her husband. He lets the paper fall onto his knees and, turning to Mr. Smillie, the advising attorney to his firm, says: "What can you do about it?"
Smillie, a little old man, quiet with quick movements. Next to him is Katchuman, important looking, in a frock suit, with a dull face, and brilliantined hair.
The family conference of the Griffiths is taking place in

the hall of their luxurious home. Piles of newspapers are heaped about the place, on chairs and on carpets, and on the first page of each is Clyde's portrait, the family name *Griffiths* and the dreadful word *arrest*.

Samuel Griffiths speaks, with his usual slight self-importance:

"If he be innocent, he shall have every possible aid in proving himself so, but if he be guilty I have no wish to aid him in any way."

Smillie talks:

"As far as I have been able to find out, it will be very difficult to prove his innocence. All the circumstances are against him."

Katchuman rises importantly and, with the expression of genius making a fundamental contribution to human knowledge, makes a proposition:

"There is one certain way of extricating him from this case. We must prove him insane —"

"You mean mad?" asks the frightened Mrs. Griffiths looking at Gilbert.

Katchuman answers:

"Yes, mad, if you like."

"No, I will never allow that. There has never been any madness in our family, and we do not desire that there should be!" says Mr. Griffiths.

Katchuman helplessly gestures with his hands, as he sits down on his chair.

An awkward pause.

Then Smillie makes a suggestion. He points out that the prosecuting attorney is running for office in the next elections and is sure to endeavour to use the case to advance his political career. If strong political opponents of his can be obtained, they can be relied on to spare no effort to discover the truth. And he knows two such men. They are Belknap and Jephson.

"And how much will that cost," asks Gilbert ironically.

And from the haughty, ironical face of Gilbert —

5.

— We turn to the bewildered, harassed face of Clyde — a replica in feature but so different in expression — with bars across it, in the prison. He sits in his cell and, as he sits, in some degree exposed by the light of the window, a stream of curious visitors passes, staring from the greater shadow of the corridor.

Different people look at him with different eyes. Some with pity, others sadly, others smile at him, others again ask him about his health, want to know his age, to know about his parents. Some ask him what psalms he sings in the evening, does he go to church, does he think of God.

All, all are selfish. Three girls titter and ask: "Was there another girl in it?"

A psychologist taps the bars to make him jump and notes the reactions in a notebook.

These constant stares and questions annoy Clyde. He nervously and ungraciously gives his answers, turns away from the pitying looks, and hides his head in his hands.

By the opposite wall stand two men. They watch the visitors, listen to their questioning and, dissatisfied with Clyde's behaviour, shake their heads .... They are Belknap and Jephson.

Presently the corridor grows deserted, but the men do not come out of their hiding place.

Clyde, seeing that he is alone, throws himself onto his bunk, and is shaken with sobs. Now one of the men approaches his cell, looks at him, gestures to the guard to open the cell up for him.

The man throws away his finished cigarette, and, taking off his hat, enters the cell. He sits down on the edge of the bunk, and slapping Clyde on the back, says kindly:

"Come, come now —"

Clyde turns his surprised and tear-stained face to him.
The man speaks:
"Hello, Clyde, my name is Belknap. Your Uncle Griffiths has entrusted me with your defence. You and I must be friends."
The kind words calm Clyde, and he stops shivering, rises on the bed. The defence attorney continues: "And listen — you must be more courteous to visitors, it is important for you."
The second man has come over close beside the cell, listening.
Clyde pulls nervously at his cigarette. Belknap stops him, takes the cigarette away, and just as kindly continues:
"You must not smoke now, that also is very important. And you must attend church regularly."
And like a father, he strokes Clyde's hair.
"And now, dear friend, tell me the whole truth."
Clyde turns his trusting face to him.

FADE OUT

6.
The exultant Mason sits in his study, surrounded by newspaper men, photographers, artists and secretaries. He opens the drawer of his desk, where two bundles of letters are lying — one tied with string — the other with ribbon, on them are initials. Mason takes the second bundle, puts it before him, plays with the ribbon, and, having awakened the interest of the reporters, says mysteriously:
"Tomorrow — I will read these letters to you, they'll be a sensation."
The reporters, journalists and photographers rise from their places.
"And today," says Mason, "I will read you these."
— and he takes a letter from the first package.

Dear Clyde, it was hard for me to come here by myself, but it is very lovely here. The trees are all green, and everything is in bloom. I can hear the buzzing of the bees under my window.

7.

Mason's study disappears, and its place on the screen is taken by the quiet home of Roberta's family. Her mother, still more stooped, yet more bowed, is washing the laundry on a porch as old as the whole house.

The same journalists who were in Mason's study surround Roberta's mother, photograph her, sketch her, question her and jot down in their notebooks her clumsy, peasant answers. They are interviewing her for their papers.

8.

Clyde's mother is singing a prayer surrounded by the congregation of her mission.

And while we hear their voices, to the door of the mission are seen approaching photographers and reporters. They place their cameras, check their fountain pens.

The prayer is finished. The mother lifts her hands to heaven in the last words of the psalm; as she does so she is illumined and the magnesium flashes of the photographers embarrass the congregation. They stop singing, and leave looking suspiciously at the journalists. The newspaper men surround the woman preacher, and rain questions at her. She speaks of Clyde as of her good little boy, as of a child, as of her son. From out of an old cardboard folder, in which she keeps documents and souvenirs, she brings out old photographs of Clyde in his childhood days, and as a youth. The men are interested in a photograph taken of the whole family on the street while singing psalms and preaching.

9.

And as soon as this photograph falls into the reporter's hands, a printing press is seen turning out copy after copy of it, and soon thousands of copies are to be seen pouring out of the machines.

10.

A page of the newspaper full screen size is to be seen, with this photograph in it. The newspaper is lowered, and Sondra takes her eyes away from it.

My Clyde is a good boy is written in heavy print under the photograph in the paper.

Crying, in tears, Sondra drops her head onto the paper. It lies on the carpet on the floor, and Sondra lies on it. Over Sondra stands her father, worried, perturbed and nervous.

"How could you write to him? Why didn't you tell us of your stupidity sooner?"

Sondra sobs. Sondra can say nothing.

"A scandal, a scandal," says her father, as he goes to the telephone, looks long at the dial and, while Sondra sobs, dials a number.

11.

Somewhere in the sleeping city in the night a telephone bell is heard to ring. In one of the houses the windows are seen to light as the lamp inside is turned on. And the voice through the telephone can be heard.

"It must be seen to that the name of our family is not brought into the papers. You have pull. Please see to this."

And another telephone bell rings over the city, and in another house the lights go on, and again there is a conversation in which the request is made that Sondra's name and the name of Finchley should not appear in the case. And still some telephone bells

Lucky Window: Jesse Lasky, Sr. (l.), B. P. Schulberg (r.) and other Paramount bigwigs transfer the window from the boss's office in the original Paramount studio to their new lot.

Upton Sinclair in 1930.

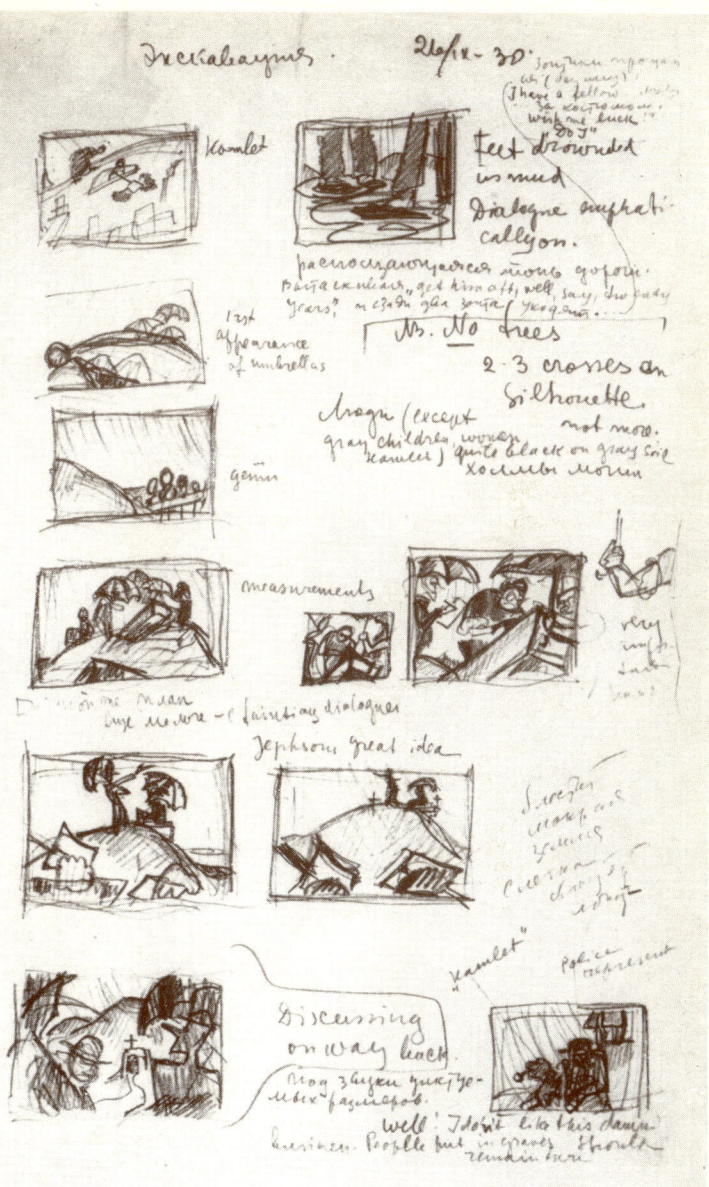

Exhumation Sequence for "An American Tragedy" (Coll. Museum of Modern Art).

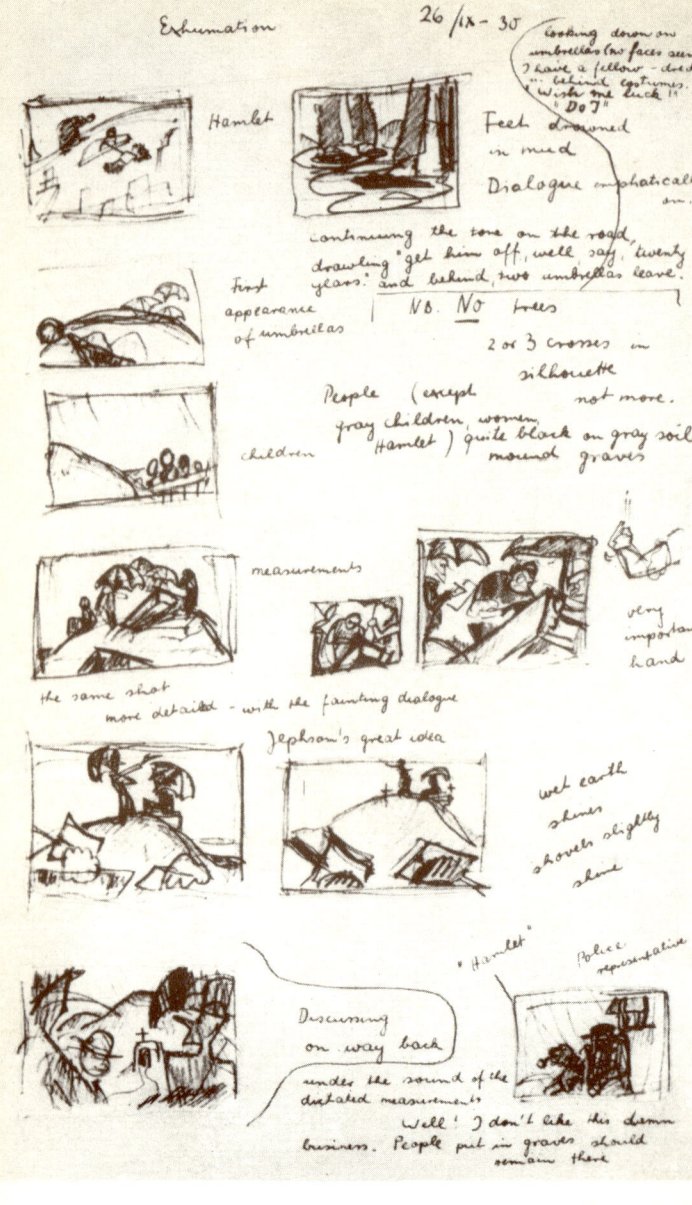

over the city and several similar conversations. And as the scene continues, the houses become more and more luxurious and larger and larger. The last light is turned on in the house grandest of all, and from this house can be heard the wanted promise.

12.

Mason is pulling up the blinds in his study — the morning light pours in. The newspaper men are waiting in an agony of anticipation.... Mason comes up to the desk, and takes out the bundle of Sondra's letters. He unties the ribbon holding the letters together, opens the first letter, with his finger passes over the initials embossed on the letterhead, smiles, with his eyes goes over all the tense, concentrated men, then takes a deep breath in order to start the reading, but a telephone bell interrupts him.

"Excuse me," Mason says, and he listens to the indistinguishable murmurings coming out of the receiver. His face becomes serious.

"I understand, I understand," Mason says into the phone. "Yes, sir, it will be done," and, bewildered, he hangs the receiver back.

"Excuse me," he says to the newspaper men once more, and ties the bundle of letters up again with the ribbon.

The journalists look at each other in amazement, and Mason, to get out of an uncomfortable spot, explains:

"I am sorry, but I shall have to disappoint you. These documents, by instruction of higher authorities in the interests of the case, are to be considered confidential, and if they are required as evidence their author will be named Miss X.Q."

and his hand puts the letters back into the drawer, and locks it.

13.

Sondra's father sighs with relief, and the sigh is repeated by Sondra.

The summer residents are closing their houses, the season has broken. Everywhere are to be seen moving vans, packed with trunks and travelling cases. The shutters are closed — the gates are locked — the blinds are pulled down and the watchmen take their places.

Sondra, in a dark veil, gets into the limousine between her father and mother. Along the wet rain-soaked road, spattering mud, the car moves off.

The reporters come, and come up to the gates of the summer residence, and look, disappointed, at the disappearing cars.... The barking of the watchdogs is to be heard behind in the grounds, and a large lock hangs on the gates of the estate.

And the locks on the gates.

14.

And on the lake, on the spot where Roberta drowned, it is raining too. The detective with the lugubrious expression is sitting in a boat, under an umbrella, watching two youths as they dive into the water, searching for something.

15.

Rain is falling in the village cemetery too, and, to the grave marked *Roberta Alden*, its gears rattling and hooting its horn, splashing through the mud, comes up a truck. The workmen, in raincoats, with hoods over their heads, throw out their shovels, and sighing and groaning get out of the truck.

Along the cemetery pathway, their collars up and under umbrellas, walking gingerly on the autumn leaves, Belknap and Jephson approach. They are talking to each other.

"I don't believe this opening-up of Roberta's grave will help in any way," Belknap tells Jephson.

"Yes, but we have to do this for the moral effect," interrupts Jephson. "We must do everything we can to postpone the beginning of the trial so as to prevent Mason using it to his advantage in the coming elections."

They approach Roberta's grave, where the workmen are preparing their tools.

16.

And on the lake, under the umbrella in the boat, the detective sits and watches the diving boys. The despairing youths dive in again. With tired eyes, the detective watches the increasing circles of water. And suddenly, from out of the water, a hand comes up with a camera in it. The detective jumps up, throws down the umbrella, and forgets about the rain. The boy swims up to the boat, and hands the camera to the detective.

17.

At the grave, under the umbrellas stand groups. The grave is being dug up. Jephson, Belknap, three doctors, police officers. The grave is half dug open, and from the hole spadefuls of earth fall with a wet thud onto the soil. Jephson and Belknap, against the background of these wet thuds and the pit-pat of the rain, are talking.

Jephson has devised a plan. He declares that the safest possible defence and the one that would best fit Clyde's own suspicious actions would be that he had never contemplated murder. "Listen," he says. "He goes up there with her, frightened, and not to marry her or to kill her but to get her to agree to go away."

With wet thuds, the earth is ever being thrown up out of the grave. Jephson is eager, his idea allures him.

"But once up there, and he sees how sick she is, and tired, and sad — he experiences a change of heart."

Belknap is not altogether convinced. "Why? For what reason?"

Jephson catches him up:

"But why? Why? Do you want to know why? I'll tell you! He felt sorry for her, see, and he wanted to marry her, or at least he wanted to do the right thing by her at the very last there."

Belknap is grudging. The pit-pat of the rain pours down. The wet earth is being flung from the grave by the constant motion of the spades.

"But it fits everything. First he wants a quiet place where they can sit and talk."

"Ye — es." This slowly.

"So they go out on the lake."

"Yes."

"And he begins to tell her about how he loves the other girl but will marry her if she still wants him to."

"I see."

"And she does want him."

"Yes."

"And he agrees."

"Sure."

"And she's so grateful that in her excitement, or gratitude, she jumps up."

"Yes."

"And that's what makes the boat rock." Jephson looks at Belknap.

Belknap whistles between his teeth.

"And now he could either have the camera in his hand or not, just as we wanted him."

"I see what you're driving at."

"And then whether he has it or hasn't, a misstep or just the motion of both of them causes them to go over and he strikes or not, as you think fit, but accidentally of course."

"Yes, I see and I'll be damned," exclaims Belknap enthusiastically. "Fine, excellent, Reuben. Wonderful really."

The rain patters, the spades delve, the wet sods and the fresh-turned earth melt in the raindrops.

"Anyway," says Jephson, mopping his forehead, "I don't see how we can find a better. That's his story and we must coach him in it. It might get him off with twenty years at the worst."

The doctors approach nearer to the grave, and look down.

"Good luck," says Belknap.

FADE OUT

18.

"This is your Bible," Jephson is telling Clyde, sitting with him in the cell. "This is the list of questions which you must learn by heart, and which you must answer the judge, as I shall teach you."

He smooths the sheet of paper out on the bed. On it, numbered, are the questions. Both bend over the pages.

19.

On the edge of Mason's desk, stands the camera found in the lake. The man who brought it, reverently extracts from his pocket his pocketbook, and takes out of it the strand of hair cut from Roberta's head.

He looks at the camera, he looks at the hair, meditatively gazing.

Satisfied, Mason is rubbing his hands together . . . .

20.

Roberta's mother is sitting on the ramshackle porch of her house weighed down by grief.

21.

In the empty mission sits the suffering mother of Clyde.

22.

Roberta's mother looks at a picture of a young girl, happy and carefree.

23.

Clyde's mother is looking at his picture. He looks youthful and innocent.

24.

The attorney Mason opens a brief case, in which are lying photographs taken of each other by Roberta and Clyde on the day of her death and now extracted from the recovered camera. He brings the photographs of the two nearer together, gives a self-satisfied wink to his secretaries, hides the photographs back in the brief case and pats it with his hand, as he says:

"This will be a sensation."

REEL 13

1.

In the autumn wind, the naked boughs of the trees are trembling... it sweeps and whirls dead leaves along the pavements... stirs the water in the fountain, around which people are sitting... and on its wings we hear the cry of newsboys yelling out their news, and selling copies of small booklets....

"Get the story of Clyde Griffiths, with all the letters of Roberta Alden, only twenty-five cents. The whole murder story."

Before the court building, a large crowd of farmers, arrived for the trial.

2.

In the courtroom filled with people is Mason (the attorney) and his assistants on their seats. The old judge takes his place. A small fellow on the left side of the tribunal cries out in a thin, little voice:

"Oyez! Oyez! All persons having business before the honourable the Supreme Court of the State of New York, County of Cataraqui, draw near and give attention. The court is now in session."

The movement of the crowds quietens in the courtroom and everyone becomes concentrated.

And the same little man gets up again, and pronounces:

"The State of New York against Clyde Griffiths."

Clyde as seen by his attorneys, nervous and hunted.

Mason gets up, and says:

"The People are ready."

Belknap stands up, bows gracefully, and says:

"The defence is ready."

Jephson bends over to Clyde, and calmly tells him:

"Whenever you feel weak or nervous, look at me, and do not forget what I told you, and what you have to do, and what you have to say. Look at me."

3.

A crowd of people who have been unable to enter the courtroom, is milling on the pavement outside.

"Full murder story — twenty-five cents."

— sound the voices of the newsboys.

A lottery bowl is turning, and hands are taking out of it slips of paper with the names of the jurors.

"Simeon Dinsmore."

— a clerk calls out the name on the paper.

A small, hunched man, resembling a ferret, goes to the jurors' bench, and sits down.

Mason, looking aggressive, in a loud voice asks Dinsmore questions:

"How old are you? Married? How many children?"

The answers to each of these are mumbled perfunctorily.
"Do you believe in capital punishment?"
Clyde shivers, and the man, who looks like a ferret, looks at him and shoots out with emphasis:

"I most certainly do — for some people."

"With the consent of the Court, the People will excuse the talesman,"

— says Mason, who feels this is a little too emphatic.

The judge glances at Belknap and grants the request.

"Foster Lund."

— cries out the clerk, and a tall, dried up individual gets up and goes to the jurors' bench.

"Who are you?" asks Mason.

"Foster Lund and Son, suppliers of cement, plaster and bricks."

But for Lund, the long jurors' bench is empty.

FADE OUT

4.

In the darkness, Mason's voice is heard:

"Gentlemen, it has been no light matter to find twelve men who could weigh the marshalled facts of this astonishing case with all the fairness and understanding that the law commands. Gentlemen, this care has been dictated only by one motive ... that right should triumph. I have no prejudices, no aforethoughts."

And under his words, from out of the darkness, we fade in on three persons, and by means of four cuts — to twelve stolid, iron individuals.

"Gentlemen, the life and death of this man is in your hands."

Clyde shrinks under the gaze of twelve enormous, sunburnt, merciless-looking farmers.

Twelve huge men, looking as if carved out of wood, sit on the jurors' bench.

Mason begins his accusations, speaking with importance. The State of New York accuses Clyde Griffiths of having deliberately, thought out and planned the cruel murder of, and of having finally drowned, Roberta Alden, daughter of a farmer in the County of Mimiko.

5.

Clyde looks out around the courtroom, and sees Roberta's family. He sees the father, a sorrowful old man, he sees her grief-stricken mother, and then suddenly his eyes open wide, and his hands clutch the arms of his chair. He sees Roberta sitting between her mother and father, a veil of mourning drawn over her pale face.

"That's her sister — that must be her sister," whispers Clyde, stealing a glance at Jephson. Then, nerveless, he drops lower in his chair.

6.

"The State of New York will produce before you substantiations of every one of these charges. You will be given facts, and of these facts, you, not I, are to be the sole judge."

Mason continues, and he starts telling his gruesome story, bringing out the highlights in sinister and dreadful colours.

And under his majestic declamation, short scenes of what he is relating flash on the screen. In endless *contredanse*, each is preceded by the stony face of its witness, seated in the court.

Roberta's friend: And we see her watching Clyde and Roberta float by her on the boat the day of their first meeting.

Roberta's landlady: And we see her as she thrusts her head out of the door to get rid of the yelping little dog, the day Roberta called out after the disappearing and angry Clyde.

The three druggists: And their refusal to comply with Clyde's wish.

The haberdasher: And Clyde's consultation with him.

The doctor: And his lecture to Roberta.

The conductor of the autobus: And the questions of Clyde.

The hotel proprietor: And Clyde and Roberta are in the boat.

The three men in the wood: And the lantern flashing in the darkness.

A Chinese cook: And he looks from his tent upon Clyde and Sondra's passionate kiss.

All these scenes pass beneath the accompaniment of Mason's words, each taking on a sombre hue. A different lighting, a different composition, and though to all appearances the same, yet in the movements and in the actions it is a different Clyde.

7.

"Not only did he kill her, he made her suffer — long and in dreadful agony. Listen to the documents that bear witness to this suffering."

Mason takes out of his brief case a bundle of letters, and picking one from them, starts to read:

"Letter No. 1 — 3rd July of this year —"

"The defence protests against this illegal playing on the emotions," says Belknap, jumping up.

"Who is leading this prosecution?" Mason wants to know of Belknap.

Then Belknap smiles, and with a movement of his hands, answers: "The candidate for judge, who will be chosen at the approaching elections if he can make himself popular enough at this trial."

Mad with rage, Mason interrupts Belknap and hurls an insult at him and Clyde. Belknap at once demands that an apology be tendered to himself and the defendant before the trial is continued. There is nearly a battle, but Judge Oberwaltzer forces them to apologize to one another. They control their rage, and officially make the necessary excuses. The Judge approves Mason continuing to read the letter: —

8.

Clyde, if I could only die. That would solve all this. And I have prayed and prayed that I would, lately, yes I have. For life does not mean as much to me now as when I first met you and you loved me. Oh, those happy days! If only things were different. If only I were out of your way.

The sun sets. Its low rays fall through the large windows of the courtroom, effectively lighting Mason as he reads.

The people, affected, wipe the tears from their eyes, little old ladies put up their handkerchiefs, the old men are shaking their heads in sign of horror. But all sit still, keeping back their breath, giving way, as Mason reads, to the sentimental mood which has seized them.

The sun has set. Behind the windows it is dark. In the courtroom, the lamp under its big shade has been lit, and Mason still continues reading the letters, which become ever more and more pathetic and despairing.

And Roberta's mother, unable to withstand the strain any longer, gives a low cry, and falls in a faint. The sister and father hastily bend over her.

Mason, taking a deep breath, says solemnly and distinctly: "The People rest."

He sits down — the screen grows faint, and in the darkness can be heard the ever fainter noise of the people.

9.
And when the screen fades in once more, we can see

slow, flaky snow falling behind the windows, and this snow carpets the roofs of the houses, the bare boughs of the trees, the streets....

And reflecting this white snow, a ghost-like white light fills the courtroom, and in this light, whiter than usual, is Clyde.

In a white, blank voice, the defence is finishing its speech —

"If I were not positive, to the very depths of my being of his innocence, I should not spend hours here trying to convince you of it. He has been called a criminal, a bearded man steeped in crime seducing an innocent girl. Take a look at him, gentlemen, this twenty-year-old-boy accused of the murder of a girl who, when he met her, was twenty-three. And did he kill her? No! And again No! And in order that you may be convinced I propose to produce before you the only living eyewitness, one who was actually present and hence knows how she met her death."

The crowd starts moving, whispering, concentrated. Everyone cranes forward.

And Belknap continues as easily as before:

"Clyde Griffiths, take the witness chair."

Disappointed, the people look darkeningly in the courtroom. The whispering dies off and the crowd sits back.

10.

And the heavy snow falls, falls evenly behind the courtroom windows.

The thick locks of the farmers in the courtroom are silvered with frost.

Jephson starts to examine Clyde, asking him questions to which he has taught him the answers.

"How was it, if you thought so highly of her at first, that you could so soon afterwards descend to a relationship that all men — and women also —" Here Jephson looks boldly round the courtroom — "so justly deplore?"

A murmur runs round the courtroom at the hinted irony. What a way to speak!

Trying to remember what he has been taught, Clyde answers: "Well, I didn't try to seduce her any time, really. I was in love with her."

Jephson: "Very much?"

Clyde: "Yes, very much."

Jephson interrupts him: "So — you loved her, but did you not think of marrying her, and strengthening your love by such a union?"

"No — I just only kind of felt that I never wanted her to leave me," slowly and uncertainly Clyde answers.

"And yet so soon after this terrible accident you were with Miss X?"

And Clyde: "Well, you see, sir, she's so beautiful, ever after seeing her I couldn't sort of think of Miss Alden in the same way."

Belknap: "I see, you were infatuated by Miss X — we might say, bewitched."

11.

The faces of three girls in the audience. Their eyes are open wide, they sigh with sentiment.

12.

Mason beside his assistants. He ejaculates: "So that's his line, is it?"

13.

Jephson: "And yet, in spite of the charms of Miss X, you decided after all to marry Miss Alden?"

And Clyde sees how all the heads are turned upon him, how the eyes of Roberta's father seem to bore into him. And Roberta's mother, her eyes dry with weep-

ing, watching him. And Clyde, with difficulty, and a
   tremble in his voice, keeping his gaze fixed on Jeph-
   son, repeats the phrases learned so well.
"Well, you see, when we met and she was so unhappy,
   and being together I sort of — I — I —"
"Ah, I see," says Jephson — "a change of heart."
An elderly lady dabs her eyes with a handkerchief.
"Well of all the bunk!" exclaims Mason.
Someone looks round at him sharply.
The faces of several members of the crowd are relaxed.
   But —
The twelve members of the jury sit, stone as ever.

14.

The snow falls behind the windows in soft flakes, and
   the window becomes frosted, so that nothing can be
   seen through it.
And the window becomes more and more frosted.
Jephson is speaking: "Now Clyde, don't shade it or try
   to make yourself look any better or any worse. This
   girl is dead, and you may be eventually if these
   twelve gentlemen here finally so decide." (Clyde
   shivers.) "Tell me now, in the shadow of the electric
   chair, before all these people and before your God,
   did you strike Roberta Alden?"
"I swear before God I did not."
A grim face in the audience relaxing in doubt.
"Nor throw her into the lake?"
"I swear it. I did not."
Sympathetic faces. A woman sobs.
"You swear that it was an accident — unpremeditated
   and undesigned by you?"
"I do," lies Clyde.
And even the face of Roberta's mother seems to show
   sympathy. But her father is ever fanatical.
Jephson looks round condescendingly and announces:
   "The prosecution may take the witness."

15.

Mason gets up like a bull to the charge. There is menace in his pause as he fixes his glance terrifyingly upon Clyde.

"Griffiths," begins Mason, in a firm and masterful voice, "you told us just now that you had a camera with you on that lake?"

"Yes, sir."

"I don't suppose in your truthful and honest way you remember telling me at your first examination that you never had a camera?"

"Yes, sir — I remember that."

"That was a lie, then?"

"Yes, sir."

And Mason's voice rises to a roar:

"So, because you lied then, because you have lied again and again ever since this case opened, you expect to be believed now, do you?"

The faces in the audience that had relaxed resume their hostility with a snap. The faces of the jury remain stone and impassive. Clyde shrinks and —

16.

— at that moment we hear a voice, speaking with sincerity and agony.

"Alone — all alone — Oh, Lord, help him." The voice booms out louder, and we can see the building of the familiar mission and the mother's heavy figure, praying on her knees.

"You are alone, Clyde, quite alone. I should be by you. The Lord will not forsake us. You must have faith. 'If ye have faith — as a grain of mustard seed, Ye shall say unto this mountain, Remove hence to yonder place; and it shall move; And nothing shall be impossible unto ye.' Oh, Lord, You know my madness and my sins are not hidden from You."

Full of faith, strong with a religious strength, big and

strong she raises her hands up to heaven; then falls face downwards on the wooden floor.

17.

The large and furious Mason comes into the camera. He stops beside Clyde.

Clyde is afraid of him. Clyde trembles. He is pale and sweating now, worn to rags. Behind Mason stands the lugubrious detective. Mason turns to him, and the man hands him the strand of hair that he cut off.

The strand of hair.

"Griffiths, you were intimate enough with Miss Alden to know the feel and colour of her hair fairly well, weren't you?"

Mason passes the hair before Clyde's face. "Is that her hair?"

Clyde looks questioningly at his defenders, sees their bewilderment, and stumblingly, says: "I think so. Maybe, yes. I don't know...."

"Yes, that is her hair," roars Mason, "it came out of your camera. That same camera, gentlemen," Mason continues, "which he tried to hide at his first examination."

"And what does this hair prove, gentlemen, tangled in the camera? It proves that not only did he not try to rescue her, but that he struck her in the face with it, before throwing her in the water."

Belknap leaps to his feet and, pulling out a hair from his own head and waving it, cries out:

"A hair can prove nothing."

Like a roar of thunder is to be heard the roar of the crowd, a mocking, contemptuous roar.

Oberwaltzer hammers on his desk.

18.

Mason comes even nearer to Clyde, and still more energetically questions him:

"How much money did you have on you?"

"About eighteen dollars" — answers Clyde.

Mason: "You are sure you had no more? Weren't you ready to run away afterwards?"

Clyde: "No."

Mason: "How then do you explain the one hundred and twelve dollars found on you at the time of your arrest?"

In the courtroom is a tense silence of expectancy. And the only sound is the wail of a rising storm outside the windows.

And in this silence, quietly, bewildered, Clyde gets tangled. "I — I borrowed them — later —"

Mason: "Borrowed them? From whom?"

Again the silence and again the wail of the storm.

Clyde: "From — from — a friend."

Mason: "His name?"

Clyde: "I can't tell!"

Together with the howling wind, through the courtroom can be heard the whisper of the crowd, from which one can make out the sense —

"Got him — Got him —"

Mason: "From whom?"

A new wail from behind the windows.

And suddenly Clyde grows bolder. He lifts his head, and hysterically cries out:

"I won't tell."

"How dare you, you urchin!" Mason yells, and lifting his hand, marches on Clyde.

Confusion, many rise up from their seats.

Oberwaltzer hammers on his table.

19.

Mason subdues his anger, and businesslike, asks:

"How much was the hire of your boat on the lake?"

Clyde, not knowing what to say, tries to evade the question: "I — I —"

Mason: "The prosecution has full knowledge of all your expenditures and thriftiness in money —"

Clyde: "Yes, my pay wasn't much."

Mason: "Come, then, remember, how much was the hire of your boat?"

A wearying pause.

The suffering Clyde tries to recollect, and cannot: "I — think — it was thirty-five cents.... Yes, I remember — thirty-five cents."

Suddenly Mason knocks his fist on the railing, and cries out: "A lie! It was fifty!"

And turning to the public, he says:

"Get up, Mr. Sissel."

From the crowd rises that same boatman who helped push their boat off the shore.

"More than that," says Mason, "you never even asked him!"

And again the mocking roar of the crowd echoes through the courtroom.

Mason continues: "And why should you have asked? You had no intention of paying."

"Ah...ah...ah...." is heard from the crowd, for it understands the trend of Mason's questioning.

"You had murder in your heart!" dramatically concludes Mason.

And suddenly, from the back row of the courtroom, a hoarse voice, the voice of a boxing M.C., cries out:

"And when will you finish with this bird?"

And another more thinly:

"Hang him!"

All Clyde's strength leaves him, and he drops back onto his seat.

Judge Oberwaltzer hammers on his table.

The police run up to the disturbers, and the yelling, the noise and the hammering die away in the

FADE OUT

20.

FADE IN

The interior of a restaurant. In different corners of the restaurant three different groups are dining.

In one corner, Judge Oberwaltzer looks at his watch, he is eating a vegetarian meal and has a book about gardening propped open before him. In another corner are Jephson and Belknap, and in a third Mason with his detectives and secretary.

"They've been hours on that verdict now," says Jephson, and through the window he looks at the building of the law courts.

21.

In a smoke-filled room, twelve jurymen, weary, perspiring and silent, deliberate on the verdict.

22.

Mason is reading a newspaper while gulping hot soup, and all his assistants and detectives keep showing him various articles out of various papers about the progress of the elections, carrying the news of the discomfiture of his rivals. The lugubrious detective says: "As a matter of fact, it doesn't much matter now what the verdict is."

Mason interrupts him, lifting his eyes from the paper: "You forget about justice, Mr. —"

"That's right, that's right," says a second man. "We forget we have before us no longer Mr. Attorney Mason, but Mr. Justice Mason!"

23.

And in the smoky room where the jurors are, Foster Lund, at the head of them, asks a man standing in front of him: "And against all our opinions, you still maintain he's not guilty?"

"Yes" — answers the man —

— and the jurors whisper among themselves, pantomiming their annoyance. And in this whispering, the phrases can be heard: "Who? A dealer in hardware — he's a personal friend of Jephson."

"So," insists Lund, "you're positive?" And, slowly emphasising each word, he continues: "Perhaps you haven't considered the effect your opinion may have on your customers. . . ." Lund hisses the last word.

And, having understood the warning, the man becomes nervous, plays with the pencil in his hand, and sits down.

Eleven focus their eyes on him, and under their gaze the man nods his head in sign of agreement.

Then the supplier of cement, plaster and bricks goes to the door, and knocks against it with his heavy fist. Three times he knocks against it . . . .

And the jurors rise heavily from their seats, and their heavy feet move along the soiled boards of the floor.

24.

And the echo of these three knocks reaches the courtroom. And quickly feet are seen running along the parquet floor, newspapers are flung aside, chairs are moved — napkins fall by the restaurant tables.

People are taking their places in the courtroom; it is filling rapidly.

The pale Clyde, and his defence encouraging him.

Accompanied by newspaper men, artists and photographers, the Judge, Mason and the latter's suite of followers enter.

25.

The clerk majestically opens the side door, and twelve heavy men stamp in. They come in soberly, their heads lowered, looking down on the floor, and, seeing this, Belknap whispers to Jephson:

"It's all up...."

The jurors have sat down on their bench, in order to rise once again. Jephson whispers to Clyde:

"Only don't let them see you're worried.... Keep going —"

— and then turning away from him, he bends over Belknap:

"We might still get him twenty years."

"Gentlemen, have you agreed upon your verdict?"

"Yes, Your Honour," answers the foreman. "We find the defendant guilty of murder in the first degree."

Clyde drops into his chair, and in his imagination "Yes" sounds in his ears eleven separate times as though in confirmation of the decision. Only the eleventh, a "Yes, yes" as though from the hardware dealer sounds out of tune with the others, coming a tiny bit too quickly and too eagerly.

26.

And by degrees, as the human voices in the courtroom grow fainter, the noise on the square before the court building grows stronger, and when, out of the doors of the building, Mason appears, a thunderous "Hurrah" is heard, and greetings are roared out by the crowd. Mason is carried across the square on their shoulders. "Hurrah for justice!" — "Hurrah for the new Judge!" — "Hurrah for Mason!"

27.

And in an empty room of the courthouse, from whence the joyous cries of the crowd can be heard, Clyde is dictating a telegram to Jephson.

Mother, I have been found guilty. Come. Clyde.

28.

And fresh yells are to be heard: "Hurrah for Orville!" — "God is with you, Judge!" — "Hurrah — Hurrah — Hurrah!" —

REEL 14

1.

A train pulls into the dark station. The lonely figure of Clyde's mother descends the steps of the carriage. She goes through the empty station — the dark empty street — the dark courtyard.

2.

The dark building of the prison. A lantern over the prison gates, and the mother enters, and once again it is dark on the screen. Out of the darkness appears a prison cell, in which Mrs. Griffiths is sitting, holding her son's head in her huge hands. Like a little boy, Clyde sobs, as he says:
"I — didn't do it —"
And the mother's large hand strokes the boy's hand, and tears well up in her eyes.

3.

The barely visible structure of the prison building fades out completely in the darkness.

4.

And a train comes directly forward into the camera. And the wheels are beating their normal rhythm, and its bell chimes out in its normal way, but it seems as though the wheels were repeating "Death — death — death" and as though the bell were tolling at a funeral. And in a compartment Clyde is sitting, joined to a guard by manacles.

5.

The train stops at a station. Clyde looks out of the window and a crowd of young girls and boys assemble, snapping him with their cameras, bringing him bouquets of flowers, and greeting him. The girls look at him with admiration — is he not the hero of a tragedy of love?

"Good luck, Mr. Griffiths." "Good luck, Clyde."

And Clyde smiles at them, smiles a boyish smile.

"Your mother will help," someone cries out from the crowd.

Smiling proudly in their importance, the two detectives pull Clyde away from the window. The train leaves....

6.

In the office of Belknap and Jephson. Belknap is seated, Jephson standing. Before them is Clyde's mother. The crudeness of her clothes has been effaced for them by the earnestness of her manner. Jephson is explaining to her that there are no funds for appeal. The Griffiths of Lycurgus have withdrawn their support. She listens taking in only a part of what they are saying. Then suddenly rises to her feet:

"The Lord will not desert me. I know it. He has declared himself to me. I will trust him and he will guide me."

In pagan astonishment and some admiration Belknap and Jephson are taken aback by this evangelistic fervour. Then —

Why not? Jephson strikes his hand to his head, and speaks animatedly to Belknap. It could be done. Why not? The only chance to raise the money. There are religious people, people of faith, everywhere. Let her speak for her son and take a collection.

FADE OUT

7.

"I am trying to gather enough money to pay for an appeal for my son."

— says Clyde's mother, turning to two men. She sits in the small confirmation room of a church.

"I should like to preach in your church."

"We cannot help you," answers a grey-haired man. "Even if he is innocent of murder — there is the adultery — that we cannot endorse in our community."

8.

Out of the doors of another church comes the sorrowful mother.

And within two grey-haired women talk of her.

"Her teaching is suspicious. She belongs to no congregation of any official church and we did right in refusing to let her preach."

9.

"I am sorry, sister," a well-built Negro preacher says to Clyde's mother. "Our church cannot give you its hall. It is only for coloured people."

And, ever more discouraged, she leaves the room.

10.

The apple trees are in blossom — ivy is crawling up the walls — the grapevine curls itself about the iron railing. The white flowers of sweet peas and the yellow of nasturtiums crowd around the prison-cell window. The white building of the prison is set in the midst of green shrubs and moss.

11.

Again the moss-covered window, and behind the window, in his cell, sits Clyde. He is dressed in the striped uniform of a prisoner, and on his back is number 772. He feels his shaved head, his sunken cheeks and trembles as if cold.

"Where am I?" — asks Clyde.

And from the next cell a voice is heard:

"In the Death House, on Murderers' Row."

And Clyde shuts his eyes, and helplessly falls on his bunk.

12.

Over the sign *Burlesque Show* above the undraped figures of women, workmen are suspending a cloth sign, on which is written:

A Mother's Appeal for her Son.

And boys in the street are handing out leaflets on which is advertised the plea of Clyde's mother.

13.

A sombre, serious crowd of people pass through the tawdry entrance of the Burlesque theatre, pass the posters of indecent, undraped women. And on the scene, with a background of the Burlesque drops on the stage, among plaster statues of gaudy women, Clyde's mother speaks in her sincere way, her large figure in bleak contrast with the surrounding atmosphere.

She speaks with faith, feelingly, touchingly, as a mother can speak of her son, and it makes the Burlesque girls clad in their sparkles and feathers cry as they wait at the back for rehearsal; even the electrician at his signal board is intent.

A tray is passed through the congregation for offerings.

"What is this — a church?" asks a merry young girl, coming late for rehearsal, as she enters backstage.

"Hush," the others quiet her, as they blow their noses.

14.

And when Clyde's mother leaves the theatre, she has to pass a row of burlesque girls ready for the rehearsal.

In her hands she holds the bag of money, two girls break line and ask respectfully to offer coins.

Clyde's mother smiles as she passes through the exit door and she hears neither the cheap music, nor the hoarse singing of the rehearsal which has started.

15.

"Clyde," a voice is heard saying in the dark.

Clyde jumps off his bunk in his cell. "A note for you," a voice says, and a hand gives him an envelope.

16.

He unfolds the note. It is typewritten and reads: *Clyde — This is so that you will not think that someone once dear to you has utterly forgotten you. She has suffered much, too — Sondra.*

He presses it to his lips, runs up to the window, looks out at the sun and repeats words that he said once before, long ago:

"To live — how good it is."

17.

"Hello, Clyde, hello, son," he hears his mother's voice and sees her come to him.

His mother forces herself to show no anxiety, she says:

"The Governor has promised to see us, son, and we have a little money together, not much —"

He throws himself into her arms, and presses his head upon her lap, once more a boy.

"Everything will be all right, Clyde," she croons, stroking the head in her lap. "Everything will be all right. You didn't do it. You didn't do it."

"Yes, mummy, I didn't do it." The warmth of her faith, the tenderness of her protecting hand, her soothing voice envelop Clyde. He is a child of years ago.

"You didn't do it — the Lord will deliver you," soothes the mother. "My boy could never think of such a thing."

Clyde snuggles closer. Gone is the tension of his long ordeal. His soul relaxes. The comforting hand caresses him.

"I did — think of it, mummy," says Clyde. And the mother's caress slows, her fingers have become stiff and her face set. And Clyde rubs his cheek against the hands that are now of wood.

"But I never — never — never did it, mummy."

18.

The door opens and Jephson enters. He speaks hurriedly to Mrs. Griffiths.

"We must go now. We are due at the Governor's. Come."

The mother rises, she presses Clyde in her great protecting arms and responds to his kiss. With a trace of absentness she leaves the cell with Jephson.

"Good luck, mother, good luck," Clyde calls after her. And once more Clyde goes to the window, Sondra's note in his hand and tears of happiness in his eyes.

19.

The unfriendly house of the Governor.

20.

The great study of the Governor.

In front of a great desk stands the Governor compassionately by the side of the mother. Quietly he asks: "Can you, Mrs. Griffiths, can you from the bottom of your soul tell me that you believe him innocent?"

She turns to him to say "Yes", but having said: "My son . . . ." she stops.

Her eyes open wide as she hears the voice of Clyde, softly: "I did — think of it, mummy —"

— and she closes her eyes. Her head drops on her chest, there is silence in the room.

The shrill sound of a bell. The mother starts, opens her eyes. The Governor removes his hand from the bell. He stands on the other side of the desk. He is important, full of power and unapproachable.

"Excuse me," he says, "but there is no reason to reopen the case. God will help you, mother. My prayers go with you."

The door is opened and automatically she leaves the room, but, as the door closes behind her, she comes to herself, cries out, and turns back towards the door.

"My son is innocent," she says.

But the door does not open.

21.

Darkness spreads over the screen, and at the same time, with a fierce rattle, an iron shutter is drawn up, disclosing a cell window. On the floor is a clean brass cuspidor. A soft broom is carefully cleaning the space around it. The broom is sweeping between the feet of the chair. And —

— on these feet hang leather thongs with heavy buckles, and from the chair onto the floor falls a shadow.

There is a heavy iron door in this room. And from behind the door can be heard a song.

Clyde and his mother are singing psalms. In the condemned cell, clad in black, sing Clyde and his fanatically exalted mother.

And suddenly Clyde breaks off in his singing, and at the knees of his mother he clasps her with a cry:
"To live —
I want to live!"

And through the window is the bright sunlit courtyard of the prison, all in green and in flowers, and on it is heard:
"To live —"

And again we see the cell window, and within it is the mother praying, and the camera receding discloses to us that now she is alone, on her knees and singing; more faintly now, but more majestically.

Slowly the heavy iron door closes.

And against the background of the spring fields and sky slides from left to right the barred gate of the prison. And from right to left the solid inner gate of the prison.

And the blinds and shutters of the windows come sliding down and sliding down, shutting out the landscapes and the sky — light — life —

And with their closing, cease the trilling of grasshoppers in the meadows, the singing of the birds and the sound of human voices, and as the last sound is gone the last shutter descends closing out the prison bars against the white and there is blackness.

Blackness and quiet.

A sharp crackle and the sharp light of an electric contact — and again quiet — again blackness.

22.

Grey smoke rises against the dull sky and loses itself in the quiet air.

A tall chimney, a roof; the camera descends past the windows and balconies of a mean building, and the lower descends the camera the stronger sound the voices of a little choir singing psalms.

In a dirty lane by a mission, surrounded by a crowd of curiosity seekers, to the sound of a harmonium, some street preachers are singing, as at the beginning of the picture. There they stand, but now the hair of the mother is white as snow, the father is old and ailing, and Esta is grown to a sickly woman and, instead of Clyde, as small as when we first saw him and resembling him, is her little seven-year-old son.

How long since you wrote to Mother?

— says a notice by the entrance to the mission.

"Everbody's happy"

— sings the white-haired, broken mother. Pitifully wheezes the harmonium and the strains of "Everybody's happy" fade distantly as the scene FADES OUT.

NOTE ON SCRIPTS

The scripts were written in the following manner:

1. We all read the novels.
   Eisenstein marked his copies with notes.
   I made a précis of *Sutter's Gold*, singling out and listing the principal characters and incidents for Eisenstein's convenience.

2. We discussed them. Of *Sutter's Gold*, we made a first broad division of the material and incidents into reels. This, written out by me, was at first in 9 reels, not 7.

3. We visited San Francisco, and the Sacramento Valley with the deserted gold rush cabins. Eisenstein made sketches, Alexandrov took photos, I analysed and noted details of character and incident from the reminiscences of those we met, and listed names and addresses of those with useful recollections.

   A similar visit was planned for Upper New York State after *An American Tragedy* was written, but the contract ended before this could be carried out as planned.

4. *Sutter's Gold* and *An American Tragedy* were both written straight off in a single operation lasting many hours, without sleep or rest.

   (a) Eisenstein outlined the action to Alexandrov who wrote it down in Russian.

   (b) Paramount translators, standing by, immediately made a literal translation.

(c) I took this translation to Eisenstein. We discussed it, changed it, I made notes on it.

(d) I wrote out in longhand an exact copy of the corrected and noted translation which then became the final script.

(e) Hell, who alone could read my writing, typed this MS.

(f) More copies were made by Paramount typists, standing by. These were distributed to senior Paramount executives and some retained by us. (The Museum of Modern Art, New York, made copies of copies of this last stage presented to it by Eisenstein).

All phases of this work proceeded simultaneously, a cross between multiple chess and a conveyor belt system. Thus Alexandrov would be writing down reel 6 (details of which he had just received from Eisenstein), while the Paramount translators were working on reel 5, and while Eisenstein and I were discussing reel 4 (just received from the translators) and the Paramount typists were following Hell's pages of reel 3 (just received from me).

5. After the scripts had been got down in this way, Eisenstein made his production sketches and costings of *Sutter's Gold* and sketches, notes and caricatures of *An American Tragedy*.

The material referred to in the above is at present preserved in the following collections:

The Museum of Modern Art, New York

1. Eisenstein's marked copy of *An American Tragedy*, Vol. II
3. Eisenstein's sketches of *Sutter's Gold*
4. (f) Copies of scripts as completed

5. Eisenstein's production sketches and costings of *Sutter's Gold* and sketches, notes and caricatures of *An American Tragedy*

Private Library, Ivor Montagu

1. Précis of *Sutter's Gold*, typed copy
2. 9 reel division, *Sutter's Gold*, typed copy
3. One Eisenstein sketch for *Sutter's Gold*
3. I.M.'s location visit notes for *Sutter's Gold*, typed copy
4. (c) Microfilm of noted translation, *Sutter's Gold*
4. (d) Longhand MSS of *Sutter's Gold*
4. (e) Typed MSS of *Sutter's Gold* and of *An American Tragedy*

Eisenstein Archive (now maintained by Gosfilmfond, Moscow)

4. (a) Eisenstein's first outline of both scenarios written in longhand by Alexandrov
4. (b) Copies of scripts as completed
4. (c) Noted translation of *Sutter's Gold*

NOTE TO PAGES 101 AND 105

In the otherwise admirable booklet on Eisenstein's theatre productions, films, drawings, projects and books issued recently by the Soviet National Film Archive "Gosfilmfond" (see Bibliography, item No. 14), not two but four subjects are listed as having been turned down by Paramount.

This is quite a false impression.

Of "The Glass House" it is said: "Eisenstein wished to create a satirical film of the isolation of people in capitalist society based on Eugene Zamyatin's novel *We* and worked out an outline sketch of script, direction and set solutions of the idea. Libretto refused by Paramount."

This is not so. I have read elsewhere, also, that S.M. derived the idea from Zamyatin's novel. If so, he never told anyone of this at the time. If he worked out any sketches he kept them to himself, which would have been unlike him. (If any exist, I should guess either that they were made later, as an exercise, or earlier, and that before coming to Hollywood he had for some reason dropped the line they represented.) A satirical approach was never considered or spoken of. No "libretto" or any other treatment was either written or proposed to Paramount, nor was any turned down. The idea was abandoned on our side, by S.M. himself, and the circumstances were exactly as described in the text.

Of *Black Majesty* (the novel by John W. Vandercook, Harper & Brothers, 1928), referred to in the text as the Christophe-Dessalines story, again a misleading impression is given by the booklet's words "Paramount refused the scenario." It is true we got the book from the Hollywood Bookstore while we were still at Paramount, and talked about it then, and corresponded both with the author (I think) and (certainly) with Paul Robeson. But it was simply as an attractive subject that might become possible under other circumstances. We knew much too much about the Hollywood set-up to imagine for a moment that such a subject could be acceptable to a big Hollywood corporation, or that proposing it to Paramount could do anything but diminish our reputation for practicality in its eyes. (The first Hollywood picture with "all-Black" cast — "Hallelujah" — had just been completed then as an exceptional novelty. Though a great success, but for a very few successors — e.g. "Green Pastures" — an exception it has fortunately remained.) The idea, and it did not get any further at that time than an attractive idea, was never put to Paramount but only, as the text mentions, came up again as a wild possibility for independent finance when we were clutching at straws after Paramount had given us the sack. But we did virtually nothing about it. There was not time.

In Mexico Eisenstein worked out production sketches for it as a relaxation. But the detailed scenario ideas worked out in the book *Lessons with Eisenstein* (see Bibliography, item No. 11) belong to S.M.'s post-Hollywood, post-Mexico period at GIK (the Soviet state film school).

All else is romance.

NOTE TO PAGE 134

It is hard to compare exact costs of pictures made under dissimilar circumstances, for different production, promotion and distribution set-ups may use different accounting methods or different criteria in assigning different categories of cost to "production".

Marie Seton in *Sergei M. Eisenstein* quotes the original contract between Mrs. Upton Sinclair and S.M.E. as providing for a picture taking 4 months to make and costing $25,000. Eisenstein, when the picture was stopped wrote that in 11 months he had spent $53,000 and needed only $8,000 more to save it from being like a play cut off "before the fifth act". Sinclair later spoke of 13 months working and said that the cost had been $75,000. A higher figure than this — $90,000 — was set to Amkino as a price at which the material might be rescued and sent to Moscow, but this undoubtedly must have visualised some compensation for wear and tear to the nerves of the investors.

At the then rate of exchange, therefore, the Sinclair expenditure on the film must have been around £15,000 — £16,000.

Sir Michael Balcon, without exact figures before him and writing to me from recollection, sets the advance budget of the project for "Man of Aran" as from £8,000 to £10,000, adding: *Only on that basis was it possible to persuade the Directors to go ahead.*

He continues: *The film escalated in cost (probably because of the introduction of the sharks — you will re-*

member that Flaherty did not know about the sharks until he had settled in Aran) and to the best of my belief ended up at least twice as much as originally intended: probably in excess of £20,000 and thus creating a great deal of trouble ....

(In fairness I should record a slightly lower figure from the recollection of John Monck, the editor employed on the film, quoting information from the production manager, Ted Black: £17,500.)

Production costs generally have markedly advanced since those days, but the chief increase has been since the war. In the few years between the two productions there was not a big change.

There can be no comparison at all in what are called "production values", that is, the costliness of appearance of the material taken for the two projects: on the one hand a few fishermen and their families in a single location, on the other an epic epitome of the social and ethnographical-historical variety of a whole nation, with "a cast of thousands".

Making allowance for all uncertainties these figures must be taken as conclusive that:

(1) It can only have been innocent folly in Sinclair to imagine that the most modest Eisenstein picture could be made in Mexico for the derisory cost that Eisenstein guessed;*

(2) It was a misunderstanding of the nature of filming a documentary in an exotic location to imagine that all that is worth while shooting can be properly foreseen or that the pressure of an artist to be allowed to extend his treatment is necessarily a sign of egotism or perversity, or even betrayal of his backers' interests;

(3) Contrary to what Sinclair believed (and said at the time), Eisenstein not only was not extravagant, megalomaniac, impractical, but must in fact have been extra-

* An outline scenario was later approved, after Eisenstein's arrival in Mexico.

ordinarily moderate, careful and efficient to have obtained such amazing material results at such comparatively low cost;

(4) Nonetheless, granting Sinclair's innocence and his initial mistake, his distress, suspicion, frustration and — ultimately — fury were entirely comprehensible.

The length of exposed negative quoted in the text — 35 miles — is the figure stated by both Sinclair and Eisenstein at different times (180,000 ft.). I have noted negative used by the first Shepherd's Bush studio production, a long-forgotten run-of-the-mill programme picture, as having amounted to 40 miles (over 200,000 ft.). In Sinclair's autobiography (quoted by Seton *op. cit.*) he recorded Mrs. Sinclair as thinking "35 miles is enough for any picture" and clamouring (his verb) "Bring them back!" Sir Michael Balcon writes of "Man of Aran": *It was only the intervention of Mrs. Isidore Ostrer* that enabled the film to be completed. She happened to visit the studio on a Saturday afternoon when I was viewing thousands of feet of sea and was captivated.*

Of course any comparison of the reactions of the two ladies to their respective "rushes" would be completely misplaced. The one did not have to bear any of the agonies and anxieties which — as a result of a simple goodwill plunge that had carried her and her husband so far out of their depth — lay so heavy on the other. Yet the contrast sheds an ironic gleam on the haps and mishaps that may make or mar a masterpiece.

* The wife of the chairman of the production company concerned with the Flaherty project.

SELECT BIBLIOGRAPHY

The making of books by and about Eisenstein has long been quite an industry in many languages. The following list does not pretend to be complete, but it includes most of the more interesting ones in English, and one or two others — enough anyway to guide further exploration of any avenue a new *aficionado* may wish to follow. There are also, of course, innumerable scattered articles, many of which are detailed in the British Film Institute Library Bibliography of June 1963.

Works by: S. M. EISENSTEIN

1. *The Film Sense*, translated and edited by J.M. Leyda (Harcourt, Brace, New York, 1942; Faber & Faber, London, 1943).
2. *Film Form*, translated and edited by J.M. Leyda (Harcourt, Brace, New York, 1949; Dobson, London, 1951).
3. *Film Essays*, translated and edited by J.M. Leyda (Dobson, London, 1968).
    These three books contain most of the principal theoretical essays available in English to date. Jay Leyda, a former student of Sergei Mikhailovich at G.I.K. (the Moscow film college) is his best and most scholarly interpreter. The first two are also combined as a paperback by Meridian (New York, 1957).
4. *Notebooks of a Film Director*, translated by X. Danko, edited by S. Yurenev (Russian edition

1956; first English edition Foreign Languages Publishing House, Moscow, 1958; republished Lawrence & Wishart, London, 1959).

> Some additional essays, with some of those above, including S.M.'s own brief account (pp. 98—106) of the circumstances of "An American Tragedy" and photographs of his visit to the U.S.A.

5. *Drawings*, edited by L.A. Ilyin (Iskusstvo, Moscow, 1961).

> A splendid collection, in colour and black and white, with essays and captions in French and English as well as Russian.

6. *Que Viva Mexico*, introduced by Ernest Lindgren (Vision, London, 1951).

> One stage of the scenario, preceded by Lindgren's excellent brief account of the circumstances.

7. *Ivan the Terrible*, edited by I. Montagu and translated by I. Montagu and H. Marshall (Simon & Schuster, New York, 1962; Secker & Warburg, London, 1963).

> The screenplay of the whole, including the unfinished third part.

8. *Izbrannye Proizvedennya* (Selected Works), edited by L.A. Ilyin (Iskusstvo, Moscow 1961—   ).

> The full treatment, superseding the earlier one-volume edition, to be completed in seven volumes of which four have appeared so far. (*Russian.*) An English edition, under the general editorship of H. Marshall, is planned by Dobson and the Massachusetts Institute of Technology.

9. Forthcoming Moscow publication:
Autobiographical Sketches, translated into English by Millman.

10. LEON MOUSSINAC
    Sergei Mikhailovich Eisenstein (No. 23 in the series *Cinéma d'Aujourd'hui*, Edition Seghers, Paris, 1964).
    A short study written by a close friend. It includes S.M.'s own, more lively, account of La Sarraz and two letters from Hollywood. (*French*)

11. VLADIMIR NIZHNY
    Lessons with Eisenstein, translated and edited by I. Montagu and J.M. Leyda (Allen & Unwin, London, 1962; Hill & Wang, New York, 1963).
    A vivid account of the master's teaching, reported by a former student at G.I.K.

12. MARIE SETON
    Sergei M. Eisenstein (Bodley Head, London, 1952; Evergreen paperback of the Grove Press, New York, 1960).
    The only biography. Invaluable, despite a liability to take Sergei Mikhailovich seriously in some of his most leg-pulling moods. An augmented revision is in preparation for Dobson.

13. VARIOUS
    Sergei Eisenstein, Künstler der Revolution (Henschelverlag, Berlin [G.D.R.], 1960).
    Proceedings of the Eisenstein Conference held in East Berlin, April 1959. An important set of reminiscences, documents and essays. (*German*)

14. ANON
    Sergei Mikhailovich Eisenstein: Spektakli, Filmi, Risunki, Zamysli, Knigi (Scientific Research Bureau of Gosfilmfond, Moscow, 1966).
    Admirable and essential brief listing of important dates and activities, with cast lists, short synopses, photographs, etc. (*Russian*) (See however Note, p. 345)

INDEX

Academy of Motion Picture Arts and Sciences 82
Alexander Nevsky (1938) 138, 143
Alexandrov, Grigory;
    at La Sarraz, 14–17;
    in Russia, 24–29, 139;
    in Europe, 28–34;
    in Hollywood, 75–128
All Quiet on the Western Front (1930) 70
Amercian Tragedy, An 110
American Tragedy, An (1931) 115, 207–341
Amkino 77, 96, 135, 347
Arliss, George 62
Aron, Robert 13, 16
Attasheva, Pera 139

Bachmann, J. G. 50–53, 62, 71, 75, 121, 128
Balász, Béla 14, 24
Balcon, Michael 347
Battleship Potemkin (1925) 15, 24, 25, 28–31, 65, 122, 143
Beckett, Joe 21
Belfrage, Cedric 47, 67
Bennett, Arnold 22
Bennett, Constance 74
Bergman, Henry 92
Berlin – Sinfonie einer Grossstadt (1927) 14
Bern, Paul 54
Bernstein, Sidney 31, 86, 128
Bezhin Meadow (1937) 138, 144
Big Trail, The (1930) 83–84
Black Majesty 101, 345
Black, Ted 348
Bluebottles (1929) 20, 23
Bouissounousse, Janine 16
Brunel, Adrian 18, 19, 23
Buñuel, Luis 89

Caesar and Cleopatra 63–65
Campbell, Mrs. Patrick 62, 139
Carstairs, John Paddy 126
Cavalcanti, Alberto 14
Cendrars, Blaise 12, 101
Cerf, Bennett 42
Chaplin, Charles 35, 49, 65–67, 73, 74, 86–97
Charley's Aunt (1931) 125
Chicherin, A. N. 68
Christie Brothers 125–127
City Lights (1931) 87, 89, 91, 93, 95
Clarke, Louis 32
Coleridge, Samuel Taylor 30
Cook, Ted 75–76
Cruze, James 115

Daniels, Bebe 75
Daydreams (1929) 19–20

Dean, Basil 35
Devil's Disciple, The 35, 101
Disney, Walt 82
Dobb, Maurice 32
Dr. Zhivago 24
Doctor's Dilemma, The 146–147
Dovzhenko, Alexander 123, 143
Dreiser, Theodore 12, 110, 117
Drifters (1929) 31

Einstein, Albert 32
Eisenstein, Sergei;
 at La Sarraz, 14–17;
 in Russia, 24–29, 138–139;
 in Europe, 28–34;
 in Hollywood, 75–128
 in Mexico, 131–137
End of St. Petersburg (1927) 90
Evans, Montgomery 14
Experimental Cinema 82

Fairbanks, Douglas 28, 35, 48, 63–66, 75
Finnegan's Wake 29
Fish, Hamilton 121, 135
Flaherty, Robert 134, 348
Fraenkel, Heinrich 47, 68, 73, 85
Francis, Kay 56, 59–60
Frauennot – Frauenglück (1930) 33
Front Page, The 43

Gabo, Naum 37
Gainsborough Company 20
Gang, Christel 82
Garbo, Greta 53–55, 85
Garrett, Oliver H. P. 104
General, The 55–63
Gert, Valeska 72
Gillette, William King 83
Glass House, The 102–105, 345

Goehr, Alexander 108
Gold Rush, The (1925) 91
Goldwyn, Samuel 122–123
Granovsky, Alexander 72
Great Dictator, The (1940) 94, 127
Grierson, John 31

Haire, Norman 21
Haldane, J. B. S. 130
Hale, Georgia 91, 95
Hallelujah (1929) 346
Hellgren, Nora 68
Herzbrun, Harry 62
Hirschfeld, Magnus 29
Hitchcock, Alfred 90, 108
Hoover, Herbert 40
Huston, Walter 56, 59

Ingster, Boris 72, 77
Isaacs, Jack 14, 16–17, 31
Israels, Josef 38
Ivan the Terrible (1944–46) 138, 140, 143–144

Joffre, Joseph 41
Joyce, James 29

Kaiser von Kalifornien, Der (1936) 115
Kapitza, Peter 32
Kellino, Roy 20
Keys, Nelson 126
Kimbrough, Hunter 132
King Solomon's Mines 140, 145
Kitchener, Horatio Herbert 30
Koch, Carl 23
Kohner, Paul 68, 70
Kono 73, 87–88
Korda, Alexander 68

Laemmle, Carl 70–71
Lanchester, Elsa 19–21
Langmuir, Irving 38
Lapworth, Charles 47
Lasky, Jesse 41, 49, 61, 79–80, 110–115, 120–121
Laughton, Charles 19–22
Lee, Rowland V. 56, 59–61
Lenin, Vladimir Ilyich 27
Levino, Albert Shelby 50, 54–55, 57, 61, 111
Lindbergh, Charles 43
Liveright, Horace 110–118
Lloyd, Harold 87
Loftus, Cissie 30
London Film Society 14, 17, 30–31
Londres, Albert 33
Lopokova, Lydia 32
Lubitsch, Ernst 68
Lyon, Ben 75

MacArthur, Charles 43
Man of Aran (1934) 134, 347, 349
de la Mandrot, Mme 13
Marshall, Herbert 31
Mayer, Louis B. 94
Mei Lan-fang 38
Meisel, Edmund 31
Metro-Goldwyn-Mayer 54–55, 93
Milton, John 30
Mr. Proback 22
Monck, John 348
Monosson, Leon 97
Montagu, Lionel 34, 128
Moskowits, Mrs. Henry 37–40, 73
Moussinac, Léon 16
Much Ado About Nothing 58

Nizhny, Vladimir 31

October (1927) 106, 143
Old and New (1929) 143
Once in a Lifetime 122–123
Orlova, Lyubov 139
Ostrer, Mrs. Isidore 349

Pabst, Georg Wilhelm 15
Paramount Pictures 35–36, 41, 48–71, 77–80, 104, 106
Parker Brothers 124
Parsons, Louella 71
Passing of the Third Floor Back, The (1935) 85
Pease, Frank 121
Piccadilly (1929) 19
Pick, Lupu 15
Pickford, Jack 48
Pickford, Mary 28, 35, 64–66
Place in the Sun, A (1951) 115
Pudovkin, Vsevolod 17, 26, 42, 90, 123, 137

Que Viva Mexico! 128–137, 143, 347–349
R.C.A. (Radio Corporation of America) 35, 42
Reeves, Al 66–67
Reiniger, Lotte 23
Reynolds, Dr. 104
Rich, Lionel 19–20
Richter, Hans 14, 16
Road to Buenos Aires, The 33
Robeson, Paul 101, 346
Robinson, Carlyle T. 67
Romance Sentimentale (1930) 33
Roosevelt, Franklin Delano 40–41
Rowson, Simon 19
Ruttmann, Erna 71–72
Ruttmann, Walther 14, 16, 72

Sarnoff, David 35, 42
Saturday Evening Post 42, 125
Schulberg, B. P. 48–49, 56, 59, 79, 109–111, 120, 140
Schulberg, Budd 111
Selznick, David 71, 120, 140
Selznick, Myron 74, 111
Seton, Marie 136
Shakespeare, William 30, 58, 95
Shaw, George Bernard 32, 35, 42, 63–65
Simon & Schuster 42, 125
Sinclair, Upton 86, 128, 129–137
Smith, Alfred 37, 40
Sorbonne 28
Stalin, Joseph 116, 136, 138, 144
Stern, Benjamin 42, 124
Stern, Seymour 81
Sternberg, Josef 79, 116
Stevens, George 115
Strike (1925) 143
Sutter, Johann August 101
Sutter's Gold 83, 101–103, 105–110, 148–205

Taming of the Shrew, The (1929) 64
Thalberg, Irving 54
Thomson, J. J. 32
Thunder Over Mexico (1933) 134, 136
Time in the Sun (1939) 136
Tisse, Eduard;
  at La Sarraz, 14–17;
  in Russia, 24–28, 139
  in Europe, 28–34;
  in Hollywood, 75–128

Tisse, Eleonora 139
Tonic, The (1929) 19, 21–22
Toulouse-Lautrec, Henri 30
Trenker, Luis 115
Tully, Jim 92
Twelvetrees, Helen 65

Ugarte, 89
Ulysses 29
Universal Film Company, 68, 70

Vandercook, John W. 345
Vidor, King 85
Viertel, Berthold 85
Viertel, Salka 85
Vigo, Jean 143
Vishnevsky, Vsevolod 140
Vormittagsspuk (1928) 14

Wallace, Edgar 45
War of Worlds, The 36, 40, 71; 101
Warner Brothers 123
Warrender, Harold 19
Weaver, John V. A. 61
Webster, John 30
Wells, Frank 18–19, 21–22
Wells, Herbert George 18–20; 22, 35–36, 99
Western Electric 35, 38
Wilde, Oscar 32

Young, Freddy 20

Zukor, Adolph 35, 41, 48, 49

Briefly,
ABOUT THE AUTHOR

Ivor Montagu was born in London in 1904. He was educated at Westminster School, the Royal College of Science, London, and King's College, Cambridge. In his long career in films there is almost no phase of the industry that Ivor Montagu has not had a hand in: as film editor, importer, distributor, exhibitor, script writer, director, and associate producer. He has worked with Hitchcock in England and *With Eisenstein in Hollywood*. He filmed in Spain during the Spanish War and in World War II for the Ministry of Information. A documentary which he co-directed won an Academy Award and a feature which he co-scripted was chosen for a Royal Command Performance. A founder of the Association of Cine and TV Technicians, Montagu served on its executive committee for twenty-eight years. He is also an Honorary Member of the Screenwriters' Guild and was co-founder and Chairman of the Film Society during its lifetime. He was the first film critic for *The Observer* and *The New Statesman*. A partial list of Mr Montagu's published works appears on page four of this book. A listing of Ivor Montagu's many other activities would run into more pages than this volume allows. But the reader will gather that he is a man of many talents — with interests that circle the globe....